Horton John] [from old catalog] [Gibson

Letters received in my two widow-hoods

Horton John] [from old catalog] [Gibson
Letters received in my two widow-hoods
ISBN/EAN: 9783337374648
Printed in Europe, USA, Canada, Australia, Japan
Cover: Foto ©ninafisch / pixelio.de

More available books at **www.hansebooks.com**

Letters

Price, 50 Cents.

RECEIVED IN MY

Two Widow-Hoods

By AVERELLE LOUTHOOD.

NEW YORK:
MYRTLE PUBLISHING COMPANY.

LETTERS RECEIVED

IN MY

TWO WIDOW-HOODS.

If words
 Were birds
  And swiftly flew
   From tips
   To lips
  Owned dear
  By you
 Would they
 To-day
  Be doves
  Of love?
  Yes!

WITH PORTRAITS.

By AVERELLE LOUTHOOD.

MYRTLE PUBLISHING COMPANY,

NEW YORK.

INTRODUCTION.

Having read Marie Bashkirtseff's Letters, I thought to myself, why should not my letters, received during my two widow-hoods, be of interest?

The Bashkirtseff letters are those of a school-girl; mine are to a woman, and they show how much, even in this nineteenth century, a woman can be thought of, admired and loved. They also show that all women do not, as men think, grasp at the first offer of marriage.

I have never read a book of this kind, nor have I ever heard of just such a compilation. The new "Abelard," like the old, was a mere brain-child, "Clarinda" high-strung, the Lytton letters childish, the Piozzi case an affair of second childhood. Those who might have given such a work to the world may have been deterred, either by the feeling that such "human documents" would not attract, or by scruples on the score of honor. There is, however, no real violation of confidence in my case, as I have substituted aliases for actual names.

That these letters may interest and help to while a few hours away is the wish of,

Cordially yours,

ALICE.

Alice, sweet Alice, so smiling her face,
Love basks in her beauty, her exquisite grace;
Ideal her eyes are, bewitching and bright.
"Carissima mea!" I live in her light,
Earth having no charms with her form not in sight

In My first
Widow - Hood
Alice

HAST THOU A FRIEND.

Hast thou a friend? Oh, hold him fast,
Fling not his hand away:
Thou of a treasure art possessed
Thou'lt not find every day.
Oh, let no hasty word or look
Blot out his name from memory's book!

A friend! to man the noblest gift
That heaven has in its power,
Stronger than death, and yet—most strange!—
Feebler than frailest flower;
For that which braved the storm severe
May yet be blighted by a sneer!

He may have errors—who has not?
Who dares perfection claim?
God gave thy friend some worthy parts—
Fix all thy heart on them!
His virtues rightly drawn, I ween,
His faults in shade will not be seen!

If thou wouldst keep thy friend thine own,
Be open—be sincere!
What thou unto thyself art known,
That to thy friend appear.
'Twixt him and thee have no disguise;
In this true friendship's secret lies.

Thou hast a friend! oh, hold him fast:
Fling not his hand away.
Thou of a treasure art possessed
That's not found every day.
Oh, let no hasty word or look
Blot thy friend's name from thy heart's book.

TABLE OF CONTENTS.

FIRST WIDOW-HOOD.

	PAGE.
Introduction,	3
Poem "Hast Thou a Friend,"	5
From Robert,	9
From B——,	45
From Ollie,	46
From Leon,	48
From Doctor B——,	102
From Theodore,	103
From L——,	108
From B——,	108
From C——,	109
From E——,	113
From F——,	113
From E——,	113
From Winfred,	122
From Paul,	124
From Seth,	127
From Neville,	127
From George,	128
From Jack,	129
From Lemont,	130

TABLE OF CONTENTS.—*Continued.*

SECOND WIDOW-HOOD.

	PAGE.
Poem "Last Night,"	147
From Robert,	148
From Leon,	148
From Theodore,	150
From Seth,	160
From Your Friend,	161
From F———,	167
From Winfred's Brother,	167
From B. B———,	170
From Leonard,	174
From Basil,	190
From L. L.,	203
From Bob,	204
From Nap,	209
From Dave,	213
From Will,	218
From Harold,	219
From M. Harris,	229
From Dey,	230
From Fred,	254
From D———,	257
From Nell,	258
From X———,	266
From Bob,	267
From T———,	271
From J———,	272
From M———,	273
From C———,	274
From G———,	279
From J———,	283
From F———,	284
From L———,	285
From 8 Years Old,	286
From E———,	287
From L———,	288
From Jean,	294
From C———,	295
From Your Friend,	297

LETTERS RECEIVED

IN MY

TWO WIDOW-HOODS

New York, July 23d.

My dear Alice:—

Your two letters—one from Montreal and one from Three Rivers—are received, the last one to-day, and glad was I to get them and learn of your safe arrival and your very kind and hospitable reception at Three Rivers.

I do not see, dear one, how any one who knows you could receive you otherwise and so I cannot say I am at all surprised, but nevertheless it is pleasant to hear how others do treat you and to find you are welcome and loved wherever you go. Don't let those complimentary speeches of the gentlemen turn your head.

My friend, keep cool and discreet, and that I feel sure you will. I am going to start for Cape May to-morrow, but the great railroad strike that is extending all over the country makes it doubtful whether we could get there or get anywhere we wanted to, and so our plans are all at sixes and sevens.

We shall probably go somewhere to-morrow and as soon as I get anywhere will write you how to direct your next letter. The weather has been very warm and oppressive since you left, but I have been quite well so far. Do not worry for me, my dear one, I shall take good care of myself and await your return as patiently as possible though you may be sure of one thing — that you are missed and that New York is not the same place without your sweet, bright face, and I don't care how soon September comes and brings you back again.

I did not write you at Montreal for the reason that I thought it possible you might not remain there.

Good bye, give my kind regards to your mother, who has my best wishes for her health and happiness, and believe me
Ever your own
Robert.

I sent you a Graphic to-day containing a picture of the hotel at St. Albans and other interesting illustrations, one of an old fellow with a young wife and what follows.

Cape May, July 26th.

I wrote you, my dear Alice, from New York the day before I left, acknowledging receipt of two letters and saying I was going to Long Branch. I went there the next day, going down the bay in a steamboat and getting to the hotel to tea. The hotels are well filled; at the one where we are stopping one of the colored waiters at the table asked me if he had not seen me in Savannah last winter at the Palaska House. It appears he was a waiter there. We came on next day to this place, not intending to remain at Long Branch, which I never liked much. We had a rather tedious time coming down here, hot, dusty and slow arriving at about seven o'clock. The hotel we first went to we did not like and changed this morning to Congress Hall, one of the best here. The beach is splendid and the bathing very fine and safe, as the shore shelves off very gradually. There were a multitude of bathers in the water this morning and we shall probably try it tomorrow, some of us at least. I wish there was one more here to be of our party. Can you guess who? The moon last night was beautiful, and I went down to the beach alone after ten o'clock and gazed at the rolling billows and the shining silvery moon and thought of one seven hundred miles away. I wonder if she was thinking of me. Perhaps so, if she was awake and not entertaining some other friend. We have music at this house morning and evening, and I believe frequent hops. A vocal concert occurs this evening. I shall walk on the beach again and make the most of the moonlight while it lasts; concerts can be heard in New York.

Write me, dear, and tell me what you have been doing these lovely evenings and how you are, and whether you are enjoying yourself among friends so kind. I think you cannot help but be passing your time pleasantly. This watering place is filled chiefly with Philadelphians (Philadelphia is, I believe, only about 80 miles distant); many of them have cottages here of their own where they reside several months. The great railroad strike appears to be somewhat subsiding and it will, we hope, soon come to an end as we may wish to go elsewhere. For the present, however, we shall probably stay here, and on receipt of this letter I want you to write me, directing as you did last, but to this place, Cape May, New Jersey.

Ever your
Robert.

Cape May, July 29th.
Sunday afternoon.

This is my third letter to you, my dear Alice. Your number three I have not yet received, but shall look for it about Wednesday next, as my second epistle, telling you where to write me, will, I think, reach you to-day or to-morrow. We have now been in this place since Wednesday, long enough to judge pretty well as to whether it suits us, and we find it exceedingly pleasant. You may remember my telling you we were here a few days some years ago, but that was at the close of the season when about every one had gone home. Now the town and hotels are overflowing, this and the next week being considered as the culminating weeks of the season. I have gone into the bathing business, going in the third time this morning. The water was quite warm, the many hundreds in the surf presenting quite a lively spectacle. All kinds, lean, graceful and awkward. Many of the ladies wear stockings, whether because of homely feet, bunions or modesty I cannot say, perhaps because of all these. The last time I went into the surf was at Rye Beach, New Hampshire, where the water was very cold, and I was so dizzy and exhausted after coming out that I almost determined never to try it again. But here, I think, it is doing me good, and I shall probably follow it up as long as we stay here.

The beach is a splendid one to ride on, and we had one good, long ride on it. The day passes without tediousness when one gets the right idea how to spend it. I breakfast about 8 o'clock, sit on the piazza and listen to the band, which is a good one—Bernstein's of New York—for an hour or so, bathe at 12, dine at 2, music again at 5, supper at 7, music again at 8, and there is generally a concert or something of the sort in the evening, commencing at about half-past nine after the band stops playing. The day's programme can be varied by riding and sailing. We have had two rides, but no sails as yet. There is one other pleasure for me every day which nobody else here has—thinking of a sweet, bright, lovely and loved friend far away from here to whom I am now writing and whose presence here would double my happiness. Can you guess who that dear friend of mine is, Alice? They take every morning a photograph of the people on the piazza when the band ceases playing. I have appeared in two and shall get a copy of the last one to-morrow and will send you the best of the two if either appears to be good enough to make it worth while, and I am going to send you also a little box of what they call here Cape May diamonds, being little, semi-transparent pebbles picked up on the beach. We rode over to the beach where they are found about five miles distant. They call it Diamond Beach, and I took pains to get some of the very prettiest ones there for you. There are white and colored ones also, but the transparent ones only are the diamonds. They tell me they can be cut and are really quite brilliant; one person said nearly as lustrous as real diamonds, but of that I have great doubts. The people here seem to be sensible sort of folks, very little loud dressing, and I have not seen one rouged face. Such there may be here, but they are not at Congress Hall. Would you like to have the Graphic sent to you while in Canada? Please say when you write. I had a headache for two or three days after getting here, but am now feeling very well. I hope you and your mother are enjoying yourselves and are well.

With my best regards to your mother,

Ever yours,

Robert.

P. S.—The Cape May diamonds will be sent by next mail.

Cape May, August 2d.

I am just in receipt of your letter of the 29th (Sunday), my dear Alice, and am happy to hear that you are well and passing your time away pleasantly.

Since last writing you—on the 29th—I have sent you some Cape May pebbles and a package of stereoscopic views of this place by mail, and a couple of mems and papers, all of which I hope may reach you in safety.

We are having to-day an easterly storm which is rolling in the breakers on the beach in magnificent fashion. How I wish you were here to see them and me. You would don your water-proof and we would start out into the rain together, walk up and down the ocean shore and talk things over. How much better we could do it than write, my dear.

I send you with this a bill of fare—mine of yesterday. You will see I continue to live. I believe I have not told you that this hotel is carried on by the same man who conducts Willards at Washington, and you know he keeps a good one. I continue to bathe every day and am careful of myself—don't go out very far and stay in but a short time, so that when I come out I don't feel at all chilly or fatigued, and it agrees with me. We were to have sack-races, pole climbing, foot and hurdle races this afternoon, as you will see by the programme of sports for the week I sent you in the paper, but the weather compels a postponement. Do you remember the afternoon of similar amusements at St. Augustine? I guess you do. I think you are wise in getting the new black silk; it is much cheaper or ought to be in Canada than New York, and it is always useful. You say, my dear, you dream of me so often. My dreams of you are in the day time and many times a day. The third week of our separation is now coming on, and we shall presently be on the last half of it, and then—and then—

I should have liked so well to see you dressed in your blue suit for church, but my imagination must supply your image as you then looked. Mrs. R— is right about that mouth of yours. There is none prettier, and in this hotel there is none half so sweet to my mind. We have not yet decided how long to remain here, but shall do so for a while yet, and I will write you in time to change my address when we conclude where to go. Meantime write me every three days or so; to-day I am going to write to the Graphic people in New York to send it to your address daily for two months, so it ought to begin to reach you within a day or two after this letter and your mother will have the benefit of it after you return home.

The card of this hotel which I enclose herein will give you, perhaps, a better idea of the house as to its location by the sea than any of the views I sent you. The little cabins by the beach are bath-houses. If your friends do not happen to have a stereoscope you will have to buy one to look at your views with. The storm is now clearing, and I hear a great shouting on the lawn which gives me an idea that some of the promised games may be in progress after all. So I guess I will bid you good bye once more and with kind regards to your mother remain

Ever your own
Robert.

Cape May, N. J., August 4th,
Saturday evening, 10½ o'clock.

There is a ball here to-night, dear, and as it is free, all creation are at it; it is in the dining-room, a view of which I sent you, and I have left it and come into my own room to sit down and write to you, my friend. In acknowledging your letter written on the 29th of July, Sunday, I did not speak of the little plant "Love in a mist," which you sent me. It came safe and is safe, and love in a mist is much better than no love at all. I continue to bathe every day and probably shall till we leave. I don't see any gain in flesh so far, but perhaps that will come when we get away from the salt water. In the views of groups which I sent you, did you find me? I was in them both. The glare of the sun on the beach and water is so great here that many persons wear colored eye-glasses and spectacles. I have a pair and find them a great comfort, being a great relief to the eyes. For the last few days there has been a great visitation of mosquitoes and at one of the large hotels they have been so bad that the people have been compelled to leave. Our house stands a little higher and is not so near low-land and has not been so bad. This is Saturday night and the afternoon train brought in great numbers of visitors. Many were turned away from here. They come in many cases just to spend Sunday. For the next two weeks the crowd will be pretty well maintained and then will begin to dwindle, and by the first of September the large hotels close. Your valued letter of Tuesday, the 31st, I got this afternoon and it was very welcome, you may be sure. It seems a long time to me as it does to you since you left, and the days don't skip along very lively. I am very sorry to hear of Mr. R.'s sickness and trust he may recover. In case he does not and his wife is really desirous to have you remain with her, I see no reason why you should not do so till you have made your visit out at least, and then, of course, you will go to Mrs. L. on the visit she invited you to pay her. I do not believe, my dear, I shall get back to New York much before September 15th. It is very warm usually there until then. Do not be impatient. The last half of the time will glide away more rapidly than the first and then again, perhaps, I can manage to have you join us somewhere before our return to New York. I do not know whether this can be accomplished, but nothing would make me happier if it could be done. You tell me you go looking for eggs every morning, won't you take me with you, my dear? Do so in your thoughts at least. We shall probably leave here by Friday, the 10th, and go to Philadelphia for two or three days. I will write you again from here and also from there. Do not write me here again.

Yours ever,
Robert.

Cape May, N. J., August 8th.

I wrote you, my dear, on the 5th, and yesterday received yours of the 2d, which I was not sorry to get. I see you do have lots of company and cannot well be lonely for lack of that. If Mr. B. and sister, the musicians, take you in hand, I expect you will be warbling Italian operatic airs the day long when you return to New York in place of the Dutch ballads which you used to sing among the mocking birds last winter in the sunny South. I am extremely happy to hear that you did not go riding with Willie F. the other day when his horse ran away, and don't you go at all with him if that is the sort of horses he drives. You will be jumping out and breaking your precious neck, or getting thrown out and killed or hurt. Do not, on any account, my dear one, ride behind any horse not known to be perfectly gentle and safe. I was sorry to hear you could not have me come on Saturday, but had to make the best of it and stay here. Perhaps some other Saturday when the rush of company is over, you may be able to squeeze out one little Saturday for me. You will try one of those days, won't you? I hear of the picture of a man my friend loves set in a gold frame and am asked to guess who he can possibly be. I see a pair of beautiful soft brown eyes gazing at that picture and wish they were right before my own this moment, and if they were, I would tell the lady who owns them, who the man she loves and gazes at in the picture is, and if I thought she would not object, I might give her a kiss, or two, or three, or ever so many. Tell your friends at Three Rivers that the 15th of September will be the extreme limit of your stay and that you may have to leave on or soon after the 1st. You cannot be spared longer than the 15th, nor so long as that if it can be helped.

We are having pretty cool weather here now, comfortable and no mosquitoes. The water is quite warm and the bathers are in every day from 12 to 1 in great numbers. We remain here till Monday, the 13th, and shall then go to Philadelphia, where we shall stay two or three days and then go on to some other place of resort. As soon as I know where it will be, I shall write you. Meantime I shall get your letter I spoke about in my last while in Philadelphia. I received a letter from my sister to-day. She is unhappy and lonely as indeed she almost always is. I wish she had a better faculty to make herself happy and contented, but that will probably never be.

You say you would be happy to receive the Argus. Don't you mean the Graphic? If not you will be disappointed, as the Graphic is the paper you are probably now getting.

I think there are some ladies who might call a Graphic an Argus without drinking anything stronger than tea or coffee and am glad to believe you are one of them. I hope A. and your mother are well and enjoying themselves.

Ever yours,
Robert.

Congress Hall.
Cape May, August 8th.

I wrote you this morning, dear Alice, and now wish to add a word. When you receive this send me a letter to Delaware Water Gap, Pennsylvania. I don't know how long we shall stay there, but write me there every three days until you hear from me. Nothing new since my last, except a very warm day.

Yours ever,
Robert.

Congress Hall.
Cape May, N. J., August 9th.

This is my last letter to you, my dear Alice, from Cape May, as we leave on Monday. Yes, to-day your welcome letter of the 4th reached me, and glad was I to get it. I see you have courage enough to ride behind Willie F.'s horse. If he is at all in the habit of running away it seems to me an unwise risk, as there are plenty of gentle horses, and no lady should ever ride behind any other, as they are sure to jump out when the animal is at full speed and break their lovely little necks, and your neck is too dear, to at least one person, to risk it being broken. Therefore be careful of it and don't risk it with a runaway horse.

The sample of silk you enclose looks like a good article, and it ought to be cheap at the price you paid. I have no doubt you are having it made up becomingly and only wish I was where I could pass judgment on it the first time you wear it. But we cannot in this world have things just as we would like them and the better plan is to be grateful for the happiness we do have rather than repine over what we don't have. There is always something to fret about if we look for it. The bill of fare you send me of your dinner is a very nice one, good enough for anybody, and doubtless relished better than hotel food which is all apt to have a peculiar flavor. We are having an intensely warm day here to-day which disposes all the people to be quiet. After my bath I was so sleepy I could not keep my eyes open and had to go to my room and go to sleep in a chair.

There is a place about two miles away where boats can be had to go sailing and fishing, but we have not managed to get there yet, and it now looks doubtful if we shall. It is always too hot or too cold, or too early or too late, or too windy or too something or other. This afternoon was fixed upon to go, and it is too hot. Yesterday we were going and then there was no wind.

There is a little girl here, about three years old, just as sweet and pretty as though she were yours, and how I wish she was. She goes into the surf every day with her father and mother, and is as fearless as any grown person. When a wave breaks over her head, covering her entirely up, she is just delighted. Her mother has a very sweet face and now and then reminds me of my friend away off on the St. Lawrence river. There are plenty of other children here, many of them larger, who kick up a great row about going into the water, yelling and squealing and shrieking when taken in by their parents, as though they were being murdered. I wrote you on the 8th, asking you to write me at Delaware Water Gap every few days till hearing further. We shall probably reach there by Thursday, how long to stay I cannot tell. It will depend upon how we like it. We shall be in Philadelphia for two days at the Continental Hotel. Did you ever hear of it? Shall go and take a look at the Centennial buildings and exhibition and the mint maybe.

They will bring fresh to my mind a little girl I went with to see them some time ago. What a pleasant day we spent up at the Centennial grounds, dear. Do you remember it?

The two happiest folks I have seen to-day were two poor little boys for whom I bought a couple of those red balloons. They were eying them very longingly and I thought I would invest a quarter to make their eyes sparkle and I succeeded entirely.

Little folks are easily made happy if the older ones will but take a little trouble to make them so. I shall go to the Post-office here for a letter from you to-morrow. If I don't get it, shall expect to have that pleasure in Philadelphia. With love from

Robert.

Continental Hotel, Philadelphia.

Monday eve, August 13th.

We reached here this morning, my dear Alice, and I found your letter awaiting me, very much to my satisfaction. I am sorry it seems so very long to you to wait till the 15th, but it does not seem any longer to you than it does to me. The days crawl along very slowly and I can only hope they will slip away more rapidly on the last half, and then you know perhaps it may yet be managed to slip off some of the last days and meet somewhere on the way to New York.

I am pleased to hear you receive the Graphic regularly and hope it may serve to while away some idle hours—if you have any idle ones. The old squaw fortune-teller must be a wonderful Sibyl. I shall begin to believe in her kind. The traveling alone must be your coming home from Three Rivers. The second husband and the two children. She must have read your wishes in your soft, sweet eyes, Alice. Let us hope the real fortune will exceed in happiness her predictions, and that neither of the two little children will be taken away. I was very sorry to hear of your mother's illness and hope she may entirely recover; she seems to have naturally a good constitution and, with care, should be spared for many a year yet. I think, my dear, your reply to P— about the long walk was good. He should walk with the lady he marries for money. He may get enough of that sort of thing and marry the next time for love, if he has a chance. Don't flirt with him, dear, or anyone, W. included. Remember your friend, your true friend. My room in this house is on the floor above the ladies' parlor. The house is very nice and very nicely kept, but it is exceedingly warm here and there is not that now here to keep me contented, and I shall get away as soon as possible, I hope by Wednesday. I walked up Chestnut street alone to-day to No. 1304 to get my umbrella covered—yours was covered there. Saw in a jeweller's window a gold brooch, made like a half open fan and thought of the owner of one like it. Saw in another window a blue striped silk, just like one a dear friend of mine owns. She was in my mind all the way up and back. Our luggage did not come on the train with us from Cape May, it appears, and if it does not come on the next one—now about due—we shall be in a pickle.

Cape May is an exceedingly pleasant place, take it all in all, and I hope you will have an opportunity of seeing whether you don't think so yet.

There is so much going on that the day passes

quickly, as a general thing, except for those who sit and think of absent ones.

Had you been here, nothing would have pleased me more than remaining the month out. How long we shall stay at the Water Gap I don't know, as it depends upon how we like it. Nor have I any idea as yet where we shall go from there. If it is cool and pleasant and anything can be found to do to pass away the time, we may remain there a week or more. We may go to Niagara, shall conclude when we get to the Gap.

I shall look for a letter from you as soon as I am there and don't believe I shall be disappointed.

Continue to write me there till you hear otherwise.

You tell me you are getting fat—I am so happy to hear it, only don't outgrow your new dress, as you know you can't afford it.

It is getting towards ten o'clock, and I must go and see whether my trunks have come and have them carried up. Good night! Good night! Good night!

R.

Water Gap House.
Delaware Water Gap,
Thursday evening, August 16th.

I wrote you from Philadelphia, my dearest one, acknowledging the receipt of your letter sent there, and reached this place this afternoon.

Here I found awaiting me your delightful letter of last Sunday, which I have read and re-read and shall read again. I took it down under the trees surrounding this hotel, and selecting a spot where I could look away up this beautiful valley of the Delaware river, read it and looked off into the distance and thought of you, imagined the river to be the St. Lawrence and you to be upon it far away.

What you say of the ride and little walk afterwards will never be forgotten by me.

This hotel is very pleasantly situated high up above the river with magnificent views, and this evening is quite cool and agreeable.

We had an excellent supper and the house appears to be extremely well kept.

I was thinking this afternoon that could I but have here one whom I do deeply love, I should be quite content to spend the summer here.

We could wander through the woods, ride, row and talk, and the summer would pass like a dream.

I see your friends in Three Rivers are doing much to make your visit there a pleasant one and am very glad to know they are. I imagine from what you tell me you are causing no end of excitement among the gentlemen.

Would not you like to know or to have heard the conversation between P. and W. last Sunday morning, I fancy you would have heard your name more than once.

I wonder if Mr. P. is sick of his matrimonial bargain. If so, he is in a bad scrape, but after all a man who marries a woman for money must not complain, for he goes in with his eyes open and cannot reasonably expect any true happiness.

Your mother, I am very glad to hear, is continuing to grow better and sincerely trust she may not have another ill turn.

You do not say what was the matter. Give her my kind regards.

Do you know, darling, that when you are reading these lines the last half of your absence from home will be well under way?

I shall be counting the days one by one. September will be here in two weeks; are you sorry? I think I hear your answer. However, do not dwell too much on time to come, enjoy yourself and be happy.

I hope the Graphic comes all right and interests you. It is a nice sort of a paper, to say nothing of the illustrations, many of which are very good. I see you have been wearing your blue silk to church again. I guess it is your favorite and don't wonder at it, for it is a sweet dress, especially when it covers so sweet a girl. But then any dress would be sweet when so used.

If you get this letter in time to write me, and post the letter not later than the 20th (Monday), direct it to this place as heretofore, otherwise direct on the 21st to Binghamton, New York, where I shall stop overnight, or if I do not, will take measures to have your letter sent to where I am.

And now, dear, it is getting on towards 11 o'clock and the guests of the house are departing to bed one after another.

The Katy-dids are singing lustily but they are not saying Katy-did to me. They say Alice—dear—Alice dear—hope—you're—well—hope—you're—well— fare —thee—well—fare—thee—well—and so I will follow their example and bid you good night.

A stage load of guests is this moment coming up the mountain to the hotel from the village where they have been to a concert and they are singing and shouting, trying perhaps to drown the voices of my little singers in the trees, but they can't do it to me.

Ever yours,
Robert.

Water Gap House.
Delaware Water Gap, Penn.

Monday morning, August 20th.

I am commencing this letter, my dear Alice, with a pen I bought at the Centennial Buildings at Philadelphia which writes by simply dipping it into water.

The ink fills the inside of it in the form of paste which the water dissolves as you write. I have an idea that I shan't like it much, but will be better able to judge by the time this letter is finished.

I wrote you last Friday, or rather Thursday, and

told you that I received your first letter sent here. I have no later letter from you, but hope for one to-day, which, however, will not reach me till this is gone, as the mail comes in after the outward mail closes. This place is, as I told you in my last, beautiful; the views of the Delaware river and Blue Ridge Mountains are splendid. There are numerous mountain walks for those who like climbing, and seats in a variety of spots around the hotel under the trees for a quiet rest, or talk, or read.

With the charming moonlight nights now occurring lovers would find no difficulty in suiting themselves to little paradisiacal nooks and corners for talking and kissing.

Those, however, who have no sweet ones or whose loved ones are elsewhere must content themselves with sitting on the piazza in the moonlight and wishing their darlings here or themselves where their dear ones are.

The house we are at, 400 feet above the river, is the finest and best one here. There are, however, several others, and some of them very good, I believe. At hotels one meets, as you know, all sorts of people. There are two young ladies who sit at our table, and who are extremely dissatisfied with everything they have to eat, and as the food is really excellent and very nicely prepared, it is reasonable to conclude that they live chiefly on mush and molasses or similar provender at home and are putting on a few airs on their travels. Something is the matter with one of them. She seems to rise and sit down with much difficulty. The waiter says she has a "misery" in her side which was hurt by falling out of a swing. Then there is a slim old lady with long ear-rings, a long nose and a hatchet face who is full to the brim with gossip and reels it off by the fathom with great satisfaction to herself if to nobody else. The gayety here is not to be compared with Cape May. No music to speak of—all it consists of one pianist, common; one fiddler, poor; one cornet player, very bad, and scarcely any dancing.

They profess to have a dance every other night, but it is a very sickly affair. What with the wheezy cornet-blower, the scraping fiddler and the bang-wanging piano player the provocation to trip on the light fantastic toe is not great. And there is a peculiarity of the dancers here which I have noticed and observed also at Cape May, and that is a perfect disregard of the music so far as time is concerned. Even when the players keep good time two-thirds of the people in the round dances hop and skip about the room with no more attention to the time of the tune than if they were utterly deaf. This, of course, spoils the whole effect of the dancing however graceful the dancer may be and gives them an odd ridiculous sort of look like Jumping Jacks or Punches and Judys.

We shall probably leave here Thursday or Friday. We hardly know where to go, but shall doubtless proceed to Watkins Glen for a few days, and then it is just about an even chance whether we go on to Niagara. I trust you and yours remain well and happy, that you continue to enjoy yourself with your kind and hospitable friends and that you will come back to New York when your visit is over with many pleasant incidents to remember, but without regret and with unabated love for

Your own
Robert.

Delaware Water Gap, Penn.

August 22d.

Your precious letter of the 16th, "Carissima mea," (which is the Latin, I believe, for "dearest one") reached me about one hour ago, after mine of the 20th started on its voyage to Canada to you, and its receipt made me very happy. You say that a knowledge that others love a person makes us love the person more ourselves. This is no doubt true, but whether in my case, so far as you are concerned, is a little doubtful, for I know not if there is any room for an increase of my affection for you. However, I am entirely willing to have it grow if it is possible. You speak of quiet, pleasant rows on the St. Lawrence. I have had two on the Delaware. The river was as smooth as a mirror and reflected the mountains on each side almost as perfectly, and as we returned the other evening as it was growing dusk we overtook a party who were singing, and one of their songs was Sweet By and Bye, and who do you suppose that brought into my mind?

I trust that nothing I have ever written you has seemed to imply that I could not entirely and fully trust and confide in you.

I have never had such a feeling for one moment, never a doubt of your unwavering love and fidelity. We shall leave here on Friday, the 24th, and after stopping for the night at Binghamton, go on to Watkins Glen, where we may stay a week or so, depending somewhat upon how we like it.

I did not tell you that we brought along with us the little alligator left living at the time we left New York. A. thought it would not receive proper care, and so took it along. It did not seem to do well, however, and died a couple of days ago, the last of the three and after all surviving much longer than I supposed any of them would when we got them.

Last night was a most magnificent moonlight night, and it seemed a sort of desecration of it to have a hop in a hot gas-lit room to poor music, as we did have, and in fact it did not go off very well.

There is a woeful lack of dancing gentlemen, and the young ladies have to dance together, which is not exactly the poetical thing, you know. The sweet little girl I believe I wrote you about at Cape May is here, having come with her parents the other day. She has deep blue eyes and one of the prettiest little mouths in the world, and so bright and winning. She reminds me of an older little girl far away whose own little one I wish she was.

I was talking with her to-day and asked her if she could spell words. "Oh yes," said she, but, as I have learned, she is only about three years old.

I did not suppose she was very great in that line, so I asked her to spell "cat," which she declined to do for the reason that there was so much noise in the room. As it really was quite still, you will see her little head works pretty quickly in inventing excuses, but she is always so cunning and sweet that everybody notices and makes much of her.

To-morrow begins the last week of August, and our time of parting is getting short. When September once sets in the few days intervening will soon roll away and we shall, I trust, once more look into each other's eyes.

The last few days have been intensely warm here, and I hope you have been more fortunate in temperature.

To-day I think one of the very warmest of this summer. Would you like to pass a couple of days or so at Saratoga in case I can manage it? I don't know yet whether we shall go there, but if we do and you would like it I shall try to think up a plan to bring it about. You know you will probably pass through Saratoga on your way home after September 10th. Saratoga will not be at its gayest, but you could get some idea of the place and know what it is like.

Perhaps it would not be best to speak of this little scheme to any of your friends, as some of them might take it in their heads to come down with you for a day. Think the matter over and let me know. I will write no more to-night, as there may be another letter from you in the office by the night's mail and I want to get it and acknowledge it in this.

———   August 23d.

As I hoped, dear, I have yours of the 20th, and also another dear letter written on the 15th, and for some reason delayed on the way. I have abandoned the writing room in disgust and gone to my own room to finish this letter. There was so much confusion down stairs and, as you will see, am writing with my water pen I wrote you about in my last.

It is no improvement on the old kind as you have to dip it into water just as often as you do the other kind into ink, and it sometimes refuses to make a mark.

You do not know, dearest, how happy the receipt of your letter makes me, so tender, so loving, so sweet. Life, as you say, is a dull, tame affair without some one to love, and to be so loved by you is more than I would have dared to hope or even could wish. My prayer is that we may each be spared to the other for long, long years.

The poems you send me are in many respects expressions of our feelings for each other, notably the longer one in the beautiful language which Byron so well knew how to use. More exquisite love poems than some he has written never were penned by mortal man. There is one, his "Dream," which is equal to anything ever composed and was his own actual experience. If you have never happened to see it, I will show it to you when we meet.

You speak, darling, of your recollections of February 10th.

These occasions are forever fixed in my mind as well and will remain there so long as life endures.

Let us say, as the new year's callers do: "Many happy returns of the day." Your story of the ill success of the Sunday-school reminds me of what occurred here a night or two ago. A lady gave recitations in the parlor with her little son, and although no charge was made for entrance, it was well understood that she was reading and reciting to maintain herself and children.

Her entertainment was very good and there was no lack of people in the room, but when the hat was passed round for contributions, what was chiefly heard was the chink of ten-cent pieces, which doesn't go very far towards supporting a family. If all the mean folks in this world were to be killed off, Alice, I am afraid there would be lots of room for those left.

I expect to sleep in Watkins Glen on Friday and shall not stop at Binghamton if it can be helped, now that there will be nothing there to stop for.

Fare thee well, dearest,

Robert.

Watkins Glen, N. J., August 26th.

I am writing this letter, dear Alice, Sunday evening, having sent you a short one yesterday acknowledging the receipt of your dear letter of Wednesday last, which I got yesterday immediately after my arrival here and just before the mail closed.

There is a convention of ministers at this hotel, some hailing from various parts of the country, for mutual consultation and also, I imagine, for recreation, and who appear to be having a good sort of a time. They rest and pray and sing and compare notes pretty much all the time.

They had a long meeting this afternoon which I attended and don't perceive that any harm has resulted.

They seem to be a pretty good set of fellows and quite a number of them have their wives with them and those that have not pretend they wish they had out of compliment to their absent spouses, I imagine. It costs nothing and looks well, you know.

We took a long walk up Watkins Glen this morning and found it a very pleasant excursion. It is a kind of gorge or chasm with immensely high walls on each side and just now only a little silvery stream of water at the very bottom, where it seems to have cut into the rock like a knife. The effect would be much improved if the supply of water was greater, which it doubtless is during the winter and spring, when, however, I don't think I should particularly care to come and see it.

There are two glens hereabout—the other some four miles distant, called the Havana Glen, which we are to ride over to-morrow and look at. Some years ago when I was here before, I recollect thinking the latter glen to be quite as pretty and interesting as the glen here, I shall send you a few views if I can find any which give one a good idea of the ravine and places of interest.

This place is a hard one to get a chance to write a letter in. There are now two ladies writing and gabbling, with much more of the last than the first.

We somewhat expected to stay here a week, but have concluded it will be too much and shall go Tuesday or Wednesday.

If your second letter has not reached me by the time I leave, I shall leave word with the Postmaster to forward it to me at Niagara Falls. You mention in your last that your mother is not feeling well and frets to go home, and I do not see where she can go, at least while you are away, except to Georgia's, and I should hardly think she would wish to go there, feeling as she does towards G's husband.

Write me what her notion is. You know when she left New York her intention was to remain in Canada. Where we shall go from Niagara I am sure I don't know, but will write you as soon as I do.

I don't want to go to Montreal and be within 90 miles of you without seeing you, as this would simply be an aggravation, and I am sure you would feel about it just as I do. I prefer to worry out the time farther away. We have had some talk of returning by the way of Saratoga and I have written you about what I would like to have you do, if we do. Of course, we should see and talk with each other if this happens. And you would see the place.

Still it may be not easy to manage, and I can't tell

exactly what will be best till we get there. So, after having your ideas on the subject I will do as seems upon the whole best and most judicious.

Write me a second letter to Niagara three days after your first one, and by that time I will let you know whether we shall be there long enough for you to write a third. The parsons are now swarming through the halls and making any quantity of noise, confusion, and I really don't know whether this letter is worth sending to you.

I hope my next, which will probably go from the Falls, will be better worth reading. I trust this letter will find your sweet self in perfect health and your mother also in the same happy condition, and wondering whether this bright, beautiful moonlight night, at ten o'clock a certain darling little girl I know is thinking of me or whether she is thinking of some one else or dreaming away the night fast asleep,

I remain, ever yours,

Robert.

Direct to Niagara Falls, New York. As a rule, dear, I think I would post my letters myself, unless it is not convenient to do so. You know there are many inquisitive people in the world, sometimes more so than we think.

Niagara Falls.
Wednesday evening, August 29th.
10.20 P. M.

We have just arrived at this place from Watkins Glen, my dear one, and got our supper, but I could not rest without sending you or rather writing you a few lines that will go off early in the morning in order that they may reach you by Saturday or Sunday. We were at Watkins Glen four days. The glen is all right, a great curiosity and well worth a visit, but the hotel at which we stopped is very poor, the food very badly cooked and everything so dirty, so much so as to take one's appetite away and give you a general disgust for everything there. As I have already written you, there was a convention of parsons there, collected together to discuss the bible and compare notes as to their understanding of it. They kept up their meetings morning, noon and night, praying, exhorting and spouting.

It was quite entertaining for a while, but began to grow tiresome. Among my pleasant recollections of the place will be the receipt of your three letters sent there, the second and third since I last wrote you, and which I now acknowledge the receipt of, and my getting them all was fortunate. I will tell you why. The first one was sent up to the mountain, why, I cannot say, for they had no business to send it anywhere out of the post-office.

I happened to look over the letters on reaching the hotel and found it awaiting me. This was good luck No. 1. If it had happened to be sent to any other hotel I never should have got it.

The second was delivered to me regularly, but the third which I thought you might have written I went for this morning before leaving and was told there were none. It struck me the young snip of a clerk did not half look, and so I stopped there about an hour after on my way to the depot and asked for a letter again.

There was another clerk there this time and he found and handed out No. 3. So you see it was only by a streak of luck and good management that I received them all. I was glad to hear that your young friend, W. F., has been so fortunate as to be promised the hand of a pretty and nice young girl and hope she will prove to be as good and sweet as he deserves, for I should judge from what you say of him that he is a very good young fellow and worthy of a real nice wife.

I don't think you would run any risk in introducing me to that very, very pretty young girl you spoke of with the mouth just like a cherry. You would find me proof against her charms. There is another mouth I know of that fills my eyes so completely that there is no room for a second one. I am sorry to hear of there being so many nice girls in Three Rivers and no unmarried gentlemen.

The girls are in mighty bad luck and should emigrate West where the men predominate. I hope the views sent you from the Gap will come safely. I sent yesterday from the Glen eleven more views of Watkins and Havana Glens. Havana Glen is in my opinion quite equal to it in beauty and attraction. Look at the views and see if you don't agree with me. I was going to send twelve, but wrote a little on one, and so had to keep it back, as ever so little writing subjects the whole package to letter postage and I sent these last open at one end as printed matter.

They will probably come among the newspapers. Let me know if they reach you in safety.

The one I did not send is the bridge you speak of between the hotel and dining-room. It is right over the chasm, and if I was going to be there to-morrow night I should surely be on it at precisely nine, thinking of you know who, and knowing she was thinking of me, which would double the pleasure of the thoughts. The lady with whom you are staying, Mrs. R., must, I am sure, be a lovely woman—so kind and thoughtful, always doing something to make you happy and to love her. Such friends are rare and cannot be too highly appreciated and cherished.

You say the little turtle is doing well—it is a great little living memento of 119. I wrote you the last alligator had departed this life. P. is evidently frisky and needs the presence of his wife. Your conduct towards him, my darling, in declining walks alone, is entirely right and as it should be. It is just not only to yourself but his wife. Do not do one single act while in Three Rivers, my dear one, that can ever be recollected or recalled against you hereafter, and I am sure you will not, and while I think of it I will suggest that you do not let him know just when you are going to return home, he might devise a plan to accompany you wholly or part way, and you do not want him.

After tea to-night I stopped for a moment out on the piazza of this house, which overhangs the Rapids, and as I watched the rushing of the mighty waters just before they make their great leap, how I wished your own sweet self was with me sharing the view.

Wishing is sometimes a very pleasant business, but it doesn't bring us those we love except through our imaginations. But this is very much better than not seeing them at all, is it not? But time passes and passes—the night is getting on towards morning, 11.30, and I think they want to put out the gas and shut up the room I am writing in. So good night and pleasant dreams to you. Write me on receipt of this, directing to Niagara Falls, New York. I may be here a week or more.

Robert.

Niagara, Sept. 1st.

I am this moment in receipt, my dear one, of your letter of August 29th, and snatch five minutes to answer it at once as the mail closes very soon and there is no mail on Sunday, to-morrow, and I know you will think it strange and wrong if no word of mine gets to you until Monday. The receipt of your sweet letter makes me very happy. You are so loving, so lovable, everything in it gave me pleasure. But what you say about poor Mollie! Poor girl! I am so sorry for her. I hope you have written her a good, long, sympathetic letter. We have been about somewhat, over to the Canada side and down to the Whirlpool Rapids and over to Goat Island, but yesterday it rained hard till afternoon. I shall send you some views from here. Have you received those I sent you from Watkins Glen?

There are two chatting young girls sitting right behind me as I write, and I am not sure some of their nonsense may not get into this epistle.

There are not many people here now, and they tell me the season has been very light.

The hotel is first rate, as it has been for years. A good many newly-married couples come here on their bridal tours, and you can tell as soon as you lay eyes on them, though they try hard to look indifferent and like old married folks.

This is a glorious day and we are going over to the Sister Islands, right in the wildest of the upper Rapids, where the water rages and tosses as it goes speeding past, being as beautiful a sight perhaps as the Falls themselves.

I am so glad to hear you are all now well and that your mother has quite recovered after such a siege, and I trust she may remain in good health.

I shall send you another letter on Monday, and you must consider this as a part of that sent ahead to prevent four long days from intervening before you hear again from me after the receipt of my last. Good bye, and God bless you, darling.

After Tuesday send letters to Saratoga Springs, New York.

Robert.

Niagara Falls, Sept. 6th.

I had just put my letters of this date in the office when your extra nice, long letter, or rather letters of Saturday and Sunday, came, and in the same curious manner that the one reached me at Watkins Glen I wrote you about. It was handed to me at this hotel as belonging to some of our party. How it happened to be delivered from the Post-office is one of those mysteries that "no fellow can find out," as Lord Dundreary says.

Friday morning, Sept. 7th. The writing of this letter was interrupted where it stops on the last page, and I resume this morning at Clifton Springs, where we arrived last night at 10.30 in a slow accommodation train and in the midst of a heavy rainstorm. We had to walk to the hotel, and it was just about as light as a dark closet, and on the whole we had rather the reverse of a pleasant entrance into the town. A very good supper, however, awaited us, having been ordered by telegraph from the Falls in advance, otherwise I think we should have had to go supperless to bed as we could not even fall back on an outside restaurant, as we did at Richmond and Columbia.

It is raining this morning and we are shut up in the house, and the day promises to be about a week long. You say, Willie F. paid you quite a compliment on your moonlight ride. He is a young gentleman of taste evidently, but I thought you wrote me he had lately become engaged, and if so, how happens it that he tells you if you will find him just such a girl as you are, he will come right down to New York and marry her?

How many girls is the young Mormon thinking of marrying, or has he already sickened of his first choice? I am afraid his present sweetheart ought to keep a pretty close lookout over him.

I do remember the little gift a certain person bought for a certain little girl at Niagara Falls long years ago, and how long it was kept and when given, and trust it may never be necessary to keep another as many weeks as that one was kept years.

You speak, dear, of the weather. Pretty much all the time we were at the Falls cold weather was the rule. Some days it was very chilly and we began to talk of taking our winter walks and winter views of the sights.

September seems to have come in with a regular autumnal smash, but I dare say we shall have quite a spell of warm weather a little later on.

Your idea of the two Glens is like mine. I think Havana upon the whole is the handsomest, but would be quite contented to be showing my friend the wonderful places in either one this morning with a little less rain.

The Council Chamber is one of the very finest views in the Havana—at once beautiful and impressive. The sweet little pen picture you draw of the lady and gentleman has struck my fancy greatly.

Is it struck out of your imagination or drawn from the stores of your memory? You shall tell me when we meet, if from memory of an actual experience. What a happy fellow he must have been! But, alas, such happiness is not in store for all. Lightning does not strike a man very often. I guess you begin to wonder at getting this long letter from one who wrote you the other day that no more letters would probably be written, but if you will forgive me this time I promise not to offend again unless something important happens, and really I could not help writing after getting your third welcome long letter already alluded to. We shall not remain here after Monday, but shall go about half way home and stop over for a day, reaching New York on Wednesday for dinner. The springs here are sulphur springs, quite strong I should judge from what I hear. There is a hotel here which is also kept as a sort of water cure, an old established affair, and doing an excellent business winter and summer. We are not where there are so many invalids.

The house we stop at is used as a young ladies' school nine months in the year, and we have to vacate Monday anyhow, as it is wanted for school preparations.

In my last two letters I wrote you fully in regard to your return, so will not now again repeat.

I expect to get your Saratoga letter if you wrote me there and one other while here, and shall have them sent after me if not arriving in time. I have spoken in previous letters of your leaving Montreal by the Delaware and Hudson railroad Friday morning, because I understand you cannot come the other way (the way you went) in the morning. Of course, if you find you can come the old way and can reach New York at the same time in the evening by the Hudson River R.R., you can do so if you prefer it, but don't run any risk of detention or not making connections. And now, dearest, I will again bid you good bye till we meet, which God grant may be in safety, good health and as we have arranged in time.

R.

ONE YEAR LATER.

August 15th.
Monday afternoon.

Yours is received, and I am very glad to know you are all right and well. I hope you will continue to like your new room better than the old one.

Do not undertake the little trip you speak of with A. There are reasons why it would not be advisable, and if Mrs. B. won't go this week, let it sleep till next or some succeeding week. Thursday of next week I hope to see you in New York and the time will soon slip away.

Come down on that day if you can. Nobody could be happier than I to see you before if circumstances favored it, as you well know. But as it is, my friend must be brave and patient.

Robert.

I have less than thirty minutes to reach the train, have been so busy.

Tuesday, August 16th.

You can hardly realize, my darling, how disappointed I was this morning, when, as the train rolled up to Katonah, your loved face was not to be seen.

I was in the parlor car, keeping a seat for you, and at once began to imagine all sorts of things had happened—that you were sick or had been run away with by a horse and thrown out of the buggy, or that A. was sick. On reaching New York, however, I at once went to my office, and there your two letters awaited me. I do not know that you did quite wisely in going to a strange place alone, even with Mrs. H.'s introduction without any talk with your friend on the matter.

It seems to me, my dearest one, that the better plan would have been when you concluded not to come home just yet, to have remained at Mrs. B.'s a few days longer and come down to the city to-day with me; then we could have considered the matter of changing to Waccabuc, and I should have been saved my disappointment in coming to the city expressly to see you. My sweet girl should remember that she is very precious to her friend, and when he has set his heart on seeing her, he does not like to have her fail him, nor to make new moves and changes without counselling with him, because he wishes to protect her so far as he possibly can from all annoyances or harm, and reasons for and against a new move sometimes might occur to him that would not to her. But the thing is now done, and I hope will turn out all right, and we shall have no cause to regret it. Come down to New York, dearest, on the 9.12 train, Thursday. Take the parlor car at Goldens Bridge, and I will join you as soon as I can. If you cannot well leave A., bring him with you.

Ever only yours,
Robert.

New York, Sept. 6th.

My dear Alice:—

I cannot get away on Saturday, but expect to be able to do so on Thursday next. Will leave New York on the first morning train and hope to stay at Waccabuc till Wednesday or Thursday. I trust the rainy weather has not made you home sick.

After all this storm we ought to have some weeks of splendid weather. I suppose you had a regular deluge the day after you went up.

I expect to find you in fine rowing trim and that all I shall have to do on that boat excursion to come off, will be to sit in the stern and steer. I hope you are well and happy.

God bless you,

Robert.

THREE YEARS LATER.

New York, August 29th.

And here I am this Thursday evening, sitting quietly at home thinking of a little girl away up in the country, who by this time, 9.30 P.M., is perhaps peacefully sleeping in her little bed dreaming it may be of him who is tracing these lines. If this be so, I can only wish that her dream-thoughts may be as sweet and pleasant of him as his waking ones are at this moment of her.

I came down Monday afternoon, reaching New York at 9.20 P.M. all right. The next morning I paid a visit to the little house. It is right there, just as it was left—even to the burning gas in the little dressing-room on the second story which I put out just to be able to say I was of some service there.

But very little dust had accumulated, and in fact, I think, you will go back into it about the 10th of September and find everything in a very satisfactory condition. I had some trouble in opening the outer door, but finally found the thin key went in too far, and by pulling it back a little, could turn the latch without difficulty. I mention this to save you any bother in case I forget to speak of it when I see you. I went Tuesday evening to the new Concert Hall at corner of Broadway and Forty-first street. It is very handsome and spacious, and the music was very good, and so was the ventilation—too good, for I got what I did not go for—a cold in the head and have been sneezing ever since, occasionally, nothing serious but still not altogether agreeable.

Went to Coney Island last evening, or rather in the afternoon. The usual multitude of people were there, splendid music and fine sea breezes. I ate steamed clams at the Brighton Pavilion and sat at the next table and opposite to a party you know—a gentleman who was taking his supper with another gentleman. Will tell you more about it when we meet. I have had lots to do day times and shall not be able to get to Milton this time, and I am afraid shall not even get to Morristown, though I am expected. I shall return to Saratoga Saturday, Divine Providence permitting. Busy though I have been, I have not been so busy but that I looked over my treasures yesterday afternoon, among other things looked long at a little golden curl or lock cut long ago from the head of one whose heart is still gold and whose love is more precious than gold to me.

The little ringlet is beautifully bright and lustrous, and the little head on which it grew must have been wonderfully lovely and sunshiny. I hope your teeth have not troubled you lately and that you and little A. have both been quite well. The city up-town is as quiet as a country churchyard. Almost everybody is away, and most of those who are here are growling because they can't get away. Did you go to Luzerne as you talked of and did you enjoy the excursion?

I was weighed at Coney Island and am 162 pounds avoirdupois. Pretty good for me. You must not let me get ahead of you. Come down to Saratoga on Tuesday, you will find one there glad to see you. Till then good bye and good night.

Ever yours,
Robert.

MY LITTLE GIRL, YOU KNOW.

> She is very dear to me,
> Dear as anything can be,
> Here on earth.

Around my poor old heart,
With a simple childish art,
　　Almost from birth,
She has wound a silken chain
That has strangled many a pain—
　　My little girl, you know.

She is winsome, she is gay,
In her own peculiar way;
　　And she knows
How to play upon my heart.
Many a biting, bitter smart
　　Born of woes
Too deep for mortal ken
She has banished now and then—
　　My little girl, you know.

She's coquettish in her ways;
And her roguish look betrays
　　A wondrous art,
That can drive dull care away,
Send a warm sunshiny ray
　　Around my heart;
Whilst her magical sweet voice
Makes my weary heart rejoice—
　　My little girl, you know.

Hers a face of daintiest mold,
Where a poet may behold,
　　With rapt surprise,
A type of beauty rare,
And her sunny, golden hair—
　　Sparkling eyes—
Work a rapture of delight,
Full of sweetness, full of light—
　　My little girl, you know.

Every moment, every hour,
With her winsome winning power
　　She displays
Such a wealth of sweet caress,
Such a power to win and bless,
　　Beyond praise,
That I find a rare delight
In her presence day and night—
　　My little girl, you know.

Earth has many a bitter cup
From whose dregs we sorrow sup,
   O'er and o'er,
But in her I find a peace
Of all sorrow the surcease,
   Never found before,
Yes, she's very dear to me,
Dear as anything can be—
   My little girl, you know.

ONE YEAR LATER.

New York, August 9th.

I am just favored, Alice, with your letter from Toronto, and am happy to hear that you had a pleasant time in Niagara. I sent you a letter there which you no doubt got on your return from Toronto, although in your last note from Niagara you advised me not to write until I heard from you.

As you are to start this morning for the Glen, this letter shall reach you very soon after you get there.

There is very little here that is new and interesting. The streets up-town are deserted and look as though the city had been emptied of its inhabitants. Down town the streets make a better show. I have not been away nor can I get away just yet. Was down last night to Coney Island, where it seemed quiet and dull. The hotels there miss the absentees from the city. Had a letter yesterday from A.

I am in hopes you will find Watkins Glen all that you anticipate and will not find yourselves very much in need of masculine attendance. Don't forget the drive over to and the walk up Havana Glen. Am glad to hear you are getting so fat. Stop just before you begin to grow pursy. Corpulent ladies are not pretty ladies. Have you heard from A., and is he all right? Let me know when you leave for Philadelphia and what day you will reach there. The weather here has continued delightful and I continue, thank God, to feel very well, and so it is not so much of a hardship to stay here and work.

I hope you will both get through your trip in good health and with only a pleasant experience to remember. Give my kind regards to Mrs. W.

Robert.

Wednesday night, January 20th.

Good fortune, good health, long life and all happiness to her whose eyes these first words first meet!

That she may never have less to be happy with and thankful for than now is the earnest hope of your friend

Robert.

Ocean Bluff Hotel.
Kennebunkport, Me., July 31st.

Dear Alice:—

I wrote you on Monday enclosing a check—a wedding present which I trust reached you safely. Have just received a line from you asking me to pay Tiffany & Co. for your wedding cards.

This I will do, and will you please consider it as part of the wedding gift.

With love. Your friend,

Robert.

A Personal Once Intended for Me.
In the New York Herald.

I dreamed of you the other night, my friend. You stood before me and as I approached to speak, gazing into your dear, bright face, a hideous creature rose between us in a black cloud, shutting you out from view. Her picture is burned into my memory. She was a fat, squatty damsel, about four feet high, with one great squinting green eye, with a red edge like a Lima bean

cut in Malachite and set in coral. Her hair was the color of the setting sun or the rising moon and flowed like a bunch of radishes or young beats down her downy neck. Her nose was like a dab of soft putty thrown against a door and her mouth resembled a hole in a kid glove, bursting from overtightness or a weather crack in a white oak log or a ragged edge break in a little boy's trousers. Her teeth stood along zigzag in that mouth at intervals like a line of antique fence posts. Her cheeks, owing to early misfortune in the small pox line, looked like twin buckwheat cakes in their first griddle agony or two rows of honeycomb tripe, with ears straining every nerve to leave their parent head and a complexion like a New Jersey road in a dry time or a pile of pale bricks or a Boston squash, a waist fully five feet round and a form taller when she lies down than when she stands up. Such was the aspect of this lovely being as fixing that fearful eye upon me and with a countenance ashen with fury and jealousy she shrieked out to my intense relief: I hate you. Had she loved me, my funeral would have occurred the second day afterwards. She vanished behind a roseate cloud which slowly fading away into a silvery mist revealed your own beautiful self, my friend. Taking my hand between your own, you uttered these memorable and golden words: "I confide in you." Let us ever be friends.
B.

Alice!

My beautiful and real heart's love—I cannot give you a name that will commence to express my great love for you. I love you from the bottom of my heart, my soul responds to thy sweet spirit as doth the harp to the fingers of the maiden. I love you and think of you in the busy hours of day, in the stillness of the night. You are my sun. You have seen the flowers turn towards the sun. The little birds sing and dance at its coming. The running brook sparkles under its bright glance; all nature indeed rejoices and grows glad; even the falling rain drops will form an arch of radiant beauty across the sky at its coming. Your presence is more to me even than the sun is to all these. How beautiful your face, how brilliant your eyes, how airy your carriage is to me. Your voice is to me like ringing of sweet bells. You may think this a fancy picture. But I tell you, it does not picture my love for you. No words wealthy enough to express my love for you. I adore you and worship you. Were I dying, I could die happy were you near to comfort me, to kiss me, to say you love me. I pray for you every night, the sweet word Alice is heard in every prayer I offer. I hope you will soon learn to pray, so you two can pray for me. I can never tire of you. Your voice is melody to my ear. In your dear presence my joy is unspeakable. You ask me, do I love you? and this is my answer: No word to offend has ever passed my lips, how could you? How could you think of it? Recall my words and you will remember and be satisfied. But this is explained. Don't speak hastily, weigh well your words for they sink deep into my soul. What is earth without the sun? All darkness, gloom and death. Always remember you are my sun, my light, my joy; without you, I, too, would be in darkness and gloom.

God bless you,
Ollie.

Light of my soul, Alice!

A bird sings to me to-night, my heart leaps with joy, I feel like a prisoner just escaped from a pent-up and narrow cell, now out in the broad earth, fresh air and sweet flowers. Great fields filled with daisies and wild flowers, tufts of living green orchards and great oaks, a stream runs babbling along on its gleeful way to the ocean. Birds of elegant plumage singing the sweetest carols, filling the air with notes which, ascending up to heaven, cause joy among the angels. This expresses but faintly the feeling of my soul to-night.

What a happy day it has been. Although up very late last night, or I should say not getting to sleep until the small hours of morning, yet I feel as fresh as if from a long sleep—my mind as clear as crystal, my heart full of love. I have found a gem of great price, a jewel of sparkling beauty.

Her breath is as the perfume of roses—her voice is music to my ear—her soul looks out to me through the windows of her bright eyes—her smile is my sunshine, my rainbow of light and promise. She smiled on me and I was happy. To-day earth was a heaven, I could have died in her presence happy. How I adore thee! Oh, cast out all fear, love me with all thy power, for no woman was ever loved by man more than I love thee. Heaven bless and protect thee and save thee from all harm. May thy guardian angel ever be on the watch to protect thee. Long life and happiness be thy lot and when thou departest this life, may a cloud of angels take thee straight to the throne of God. There may we meet and never know any more sorrow and forever lead lives of joy and gladness. You say leave me. I thought of the root of the tree that sometimes winds around a stone, throwing tendril after tendril until at last the stone cannot be seen—all is roots and tendrils. Imagine the tree looking down and saying to the helpless stone, leave me. You are the tree, my heart is the stone; how can I leave you? The words pierce my very soul.

Good night,
Ollie.

New York.

My dear Mrs. Hutton:—

I wonder who will get the first letter—about time I began to write anyway. The reason why I am so tardy in letting you know that I am just feeling elegant is, because I have been what they vulgarly call humming, but properly speaking, enjoying the beautiful evenings and lovely weather in general. Oh, this has been a bad week thus far for staying at home. You know where I was Monday evening—Tuesday night 12.30 A. M.—To-night, well, cannot say as yet. It is now 11.30 A.M., and at 12 my colleague and myself are going to start out on a little touring expedition, going to Brooklyn and there take a train and run up to some beach. Do not know yet where. Dr. F. called on me Monday afternoon and I am going to see him Saturday evening. Dr. J. wrote me a note asking me to call; hardly think I shall have time to call there this week. Will go to a party on Thirty-fourth street to-morrow evening. I am feeling splendid and am in prime condition. This weather is just bringing me back to base-ball days as quickly as 5 or 6 o'clock can make me leave my bed. If I am down your way I shall come in and see you.

Lovingly yours,
Leon.

New York.

My dear Mrs. Hutton:—

    O! that I were what I should be,
      Then would I be what I am not,
    For what I am I must be,
      And what I should be I am not.

Yours received.

How glad I was to hear from you. From the very beginning your letters were a cheer to me. I feel that you have suffered a little disappointment caused by my delay in answering. Whenever this should happen, why, always think that the longer the interval of time the more is my mind taken up with pleasant thoughts of my dear loved one. I have been busy with one thing and another, looking over letters—unanswered letters six and eight weeks back. Now, I never used to do that, always responded promptly. But this must be in the eastern atmosphere—sea breeze, you know. They say eyes have a language; I rather begin to think that they have. For the first evening that I had the pleasure of meeting you this queer idea was brought to my mind. I know that there is a language of flowers, but as to a comparison to the language of eyes it would be like Latin and Greek. This cupid is an artful little fellow anyway. I know he is innocent but so reckless. I remain,

Most sincerely yours,
Leon.

New York.

My dear Mrs. Hutton:—

Did I answer your two letters from the 31st of last month? An epistle dated 31/1, I received yesterday at 7 P. M. Was just going out, so you see I was entertained on my way very pleasantly, indeed. You did not assuredly suffer a little disappointment caused by my delay in answering? It has been a long time since I have seen you. This won't do at all—will it? Not for my part, I assure you. I see you have had lots of company—that's nice? ? ? I've got to copy again. This friendship is for a short time only, and so, while it lasts, we might as well be friends and make the best of all—oh you—dear Mrs. Hutton. During the course of yesterday afternoon I went over to the lake and took a little skate. The ice was just lovely. To-day I was kept too busy to allow myself any time for pleasure. My evening I shall devote to answering letters which should have been answered long ago—to the romantic West—a country full of song and poetry. Shan't I come on Saturday evening? I sincerely hope to. You may expect me early, provided nothing interferes. Permit me to reverse a sentence in your letter—now it's not copying. I do not know how badly you want to see me, I only know how badly I want to see you.

Lovingly yours,
Leon.

Oh! my darling:—

Returned last night—Found your letter on my desk this morning—Left for Washington Tuesday night—Trip, including everything, very pleasant, my only regret being the limitation of time. Stopped off at Philadelphia for six hours. Professional business only, my love. How anxious I am to see you. Think of calling on my darling Saturday afternoon. However, I partly think I can call Sunday afternoon, but fear that your company will be taken up with visitors who call less frequently than a certain doctor does. So this week may pass without ever getting a glimpse at the very pleasant countenance and the lips I have so often kissed.

You're hoping that I am "well." Well, quite well, thank you; never felt better in my life. Oh, how could one feel different that can ever picture such a smiling face as I have met on the eve of December 26th?

What happy and pleasant remembrances, so cheering.

Ta, ta, my loved one.

Leon.

Friday, 5.05 P. M.

Alice, my dearest:—

Am delighted.

Since you have stated in your epistle that should you not receive a message by Saturday morning you would expect me Saturday evening.

I would like to say that you really cannot imagine how it cheers me even to grant you a few lines. I am almost certain that you will receive a note by Saturday morning and that it will not be a holograph which shall say—No, I cannot see my love Saturday evening.

My dear, expect me; I will try and be there by your appointed time. Will be kept very busy to-morrow, in fact, more so than to-day, and should I come a little late I do hope you will pardon me.

I must come, for you do not know how anxious I am to see you, dearest. On Sunday I am on duty and must stay in. Monday, Medical Society meeting. Tuesday I want to go to a dance. Wednesday, must call on Dr. S. Thursday, on Dr. H. Friday, duty again. Saturday I want to see—oh, you know who—oh, you sweetness. I am just looking at your picture, your photo; I like it very much, I just think it's splendid. The only way I can thank you for it is to present my photo to you.

Oh! I must see you to-morrow evening.

Next time I will write nicer. You will excuse me this time, my dear; they have called me twice.

Yours lovingly,
Leon.

My dearest and sweetest:—

Your delightful company I have longed for this evening. Friday seems so long to me, although I had seen my darling but yesterday. To think of our walk in the Park fills my heart with joy. Why, with what could it be filled otherwise? How beautiful and how charming you looked that morning! Can you imagine what thoughts flashed through my mind when I bid you good morning? I cannot recall a happier or pleasanter Sunday morning spent. How we were favored with such a delightful day as it was. What would Dickey Birdie say to a kiss in the Park? A splendid morning, a most pleasant pastime. Just think, in broad daylight, the lawn and waysides spotted with "blue" not violets but coats. What would this come to in a moonlight night? Did we care for anybody? No, nobody! I had about thirty minutes time yet when I left you at the L. Wish I had known it. Should I happen to be down town during any of the afternoons this week I shall not fail to call on you. With the assurance of my love for so dear and charming a companion I can offer no other final than

    My very best love,
            Leon.

         6/21, 5.20 P.M.

My darling Alice:—

Your very kind invitation to hand. I just wish I had a little daisy here. "Shall I or shall I not?" You have already wasted a theatre ticket on me. I do just despise any waste, no matter what it may be. So nicely and so frankly and flatly you refused my invitation to Brighton Beach I shall revenge myself by accepting your "dear" invitation to the theatre next Thursday. My darling, you are doing the superintending of this, so I shall just dance after your music, i. e., all what you do suits me. Oh! how bad you made me feel last Saturday evening. I was going to obliterate the messenger boy for not delivering the message in time, but I now think that I ought to obliterate myself for not keeping to time. Did you really know where I was going that evening, my dear? I will tell you when I see you. Yes, Dr. H. was kind enough to extent an invitation to supper to me. Regretted very much that I could not come, for I was in great hopes of going, but was compelled to send a messenger instead during the evening. The next morning Dr. H. told me that he had a very nice lady there for me. He also made mention of a certain Mrs. Hutton as my friend. What's up? But, dear, had I known that you would be there I would have made more certain arrangements some time ahead. Speak about moonlight on the Hudson—speak about fun on the Hudson (last Sunday's excursion). I am beginning to think there are some right good girls in the East. Dear, you have sent me two roses; what can or should they mean? Can I go by this every day flower talk? Well, I do not know whether I should ac--

cept your invitation. Yes, I guess I will. I will try and be with you for a day or two in the mountains, but shall not promise at present.

If at all convenient, would be pleased to call on you some afternoon before you leave for the mountains. You really do not know how I long to have a nice chat with you, my dear. If mountains and rivers were between us it would and might be a different thing, but since there are but two score and ten blocks between us it can and will not be a difficult matter.

Yours very sincerely,
Leon.

July 10th.

My darling Alice:—

Yours from the mountains at hand. Did you think I was ever going to answer?

Mountain silence made you think still more so, didn't it, dearest? Then another thing. I did not know how far you have to go to your Post-office, for I doubt very much the existence of mail carriers in gray uniforms. I mean those kind that get so readily accustomed to hieroglyphic and immediately suspect or even know from "whom" it is or might be.

Well, that mail man is about as far off as the writer of this letter is—as you say, one hundred and thirty miles, "kinder" far to think about, but when considered in reality it just takes about that distance to bring one where mosquitoes can't picnic about them. Darling, it has been hotter than beeswax in town.

I have been wishing and hoping that I may lay myself down under trees and near laughing waters and chat with you as in happy hours gone by.

I am in strong hopes that such hours may come and tell me to go and search for one whose arms have now and then encircled me at midnight's hours in lovers' sacred dreams among the woodlands of the mountains.

It must be a most pleasant search for this little

cottage embowered at the foot of a hill, the clematis twining about each window and white roses scenting the doorway and there find my darling Alice listening to the choir of happy birds and enjoying the happiest and most delightful mountain scenery.

How much I would like to spend this very evening with you, although I do not feel as I ought to.

I know your presence would make me feel much better.

A letter from home. Mamma has been very sick again for almost three weeks and has been growing worse those last couple of days. I almost feel like doing nothing. Your letter I must answer though. My mail has accumulated to such an extent that I expect to diminish my correspondence considerably. I just do wish they would quit writing. But I think it's all my fault—for whenever I am in good humor, i. e., writing humor, I sit down and write some four or five letters in one afternoon, and quite naturally get an answer sooner or later, asking all kinds of questions, and it just makes me tired. But that's the way women are.

There I am away off, ain't I?—one hundred and thirty miles, eh?

You say I should be as good as I possibly can. Why, certainly, darling Alice. Wonder if I'll come up? Am somewhat anxious to know myself. Dr. F. has got lots of time to freshen up now. I hope he will enjoy the mountains.

You wrote your letter on the fourth of July, dear. Don't think you could have done it had you been in the city.

The infernal din I ever heard on a day like that always made me feel like taking a train for some country where fire-crackers and guns were unknown.

This has been a very quiet day. I spent from four to six P.M. in Central Park to get tuned up by Cappa, but he only made me feel worse with pathetic music.

I really do not know how I am feeling to-night, but shall make a staunch effort to go to sleep.

Now, dear, good night. Supposing this was in the mountains, what a difference there would be.

Yours,

Leon.

My darling Alice:—

Your pleasant little note accompanied by those nice little mountain flowers to hand.

How very sorry did I feel that you could not hand them in person to me.

It appears to me an awfully long time since I saw you last. Will it really be October before I can see you again?

Is the weather really so cool that it will not permit you to look after "Home, sweet home," amidst the strong structures of a city, or will it really be as hot in the city as to compel me to drive up to the mountain cottage amidst song, poetry and solitude of nature?

How is it? "Safe?"

Dearest, your last letter was received and it made me feel real good. 'T—a makes me feel so anxious.

The little paper clipping contained in it reminds me that whenever I said or used to say "Rats" I was quoting Shakespeare; well, that's all right.

Since you left the city we have been having some nice thunder storms. I say nice, because I like thunder and lightning. Some people do not.

There is also some nice sea bathing. The hot weather kept me in salt water almost daily for three hours, still I don't taste salt, it keeps me fresh, though, and keeps me from getting spoiled. The other day it was pretty hot. I do not know exactly which day it was, for there were so many of them. Well, I thought I would go and get myself a white elephant at Coney Island. A colleague and myself started out in the afternoon with one of the "Iron" boats to look at that great resort. We looked just too larky for anything in our bathing suits.

I felt proud of mine, because it did not bag at the knees, but it bagged every other place. We faced the waves boldly, but my colleague always thought he had an anchor or something of the kind tied to him. Every time a real breaker came in it would play hide and seek in his spacious and voluble suit. This was quite puzzling. I was always afraid some big stone would get lodged in mine, so I was very careful to avoid the larger waves. After we had inhaled all the salt water and air then we thought we had sufficient to give us some thirst for that Coney Island beer. We left the surf and strolled along the sand.

Coney Island is a great place. This is only a part of my holiday enjoyment.

Last Sunday I went to Long Branch. Fortunately got caught in a storm, therefore had a nice time. At one time all on board gave up their hopes as the boat was about to be blown over on one side. The boat was scared very much, I think, for it creaked fearfully. Twenty-five hundred people were as white as white ghosts.

I felt all right, for I had one-half dozen life preservers. Often I was thinking of Alice in the mountains, how glad she would be if I would not drown this time.

Got home safe. Occasionally I go to the Polo Grounds. Let me know when you are coming home.

I remain as ever fresh,

Leon.

Sunday evening, 11 o'clock.

My dear Mrs. Hutton:—

A nice time to write, is it not? I want to see you and I cannot, for you will have some company. Now, when you begin to write—a week away, seven days, seven nights—why, you make me feel as if it was awfully long since I've seen you. Do you really know how badly I want to see you??

From the contents of your epistle received Saturday I see that you were on the ice again. How very sorry I felt that I could not have been with you upon the rims of steel.

I was over about three o'clock in the afternoon, but only found a deserted pond, the ice partly covered with water, and marks upon the ice showed that but a short time previous to my coming skaters had been upon the pond.

I think I saw a big semi-circle cut deep in the ice (similar to a Dutch roll) made by your skate.

Mrs. Hutton, I will probably be kept quite busy the first part of this week, so if your leisure will come in about Thursday or some other day following, then I would be almost certain that I would not disappoint you, for I know if I do the disappointment will be as much to me as to you—if not more.

Regarding my photo I will keep my promise and fulfill it as soon as the photographer gets through with me. At present you can have my life size.

And the flowers that bloom in the spring have nothing to do with the case.

Yours very truly,

Leon.

My dear friend, Mrs. Hutton:—

Nearly all day, excepting the time I spent with the sick, I have been in my room resting either in the easy chair or on my couch, thinking about the evening spent in Fairy Land. Like Wagner, so will I say to myself, "It was but a dream." Still I am thinking about the probability of such precious dreams. Is it possible? Can it be possible? and will it be possible? Well, I should say so. How pleasant it was that we both should dream the same dream. Now dreams will come true sometimes. Will this come to be true? This is what frequented my mind so very much as I hurried out into the cold dark night deeply impressed with Fairy Land. It was about one o'clock when I got home. Feeling somewhat tired, I immediately went to bed, and in a very short time fell into a profound sleep. Those dreams, those dreams!

Next morning when I awoke, 9.10 A.M., I lay dawdling in bed for about half an hour longer. Did I think of you? Wish I had had some one to tell them about Fairy Land.

It is raining this evening. Rain is not half as charming as snow. Everything seems to be tinged with a sense of melancholy—not I, though—oh! no, that could never be if I tried. Wonder what you are doing this evening? I wish I could talk to you. I've been consuming about one and a half packages of cigarettes. After I have given you a kiss and embrace per letter, I shall hurriedly look through the wards and then go to bed.

Was trying to read to-day; read a line about four times and then did not know what it was about.

Believe me to be yours,
Most sincerely,
Leon.

28/3.

Oh! My darling!

How very charming it is to receive so kind a message from a loved one asking to call and take tea "en compagnie." I am only too glad to join you at tea, my darling, but if it can be to-morrow evening I could not state with any certainty. So do not be disappointed if I should fail to put in an appearance. Will try very hard, for I should be pleased to meet your company also. This is the reason. Two of my colleagues, as a rule, go bowling Tuesday evenings. I was to stay home to-day, but having received a letter from Dr. C., an old college chum of mine, stating that he will be in New

York on Thursday and leave for Europe the following day, I had exchanged date with my colleague B., who was to stay home to-morrow night. So it happens that to-morrow eve will be a rather doubtful one for me, as it is very likely that I've got to stay at home. Nevertheless I will not give up hopes as you cannot imagine how anxious I am and have been to see my darling and have a good chat with her. Oh! had I only known it, would not have changed for anything in the world.

I've been down town ever since 11 A.M. It will be late before I return home, so I avail myself of the opportunity to acknowledge the receipt of your kind invitation. At present I cannot wish for a more pleasant hour than the one I expect in your delightful company. How nice it is to take tea with so dear a one. Oh! I do hope that I can come. Then I will come very early, too. Well, should I be deprived of the pleasure I will call and spend the evening this coming Thursday. Shall the call be about 5.30 or 6 P.M.?

My dear, excuse me, but you must have had an attack of this most horrible distress which so often afflicts women, the "blues." I might be mistaken, too.

With the assurance of an evening with you,

Yours very truly,

I remain lovingly,

Leon.

11/3.

My darling Alice:—

Just twenty-four hours ago—Ha—Ha—Ha—'tis you and me.

Our parting was not a Romeo-Juliet affair by any means. Didn't you give me the "cold shakes" though—excuse the expression.

You just did that too beautiful for anything. I can never forget it. To slightly look back and recall some of that "darkness" brings me in a state of astonishment. I am very much surprised at myself. When

I woke up this morning I was still angry with myself. A beastly headache was my only consolation. What brought me "off" that way I do not know, but I must say this, I cannot recollect ever having been in so provoking a mood since I had the pleasure of your delightful company. Now, Mrs. H., I do not wish nor do I hope that you look at it in a wrong light. It is all personal and confided to a single person—"myself." The question, "what shall I do with myself?" will probably explain it all. A time is before me that will probably knock all happiness for some time into a cocked hat. I must now settle down to real work—work that shall bring me my daily bread. Should I not be successful it will and must be a case of try, try again. Yes, I shall keep on ploughing till I get in the right furrow. When I shall succeed, will probably depend more upon luck than anything else. You made me feel pretty cheap this night. Anybody could have bought me for ten cents, I think. Will see you soon. Good bye.

Hastily, your

Leon.

My dear Mrs. Hutton:—

It is now 10.02 P.M. This day I passed in closing up shop. When I last bade you good bye it was with the promise of a small note for this morning. Up to now that note has not come. It's coming, though, as usual not in time. Had lots of time to attend to such sweet and delightful business yesterday, but owing to the wandering of my thoughts tinged with home sickness of considerable quantity, I was not able to get a clear thought the whole blessed day.

Happily to-day I received a telegram from my cousin in the afternoon asking me to accompany her to a Liederkranz entertainment, which I did, passing a most pleasant evening. Drank Pilsener beer till 1 A.M. This tuned me up in a different key, and to-day I feel much better. Will this note catch you out? Well, I hope not. Recalling our conversation I faintly recollect having heard the word Brooklyn. This was my last day of service. I do hope they will let me depart tomorrow. How I will rest to-night I do not know yet; nevertheless there's no cause for horrid dreams and lots of cause for very pleasant Fairy-land thoughts. My dear Mrs. Hutton, pardon me for the brevity of this note, I shall tell you more soon.

Yours affectionately,

Leon.

New York, 11/18.

My very dear Mrs. Hutton:—

Your most delightful invitation to hand this A.M. Although dated the 15th, my absence from the hospital accounts for the delayed response. My dear, you may expect me for tea, in fact, I shall try and be there as early as I can in the afternoon. I have several calls to make during P.M., but I shall cut them very short. Now, my darling, you must not weep as it would make me feel very, very bad. If you do, I fear I will be unable to control my cardiac feelings which I have so long held in check by most strenuous efforts.

If you do, I'll be a "goner," sure.

Now, do not do it. We must talk of the past and only take into consideration most vivid conversational matters—such as jumping off the Brooklyn bridge, and the like. Don't think of my departure. Why, confound it, tell me I must hustle, pack up and go, something like that, you know, anything that will make matters lively.

Expect me, my darling. Good bye.

With December kisses, your

Leon.

New York, 11/26.

Alice, my best beloved darling:—

At last time has fully come upon me. It is to me a painful realization to even think of the past. Although my hour of departure has almost come, yet I can hardly think that I am leaving New York and severing connections with a friend whose kind words have nestled in my heart. Yes, darling, to think of your kindness, of your pleasantries, is enough to make me feel heavy—very heavy. I have had several "partings," but to part with one is not like parting with another.

I feel sadder than sad and can hardly control myself, although I am compelled to smile to those around me. I would write no more, only I need but say I am up at the hospital to bid them good bye and take the dinner with them to which they have so kindly invited me. I wish for you to be as happy as ever. When we will meet again I cannot say. Mountains and hills divide us. I hope God spares us that we will again see each other. I must see you again. How the West will treat me I do not know; will occasionally write to you.

Now, my dearest, may God take you in his good care so that you may live long and be happy. Again I give you my hearty assurance that my sincere friendship for you could not have blossomed fuller.

A last kiss.—Good bye,

Your

Leon.

11/27.

Suspension Bridge, Niagara.

My darling Alice:—

It is raining pretty keenly, thus adding more to my gloom. Have been viewing the Falls, Rapids and Whirlpool ever since I arrived at this careworn-looking town, 9.20 A.M. While writing these lines I am waiting for my supper.

This is a hopeless place—no decent hotel or stop-off place here. Inquired at four different places for supper, but couldn't possibly get anything warm. Will leave to-night at 12.50. Thank God, supper has come—ham and eggs. Wish some one was here to sing that song to me. Made an attempt to eat, gave it up and declared my supper off—as hungry as ever. Indeed, a grand harmony with the lovely sight I had at the Falls. I'll content myself with cake till I get to Detroit, that via West Shore. I wanted to go that way. That our meeting there one pleasant summer afternoon was recalled I need not mention. My dearest, I left New York very much against my will and with strong hopes of coming back some day. To think of such a happy future has been and will be my only delight. There is no place like New York (excluding home for a little while). Will send these lines to you with so much feeling and liking for you as only you can know. May they find you in happier spirits and pleasanter mood than that of the sender. By George, since about two weeks I am not able to catch or hold a solid substantial thought. May be Western winds will fix me all right in the course of time.

    Yours very lovingly,

              Leon.

          Laclede Hotel, 12/19.

My darling Alice:—

  Wish I could just pour out my whole heart to you to-day—no, not only for to-day, but for the days that have passed since we met—days that were filled with the thought of what might have been. You see I am still addressing you as darling mine; although the days since my departure from such a loved one as Alice have already seemed to me like years, yet I have experienced moments that impressed me as though I had seen you just the evening before.

  Am now in the city to make some calls—hope to be through by the time you may receive these lines. Ever since I have been home notes kept coming in something like this: Have you returned?—do please call, etc. In some the words were slightly varied but the sense, of course, was the same. I do not know how they ever found out I was home, for I did not stop off at St. L. at all and went right through home. While home I have been wandering around. Mamma was very, very sick. Papa did not feel well when I left his company, and so it went day by day. I cannot express to you the happiness my presence brought back home. A wonderful improvement in Mamma. I wanted to address you long before this. Ere long you may expect a long letter, my dear. Several friends are waiting for me at the rotunda and they are getting very impatient.

With sincere love and many Western kisses,
I am your
Leon.

P.S.—This is my first note to New York since I left. I have not determined where I shall settle for practice. New York is very good as yet.

Ta, ta.

How merry a Xmas could I wish you, my darling? And as to the happy new year? If I were with you I know it would be a very happy one.

L.

Laclede

My darling Alice:—

Your very kind letter was forwarded to me and received yesterday. Do not at all intimate from this that I have "located," for I am still drifting, and in fact in St. L. Have come over almost a week ago with a seriousness more acute than in former times. Should I not be suited it will be a great disappointment to me. By George, everybody is advising me differently, some say, settle in this part of the city, some say I would be delighted with Kansas City, some say I would be delighted with some other place, and all such talk. Nevertheless, it makes it more exciting for me, as I intend to dwell upon my own judgment as much as possible. At the same time I care not to slight the experience of my elders. I am exceedingly well pleased with the neighborhood of Sidney and McMair avenues, and shall eventually determine upon that locality. Hope so; once settled I shall have a friend of mine work me a motto—A Rolling Stone Gathers No Moss—this motto shall hang in my office. Plague on that kind of business anyway. When I do settle I hope to keep right at it. My New York career has been here upon the books of my colleagues and I have never seen a more envious set of people than a set of doctors; still I was complimented on my success, my good luck, the splendid likeness in Dr. W. S.'s book, and all such things which would most generally go unnoticed in the East, to a surprising extent, so that I am thinking of keeping myself in a manner that may not reflect discredit on the East. But, bah, I am here, so that can hardly be worked to its full extent. Was to a banquet of the Alumni Medical College on Wednesday night; came very near not getting home at all.

It was a splendid old time affair again with my old Professors and fellow graduates. Last night I attended the commencement exercises of the same college. Sunday I expect to go home. Dear, the letter I promised to answer has not been answered yet. I will keep my promise and respond to everything I can. There are several points I would like to dwell upon. Your last letter on your way to Brooklyn was most assuredly written while you were in one of your very best moods. But the one previous to that—well, what of it? You must have been in love. Now, with the one previous to that, what was the matter with it?

Everything mingling in itself. From the standing offer to the twenty thousand dollar young man—from marriage to a lead pill—my goodness, you are almost as in a looking glass. Now, dear, if you get your nerves strung up that way, you may not get them strung down again, and that is bad.

I like everything excepting the lead pill, in fact, I never liked lead pills. Their effects are too exciting. Now, dear, do me the favor not to scare me in a similar way again. I made an attempt to answer those letters before leaving for St. Louis but it was the humor that compelled me to desist. In your second letter you use a peculiar phrase where you remark: "I do not know it all or else, etc." I do not remember your exact words anymore—the letter is at home in my desk. That phrase twisted me. You must hereafter feel better, Alice. My thoughts are brooding seriously upon the weeks in the future and compel me to desist my lady companion's company for an indefinite time. Hands off—leap year—hard times, such short sentences will enter one's head occasionally only to increase the dilemma. I am at times so very anxious to have a little chat with you that I generally resort to some active work to drive you from my mind.

A picture that frames most frequently in my mind is the one summer evening I saw you sitting by the window watching the light, pull down its curtain and pin it with a star. That evening you were dressed in a very light garment, nicely embroidered like lace. I never could see your face sweeter than it was that evening. I often thought that you looked lovely in the Langtry, but the lawn and lace suited me better. I am a strong advocate of simplicity. To me that evening was the happiest I spent in your very delightful company. You really looked queenly. This is the picture that is Inexpugnable from my memory.

To spend another such evening with you is now my only wish. I will close with the promise of writing soon. Do not be disappointed at the interval of time, dear; I have not been regulated yet.

With kisses and a cordial embrace,
    Yours most sincerely,
        Leon.

      At home, December 28th.

My best darling, Alice:—

 All day long my thoughts have been mingling with the falling snow flakes. It has been snowing quite heavily and I have been thinking rather heavily. Writing to you brings me almost back to my second home. To spend a day like this in your very pleasant company would be all I could wish. They were angelic times in the full sense of the word. Often have I longed but for one—no but for a few moments—Tiliani —1,100 miles—it is quite a distance, I assure you, and while still in New York where my letters and missives had but a couple of blocks to travel for their destination I would, if any interruption had prevented my writing to you, think, pshaw, I'll go and see Mrs. Hutton this eve and tell my darling in person. Quite different now, dearest. By Jove, but that's the way I have been feeling ever since I left my parental roof, or rather ever since I have been old enough. This makes me think that I ain't old enough yet, nevertheless you thought me an old timer—pardon the expression.

I have a glass of punch before me that I expect to consume while cordially thinking of you and picturing my darling to be an angel in Paradise. Dear, to be with you to-day—pshaw. I hope to see you again ere very, very long. When I have settled I can perhaps make a pretty close guess at the time. I must see you again and spend so happily a time such as we had some of the evenings I called. My darling, I think I ought to have called oftener. Yes, and why didn't I? I just think I was right mean sometimes. I occasionally do think of those out of the way moments, and they do make me feel awfully bad. I hope it is different with you—circumstances, thank God, were different, so that you may equalize those on your part. My darling, your letter I can only consider a rare pleasure. It added much to my holiday enjoyment. On New Year's day I will read it again. December 26th,—how well I remember that date. It will and can never be erased from my memory. As it now is it will continue to be as brilliant as some of the evenings we passed together; ever since I have been the happy recipient of this most delightful gift I have been meditating how I could ever reciprocate. I know, though, that there will be a time when I can fully reciprocate. Thanks and thanks and a fond embrace is all that I shall convey to you in this letter. This is not the letter I intended to write—that one will soon follow. There is such a push, go and have-some-fun in our home. Brother A. always wants to go skating and is bothering me all day, long so that I can hardly concentrate my thoughts. I have about two dozen invitations to new year's dinners, but I think I shall take my dinner at home. Central Park ice was not much good, still I enjoyed it a couple of times especially.

A most happy new year to you, with loving kisses, dearest.
Embraces from
Leon.

At home, January 20th,
8 P.M.

My best darling Alice:—

It snows.

> The beautiful snow is falling
> Upon river and woodland and wold,
> The trees bear spectral blossoms
> In the moonlight sombre and cold.

A penny for your thoughts. Yes, and I would give millions of them for your thoughts that have been thought ever since my darling expected a letter from one who left the East by mistake. Oh! promiser, why art thou a promiser? Oh! negligence, why dost thou intrude?

> It's still snowing, cries the Belle. Dear how lucky! and turns
> From her mirror to watch the flakes fall;
> Like the first rose of summer her dimpled cheek burns,
> While musing on sleigh rides and balls.

My darling:—

> If words
> Were birds
> And swiftly flew
> From tips
> To lips

Owned, dear, by you,
Would they
To-day
Be Doves
Of Love?
Yes!

I have before me two letters, one dated January 3d, and the other January (?), both from a party from whom I parted by mistake. These two kind and dear epistles ought to have been answered long, long ago. Yes, long, long, long ago. You very well know and I remember it quite well yet myself that I came out of the horn at the little end with my apologies which you claimed were manufactured, very much to my disappointment in success. So I shall be very careful in bringing before you my excuse this time. I will offer an excuse, you know I will, darling, and you know, too, that if nothing would have interfered, your kind epistles would have been answered to your wish. Your disappointment is my bitterest woe. I regret very much that it just happened as it did. So, after I had again read a few loving words on a separate sheet: "Write to me about once a week"—my, my, my—and this going on the third week—makes me feel as though I wanted to fall into an everlasting embrace to make up for lost time. Do not think this sarcasm in any sense, for I fear that while you may read this letter something of that nature may pass through your mind; so permit me to recall it to you before further injury is done. Darling mine is somewhat partial to that expression anyway, judging from happy past times.

Dear, I am as frank as a man can be, at least I think so. What I say I hope will not lead to any uneasiness as to its true meaning. You may believe me that had I been at home or at any place where I could have had access to a mail box, a response—one such as I always sent to you (from my heart) would have reached you in due time.

Guess where I was, dear? Out camping—not in

the Far West, nor in the deep of the mountains, but over in old Okla Bottom, some forty miles from home. Back into old times, not quite in the scenes of my childhood; but in the scene of advanced boyhood. For two weeks I have stood the frost and cold until driven out by blizzards, but this was only fun; still my comrades thought different. Two years ago I went to the same place with my same comrades, old-time schoolmates, to camp and enjoy the winter scenery (there is not much of it, nevertheless we make scenery to suit ourselves) and hunt. I mean do some real, genuine hunting, with real genuine guns, kill ducks, geese and turkeys. It is a pleasure, I assure you. How musical the whooping of those confounded owls (opera), how melodious the shrieking of raccoons (tragedy), and how harmonious the whistling of the northwestern winds blowing through the branches of the forest trees. Still it was nice. I enjoyed it, so did my dog. Were you ever lost in the woods at night, dear? I was. It's delightful, especially when you have strong hopes for sleeping all the night and are obliged to keep yourself awake by felling trees, logs and shrubs, to insure yourself against being frozen during the night. The moon and all the lakes looked too beautiful for anything that night, but the effect it had upon me was notably small. I used to look at the moon and recite poetry, but that night I excused myself. The owls were unusually lively. I kept firing at them whenever I had the slightest provocation. Their college yell did not recall Yale or Harvard. At about 5 o'clock in the morning I ran up against our tent, very much to my relief. That night I was looking for some music from the tingling brook, but the brook was frozen up and so was the tingling. I recollect of a slight tingle in my ear. It was the cold that did it, I think. Mamma used to tell me that whenever ears tingled somebody was thinking good of you. That might be so, but where is the somebody that would think good of me? Why I can hardly do the job myself. Well, that was my luck to get to camp. For three hours afterwards a blizzard of the most pronounced type came directly from the north. It kept us busy, for our tent went to pieces. Shovelling snow was a pleasure.

Of course, we had to have something to amuse us, so we kept shovelling out snow from our tent that we might get to our beds towards night. This blizzard brought along lots of ducks and our guns sounded all day long with results of a most killing nature. Oh, but cold! My! cold enough to freeze me out of a year's growth. It was the coldest camping I ever experienced. At times we would not dare go out for a short hunt for fear of being overtaken by a snow storm with unpleasant results, that is getting frozen to death. If we could not hunt, we could certainly eat, and as we gathered about the great fire toasting bacon at the end of long sticks, with ducks in the pan and smoking coffee right from the fire, we agreed that dining was one of our favorite occupations. While thus in camp we would prepare our wood for future use, and had almost succeeded in cutting down a small forest. There was nothing small about us. I think the woods must have been lighted up for miles around. It was glorious, with our feet to the fire and well wrapped up in blankets, with my dog by my side. But it was not so glorious to wake up in the night and be obliged to renew the fire with an entire tree that we might sleep in comfort. And it was not at all glorious to find at daybreak the fire out and frost all over our bedding. There were no flies on us. But some frosting, dear, worse than frontier life. For two weeks we enjoyed this. The night before we left it began to snow, and in the morning my friend who received the nomination as firemaker, through a game of freeze out, got up to enliven the fire and came in with a small tree saying it was cold. We all agreed with him after getting up and taking in the morning glance of the day. I came to the conclusion that it might rain ere long, and as a critic in the hunting Quarterly pronounced the day an elegant one for the purpose, we started out and bagged enough turkeys for twenty Thanksgiving and enough ducks for as many more Sunday dinners.

At about three P.M. we returned in a light drizzling rain. This rain changed hands with sleet occasionally and showed itself as good for all night. During the night we almost froze in our beds and in the morning —that was a very early morning, 4 A.M.—we were up and about, everything covered with snow and sleet, so that we could hardly find enough wood to cook a meal. We hinted strongly to each other to get up and go. But as we all liked the idea it came out slick enough, and we went, and why? Why, the river froze up right before our eyes and we could not find the axe lost in the snow. Now for the wagon to haul our truck; it was five miles off. Two of us went for it. Our next railroad station was fifteen miles off. This was the toughest of all my times. In snow, rain and cold—all acting in harmony upon those poor hunters—but we got there slightly frosted.

Home again. Your two letters greeted me and Mamma said, "Here are two letters that undoubtedly need answering, they came the day following your going out hunting." Other mail was in my drawer. How this happened is funny to me—Mamma holding these two letters as long as a player holding four aces alone. I inquired why she did not have those letters with my other mail, and here is what mamma said: "I went to the Post-office in person that day when these two letters came for you, and thinking they were letters you most wanted, I kept them, thinking should I be at all lucky they must be letters you cared for more than others. So I took care of them." I had to laugh and remarked that she was just right. Brother Owen usually tends to our mail, so this was just an exceptional time. Well, by 10 P.M. I was back home. Of course, I had lots to say, my dear. I think this my last camp out and shall now make only short hunts on rabbits besides going skating and sleighing.

I have lots of time for anything. There is an elegant track out here in the country, as fine a one as I have ever seen. Just now it has an icy covering. The snow of to-night will make it beautiful. Mamma told me that during my absence I had lots of invitations to old time country sleigh rides, i. e., start from one place, have a dance at another and the sleigh ride between. Do you see how, dearest? The river is frozen and looks like glass. I am going over to St. Louis to-morrow to get some toboggans. Will try and arrange a skating party on our river for next Thursday. Shall stop off at Thomasville and invite all my young friends fond of the poetry of nature. Oh! but for a moment, darling, could I only be in that sitting room before that grate fire but for a while just now.

Well, I expect this party to have a fine time. This town of ours is a very hospitable and jovial place and not at all a stranger to the guests to be invited. For many a time have they sought its surrounding woods for pleasure and only pleasure, happy to be remembered. This brings freshly to my mind Central Park. To now cling to your arm is my longing, skate or not skate. I think if I had those times over again I would be somewhat different. We could have had times more pleasant on the ice than we really did, oftener, anyway, I may say. That beautiful and poetical park. There went the beautiful month of May when you had promised me a walk that was never walked. You see, my darling, I have lots and lots of time to think. There is not a day passes that you do not appear to me in some way or form in my mind. And so the most pleasant pasts mingle with pasts whose moments were really less pleasant than they seemed to be. As I have been away from home half of my life and now returned, I expect to remain with papa and mamma for a short indefinite time yet and then make preparations for my future.

I will find enough occupation to utilize my time valuably, i. e., outside of entertaining Pa, assisting him in his practice and following my own enjoyments. Many times the question has been put to me since my return, how I could accustom myself to such quiescence after living in New York so long? That is very easily answered, and as far as that is concerned I have not accustomed myself to life in such a way that I cannot accustom myself very easily to any place where this current of life wafts me. I do not hope that it will at all impress you that I have made an attempt to support myself in medicine in St. Louis. I shall try, and if not successful shall vacate at short notice. Still I always entertained strong hopes and always "settle to move." I expect to visit New York occasionally. A happiness that now has possession of me is that whenever I shall come to New York I will make my home with my darling during my stay.

I do wonder if this is the long letter I wanted to write to you, I wonder whether I wrote you of the delightful time I had coming home. I do not remember. I will not tack it on now if I did not. Still one remark I shall again pass, that is what a charming companion I had from Hamilton (Canada) to Detroit. A stop over from 10 A.M. to 4 P.M. proved to be a very pleasant one and helped to drown some of my "blues." Another pretty companion cheered me on my way from Chicago to St. Louis. In this way my trip seemed to be dotted with little incidents of a happy and pleasant nature, wearing off some of the moroseness that had been hardening me. Before I will bid you good night, my darling, I wish to answer your kind letter more directly, for I have been crowding these sheets with so much backwoods talk that I fear it will be of little interest to you.

In my next letter I shall be a little more considerate and write you all about my old girls, how they received me, and how they like me, what they want me to do, and what they do not want me to do, the parties they are going to give me and all such truck—excuse me— there it is again, I did not mean that word, I meant "niceties." Well, you will not write until you hear from me—that is right. "Du heim"—now, that's regular Western talk, ain't it? Yes, I had to go out in the woods for two weeks to again accustom myself to this life and living. It's a fact, and if the next two years does not find me back in New York I must have struck a snap. I agree with you that our affairs were a failure. A merry Xmas to you. Yes, my dear, some and even many, very many, convey this, a most cordial wish to parties for whom their admiration has bloomed into an everlasting bloom—not by mere words alone, be they written or spoken.

I see from all the many beautiful presents you received that you could do without an "outsider," darling. So you are going or rather went to Trenton on the 10th of this month. A letter—my! this touched a very soft spot in me; it makes me feel as bad as though I were invited to a Liederkranz dance. I expect you were very much surprised not to find a letter on your return home; however, my darling, you need not forgive me for this time, the letter is coming. Probably this letter will come in time for the opening. Yes, I wish I could be there instead. Your letter was a most encouraging one to me, and I have been thinking much ever since I read it. Had you only hinted to me of your undertaking I know I must have changed my mind before I left, providing that mamma's health would have permitted my stay. You really do not know, dearest, how I felt when leaving New York. Often since have I been in the blues.

How I do wish to see your new tea gown. Keep it, dear, until I come. If too long for you, wear it for yourself but for nobody else, understand, and have a new one when I call. I know I shall like it, for you know my taste. That flush gown a la Langtry is as beautiful a gown as I have yet seen, and you looked very pretty in it. It sets your shape off in a most lovely way—When I think of that evening you were thus gowned.—(I know I made a mistake. I should have stayed until Xmas anyway.) Oh! white silk and lace —decollette—amethysts and sapphires! Oh, you angel, you, my dearest bijou, come and let me kiss you—I do miss you so, and more to-night while I write to you—oh, I want to see you so much. Your kindness I shall ever remember and have it stored away in my heart.

Now, good night, dear. Be good to yourself, and believe me to be with a fond embrace,

Your loving
Leon.

At home, February 11th.

My dear Alice:—

You receive so very many letters from me that I suspect a surprise on your part. As you again see by this Western looking sheet, I do manage to get one up to my very dear friend occasionally and tell her that occidental air has not turned too strong on me yet, although I always wish it would blow me up towards the East to stay. Whether I have changed some since I left New York I can hardly say with any certainty, but they tell me I have. As far as Western customs are concerned one will pick them up—en passant—and almost without knowing it, too. There is a lack of aristocracy in our Western cities, but as time passes and the association becomes more frequent a Western citizen may soon find himself aristocracized to the full extent. For instance, they will never catch cold in St. Louis on account of forgetting their canes—they don't carry any. Parade gloves are about as scarce as snow flakes in summer. Low-necked dresses are only worn on retiring (to sleep). I know of a certain gentleman who wore patent-leather shoes on the street only one time; after walking about two blocks even the wearer did not know that they were of patent leather. If some of these old fogy capitalists will die off, so that the money can get square and slick into the young chaps' hands, then we will get some nice Sunday streets. Yes, just as I said, one will again accustom himself to such oddities —the only difference is that it takes somewhat longer if he's been east for any length of time. Now, I've been there, and it's just like jumping off the East River bridge for me to exist in the great inland town—it's every one for himself, with the hope of getting there. If I am not mistaken, this is a second letter to my darling since Xmas. Now isn't that mean? When I left I felt as if I must write one every day to you—now, how is this? It is very nice to depart from a loved one with such a happy idea and retain it, too, and even nicer to inform my fair lady correspondent of it. Oh, I am always frank to my "Li Liani," knowing she will forgive me. Forgiving is the loveliest and the very pleasantest language of love. Did you turn a new leaf, Alice? If you did, why, turn it back. I thought I would turn one and did so, too, but turned it back again, ever since my last letter to you, that was when I came home from camping. I have been thinking myself that the way I do and must utilize my time is about as funny, agreeable and pleasant to me as I could wish under the circumstances. Could I transform this speckled programme into color it would give a grand variegation, and any one not used to it might suddenly die of color blindness. One day will find me at home doing all sorts of things I should not do, the next day I might be out in rural districts or in the woodland with the dogs and fowling piece. By the way, Alice, I have five splendid dogs. Would I trade with your dog? That dog of yours should get the prize for eating— pardon me—I do not at all dispute his beauty, grace and accomplishments, and am very much inclined to believe that he will get a prize. He is a beautiful animal. Well, to continue, some other day I must be out on the river rowing. If people could see me they could easily picture a rising Hanlon in me. Still I consider myself a strong oarsman. Other days will bring me to St. Louis, Belleville or some other surrounding country town. Not on business, but on pleasure. When at home I generally do most of the talking, and a little brother of mine does the most asking. He is a continual drag around me, and much of my negligence I owe to him. Although yet a young chap he is almost five years ahead of his time. It's quite a time since I had myself so taken up. Judging from the struggling temperature Winter's a kinder loosing his hold. All of the last week we had a slight touch of spring. Bill Nye most assuredly would have gotten out his straw hat. I had great times those days. Got out my saddle and made calls on rustic maidens. Quite a number graduated before the holidays and remained at home. Dearest, you would be surprised to see how "New York" draws. Just like candy and flies. People out here say they never knew of so many parties having taken place. I do not know of any time where moral quiescence teamed with so many gatherings of vivacious damsels— the very juice of nature, sweetened with the fragrance of woodland violets, strong, stout and rosy. Some, having been educated in the city seminaries, have lost nothing of their "home familiarity." In St. Louis it's quite different. I generally go over in the morning and return the same evening; otherwise I go over on professional business which generally keeps me three to four days. The difference between a city and country damsel in this part of the country is not very marked. The former is more reserved when out, but every bit as wild when in confidential company. Accomplishments and refinement predominate in the city lady, but when it comes to rosiness of complexion, etc., the country girl comes to the front smiling and oftentimes displays rows of pearls that place those of the delicate city mademoiselles in a shady repose. I very often make mention of this to some of my lady companions, but they do not approve of it at all and are always willing to change the subject. Rocky Mountain air or several weeks at the sea-shore does not influence city health to any considerable extent. I have always been in favor of spending childhood's days in a pure, beautiful country and after their termination to resort to a city, provided there is an object in it which would give said being in the city something to live for during the rest of his existence.

I know of a certain lady who grew stout in a comparatively short time. She not only grew more stout and more fleshy, but more beautiful. What a beautiful shape—straight as an arrow—those beautiful arms and those tiny feet! I very often wish and long for them. The pictures varied as they may have been all fresh in my memory. I wish I could kiss your sweet lips right now. I have just gotten out your dear epistles. I keep them stored away in the drawer for fear they might lead me off the track and make me think of things too pleasant to digest at present. Letters dated January 25th, and February 2d. Before I proceed to answer several of your interrogations permit me to say that with the epistle of February 2d, I received a most lovely photograph. Wonder what you were thinking about when you had the same taken. It is splendid! How well you look! I am so pleased with the attire for the occasion. Your visage is as lovely and kissable as ever—even more so. But, dear Alice, do you not think that the smile enters too much into a laugh and thus affects the eyes to a rather undesirable extent? In pictures they naturally will be smaller than in nature, strong smiles affect them more so; still, if the artist had but given you a pose slightly inclined, your head downward, the picture would have been much better, i. e., an improvement in its superb work would have been noticeable. I must now rush. They really worry the life out of me. Glad you feel tip top. Midsummer nights' dreams on the Hudson— a beautiful theme for a novel—won't you write one? I must confess I do not understand Dr. G.'s expression about the young M. D.'s being a drug on the market. Alice, you say you have lived longer than I. How much longer, pray, may I ask? Now the servants sleep down stairs. I really do regret that such a change did not take place in 18—. Darling, I must stop with the hope of concluding before long.

Thanking you most sincerely for your kind remembrance, I remain
Lovingly yours,
With a kiss and embrace,
Leon.

N.B.—About coming in May, permit me to make mention of that in my next letter. I want to see you as badly as probably you do me.—Ta, ta!
L.

At home, March 24th.
Afternoon at 1.25.

My angelic Alice:—

Come, gentle spring! ethereal mildness, come! It takes a "woman" to say that. Why? Simply because there is more poetry in this dreaming longing than it really deserves.

The last three days were wrapped in one continual spring shower. It is now raining a drizzling rain, just enough to keep me indoors, although a little water like this could not interfere with my outdoor doings. I had already booked Saturday afternoon a week previous, rain or shine, to be devoted as a conversational one between my very sincere friend Alice and myself. Of course, it's my time to talk now. I know you would not at all hesitate in saying: "Yes, it is, and it has been your time to talk for the week past." Oh, that I am—why am I to be so negligent. What a bad habit procrastination has become (I guess I'll quit it?). No, but dear, every time I begin to address you I go fishing around for an apology. Confound such a fellow, anyway. He knows he's doing wrong—two "wrongs" make a "right" (my motto). If at first you don't succeed (my coat of arms). But, Alice dear, I must tell you that ever since I left East my time down here has been a really speckled one. In delay I have been soothing myself by thinking that in your indulgence I will be forgiven. For the future I have been contenting myself with the hope that I may become more punctual. "Write once a week to me, dear," "wake me early, mother, dear, etc." It's so nice—well, then, why in the world don't you do it?

Ye softening dews, ye tender showers, descend! Spring poetry and winter romances are incomparable. This is my first letter to you in spring, dear. With it my friendly attachment comes to you as though it were but a fresh spring. All seems so fresh to me. How can I think 'tis almost four months since. Time is passing fast. It makes me pace the floor of my room at times. Still there is no reason for it. I am ready for the plunge at any time. I fear nothing, but still I am feeling as if somebody were holding me and keeping me where I now am. Yes, 'tis true. It's the place where I spent the days of my childhood's sunny days—home—and that is what holds me. To leave a home and to make a home (for yourself). They tell me I have time. Oh, yes, but how much? I enjoy notoriety. I love the city. Almost half of my time on this earth is past. I expect to do a great deal of hustling during the next half. How long it will take me to get there I do not know. Nevertheless I expect to keep the dust off me. I am feeling almost as gloomy as the day looks. Since my last note to you I have been remaining at home doing this and doing that. Have been kept quite busy assisting papa in his practice as this change of weather always keeps doctors more or less busy getting people's "air boxes" in good working order. Do not at all infer from this that I have settled. I am only relieving Pa of some work, that's all. For this reason I have not taken out any license as yet, for Ill's, a little brother of mine who was taken sick with diphtheria in December while attending St. Louis school, causing his dismissal from school for the rest of the season, utilizes considerable of my personal time. He is very anxious to get into the Polytechnic this September and thus draws upon me for knowledge. This is a great pleasure to me. I never had my faculty as a tutor judged, but know this much that it gives me pleasure to instruct and that my instructions are appreciated. This puts me in mind that while yet a "kid," the kids appointed me drawing and painting teacher. We would assemble at some boy's home, bring our paper, pencils and paints along, and draw whatever suited our taste. This was the way we spent our Sunday afternoons for over two years. I have tried to follow a programme by properly dividing my time, but can not do it. Who is to blame? I! Last Sunday played my first game of base ball this season. It was a model day and a model game. I felt as lithe as ever. The curves came as natural as ever. It was an enjoyable day and I wished for some of my "Deutsch" colleagues. I hardly ever play ball on Sunday, but when the day comes I am very much inclined to feel like the little boy who went fishing on Sunday and was met on his way home by the Parson who spoke to the little fellow, saying: "My dear little boy, are you not ashamed to go fishing on Sunday?" The little fellow, holding his fish up to the Parson's nose, replied: "Ashamed! Why, look at them!"

Now I feel very much like this little boy, dearest. I have been fishing this season already, caught an eel and a big catfish. With me it is not so much the fishing as it is the getting up and having a spin on the river. I must have something to pull me out of bed at 5 A. M., two dozen lines generally does it. I kept it up until overtaken with a snow storm, when I was compelled to discontinue for fear of getting snow bound. What a lovely time N. Y. had during its snow storm? I'd have liked to been there. Surely I would have been snow bound at No. ——. Do you know that a peculiar sensation passed over me when I read the day and time? I could not help feeling snow bound at No. ——. Now that would have been a picnic. Just imagine some of those times you told me to go, to hustle off, and then to find myself snow bound. Things like that didn't happen in 18—. I thank you, my dear, for the papers you have sent me—enjoyable reading, indeed. What thrilling experiences! How narrow the escapes—money no object. That snow man was great. I envied the party that danced all night on the Staten Island ferry boat. What a hint to the young man that said, "It's too late to go to sleep now," and the fairy chipped in, "besides, we have no place to sleep." The day of the blizzard I was in the woods looking for violets. I was disappointed and found but leaves. It was a warm sun and I went in my shirt sleeves. What a contrast! Here spring in its glory, there the scowling face of winter. This last expression will give New Yorkers who are not acquainted with the Far West an insight into how people are dealt with a little west of St. Louis. There was no monkeying about that blizzard. From the newspaper accounts one can see how ignorant these Eastern people were as to the danger of such snow storms. Why, such people would be frozen to death the first winter out here. That people are not accustomed to such "shows," can be seen by the description of the blizzard. They are only regarded as trivial affairs out here—hardly any mention made of them—light snow storms. I would not have been surprised if some of our Western folks would not have ventured out for a sleigh ride. Well, it has not been very long since our thermometer got disgusted and dropped down to freezing point. A nice little snowfall followed, covering everything excepting the ground which was too moist to retain snow any length of time. In the course of eight hours there was no more snow.

Looking at the woods from a distance another characteristic sign of spring may be observed—a mist of a greenish tinge marks the top of the woods—everything is budding. I noticed that more closely the other day when I chased half a dozen snipe.

Alice, how you do pun! Let me now devote a little time to answering your very kind epistles received at various dates.

Do I remember a nail in my shoe? How very well! Oh, had I but a nail in my shoe every time I was to leave your delightful company. Yes, a dozen or more of them. You once remarked that you really did not know why Doctor E. does not tire of you? If Doctor E.'s feelings are such as, or similar to, mine, it is then quite easy to say why. To me your company grew more interesting every time I called. It was one of my most consoling pleasures to but think of calling on you before long. While in your company I felt happy and surcharged with an excess of joy. With all those unpleasant and disagreeable happenings at the hospital, which, by the by, are unavoidable, your presence always made me feel as though I had experienced nothing but pleasure and gratification, when it had been just the contrary. Nevertheless I hope that this may not be an excuse for not calling four times in one week like a certain party did. Now, Alice, you remarked that this was more than I had ever done. To give you my frank response I must say that any man who does that without having any serious intentions has a monumental "gall." Still, if based upon encouragement, it can be considered nothing else but a compliment.

No, Alice dear, I never ran up my record to that height. I think if I desired, too, I could beat that record with ease. Dear, what did you do to that twenty-two year old lad that said, "I love you?" He is a sensible man so far as that is concerned, but as for giving all others up, I do not think him politic at all. Quite a surprise—always to be appreciated. I hope your new undertaking will not interfere with your hours of pleasure. Do like Commodore Perry, who, fatally wounded, cried out: "Don't give up the ship! Don't let yourselves be driven to the wall!" Standing offers and lead pills are uncomfortable. Never mind the latter—consider the former. Most undoubtedly you must have been slightly indisposed when you wrote that. Could I only have pressed a kiss on your lovely lips at that time.

I had a dream which was not all a dream—Byron said that. He was a splendid fellow. I dream quite frequently of you—happy dreams of having you by my side. Still I would like again to dream a dream and know it beforehand. Oh, I have hopes, great hopes, for the time to come. I shall prepare myself for it, and when it has come it will be "heavenly." I have a sheet before me without any date. From its contents I can readily guess at the date. Here is the clew: "You will get this letter just one year from the day that you had the chill." The night you gave me the ginger tea—eh! Three more letters, amongst them the last from March 12th, will be responded to some time in the near future.

Before I close permit me to state that your last epistle made me feel very happy. To see you would be a rare pleasure to me. How anxious for such a meeting I am, I can hardly express with words. Should you reach Chicago with some spare time for St. Louis during your trip, just inform me about what time you expect to be in the city, and I will be with my darling, but should I have located during the former part of April, I will of course let you know. Will try and get the photograph you asked for, dear, as soon as possible. My regards to A. Remember me to Mr. R. Regret very much not seeing him before I left the city.

With kisses and embraces,

I remain yours lovingly,

Leon.

Do not fail to come to St. Louis if you should go to Chicago. L.

St. Louis, April 22d.

My departed darling:—

9.30 A.M. Have returned to Hotel. Oh, what a change! Your sweet voice, music to me, I can no longer hear. Your lovely face and graceful figure have disappeared from the parlors. With you, my darling, all loveliness has vanished. I must leave as soon as possible, for staying longer would be suffering to me. How I feel I could not tell you, dear. Why does your presence charm me so? In your company I feel like an embodiment of happiness. How I do regret that my train did not leave at the same time yours did. I don't care to stay a second longer. I'll go and return to the Okla and there wait until the worst has blown over. I'm no good for another two weeks. Mr. R.'s kindness I can never forget. It was an act beyond any reciprocation. And, as I have said to you before, shall remember him in my prayers. Darling, you came so far to see me. How very nice! I love you more than ever. I shall most assuredly be up East to see you at my first opportunity. Until then I shall remain true, faithful and firm to you and only you. By this time you are out of sight of this city where the heart of a Western lad has been made joyous with the company of the dearest friend.

To love you, my darling, and love you dearly and earnestly is the happiness of your

Leon.

P.S.—May God keep you in his best care. Good bye! My head feels as though it were swimming.

Hastily but very fondly,

L

At home, May 1st.

In the beautiful month of May, etc. This month has been regarded by poets as the most beautiful—it will hardly be disputed by those who are non-poets. A year ago found me in active service far away from home. Often had I wished that this year would find me in the same city if not in the same place. I could hardly say that such a change was brought about in my past altogether, still I think that a more serious consideration of my future might have somewhat altered the present condition of affairs. Not at all regretting my very pleasant stay at home, I may go as far as to consider it a loss of time for me. This might materially have shortened my starving time and, as I know, has improved my very good health, not to mention the splendid time I spent in the fields, woods and on the rivers. It has already made me tired recalling the innumerable times that I wished myself back in the metropolis, yet every time I found some cause in which I could mingle consolation, in which I could drown my regrets for leaving.

The first of May was the fixed date when I expected to be equipped for my duties of life. I desire to be my own self, my own boss and my own everything. Have had enough of supervision—can't paint these fellows in the brightest colors. It is not at all pleasant to sometimes recall scenes and incidents of that nature. I do not care a continental how I am treated when superintending myself, provided they will not let me hold my breath too long. I can quite easily and very readily accustom myself to the customs and habits of the public, but I'll be ―――― if I am going to turn blue in my face, as my friend says, "rather take to sawing wood." Ere two weeks have passed I expect to be "out." My parents are not of French descent, so if nothing interferes I will not be detained any longer. I am not going so very far—can return at short notice and within an hour. This is not so terrible. Quite often has it been a question to me why I hadn't long ago been placed in a gilt-edged frame. From to-day on the law will protect its game. My dog Leondo will be very displeased, I know. Since at home he has been an early morning visitor to my sleeping apartment, looking after the interest of a day's sport. Seldom that he was disappointed, even if it was but a short hunt in the meadows for jack snipe. It's all over. He may go along to fish now. Brother T. was out to spend Sunday with us. He came Saturday night and returned Monday morning. Sunday afternoon a game of base ball was contested. The side I pitched for was defeated. I can only attribute the loss to myself and feel sorry for playing that afternoon. Why do they not let me alone when I do not care to play? T. was all smiles. The greater part of his time was spent in talking about a certain lady from New York, a late visitor to St. Louis. He is simply delighted. I do not know my brother's kissing abilities, but think they are every bit as good as those of his rivals (so I heard); still that New York kiss must have made him feel somewhat different. At least it made him quite talkative, something unusual with him, on the subject of ladies. There was no surprise expressed at all—this somewhat surprised me. I was often told that my backwardness was much to my disadvantage. Experience teaches, or better, makes perfect. Yes, my dear; T. spoke in a quite ardent tone of you. I really do not know what a longer stay in St. Louis might have accomplished. He told me those are the kind of women he likes. During the conversation he informed me that he had received a note from you. Something quite puzzling he found in that note. Now I could not guess what that could be and felt like Adelia Harrison, "as in hot water." Asking what it could be, he showed me the signature. T. did not know what to make of it, as I had always addressed you as "Miss," talked to him about you as "Miss," and in fact never let on as to a "Mrs." Your signatures on the back of your photos were those of an unmarried lady. Mr. R. addressed you as "Allie," of course the title for a Miss, and all such little things bearing on that prefix. T. furthermore told me that I knew all about you, asking at the same time who you meant by the name of A.—the name he had heard several times was A. In response I told T.

that I did not know enough about the party in question to answer his questions, and that the young man he was referring to was probably Mr. H.'s brother (this is an extract from one of your former letters to me when a lad of twenty asked you about your brother).

Now, my darling, I could never permit the thought to enter my head that you were ever a married lady. In spite of all this it would sometimes occur to me, while enjoying that delightful company of yours, my mind would suddenly dwell upon that subject, and I assure you I felt very much provoked. Really I do hate to write about all this, but I've got to. I do not care to be too evasive in my answers. "How do you address your envelopes?" was another of the many questions put to me regarding the Miss or Mrs. "Did you ever kiss Mrs. H.?" is another. If that "osculation" had taken place anywhere else excepting in my presence, I think such a question would never have been put to me. In response I said that I had given it up for a bad job long ago.

My dear Alice, I did not feel good at all yesterday afternoon. I lost that game and would have lost dozens of them on account of that "Miss" as a prefix. I told T., the best he could do was to make a direct inquiry and thus find out. At my request he will send you his photo at the earliest convenience. Brother thought he could get more satisfaction from me than he really did. Alice, dear, did you tell him that I had three of your photos? T. wanted to see these three photos. I showed him but two. Don't show the third to anybody on account of the writing on back. Even I, when looking at it, fail to read what is written there. Now, dear, you will plunge me in sure enough. I shall always tell the truth hereafter about my best girls. But I'll be switched if one can sometimes, and then for my part I would not care to sometimes. How glad I am that you made that remark regarding A. in your letter. It makes me feel real good, and I am going to stick to it. Will drop this subject now, it makes me feel worse than yesterday. Thinking of this and that pleasant time together in St. Louis, I can only compare to eating sugar and salt together. Pshaw! I am going to abbreviate this letter. Wanted to continue, but my mind is a regular cyclone. Little things like these bother me very much. My darling, in your indulgence you will excuse me, I know. Will write to you soon again, and then take your very nice letters into consideration. This will give me a chance to record them again—one of my pleasantest pastimes. Regret you are feeling so out of sorts. Darling mine, I want you to be very, very happy. Kiss me now, and I'll bid you adieu.

By, by! Ta, ta!

Yours lovingly,
L.

>Kiss me, kiss me quickly, love!
>Where the fragrant
>Vine and vagrant
>Winds your window ledge above.

My taste differs, and I would rather be kissed slowly than quickly. There is very little satisfaction in lightning kisses.

>It seems to me like kisses wasted—
>The pleasure's gone before you taste it.
>A greater joy, a sweeter bliss,
>Lies in the long and lingering kiss—
>The melting kiss, as we might say,
>That fairly takes your breath away.

Will you agree with me in this, my best beloved darling?

Your
Leon.

Saturday, 1 P.M.
By the river side.

Dearest and sweetest of friends, Alice, my darling:—

For you to be with me this afternoon would be a divine pleasure to me. The day is a typical May day—

all is smiles. At 11 A.M. I started out with my dog, a Gordon setter, and crawfish enough to last a week, and paper and crayons to amuse myself between times in sketching. I do long for you, my most precious, so much. I am enjoying everything that nature presents, strong imagination almost conquers me. I can almost believe that life makes dreams of us—not an event that passed between you and me has escaped my wandering thoughts. Oh, those romantic visions and pleasantly painful sensations that were once so true almost compel me to close my eyes in thought. Dear me, I am just dying for an embrace. This is as delicious a seclusion as I care to be in. All is sweet silence excepting the sobbing of the breeze among the trees and the vocal and multitudinous chorus of the birds. These are not at all in any way intrusive. Looking at the river one might suspect that it was one for beauty only, so placid and clear is this streamlet. Yonder stands my boat motionless as though it were afraid to move. No smoke from puffing steamboats blurs the sky at this calm spot. It looks like a deserted paradise which I would so love to inhabit with you this afternoon. All these pretty clumps of trees with their cooling shades and the clusters of flowers that fling their perfume with every passing breath of wind would be far nicer to me could I have you here with me, Alice dear; it is a longing from my heart. I expected to do considerable sketching, but I shan't. This lovely afternoon I shall devote to conversing with you. Just wish that I could always feel as I do now. Dearest, parting forever is a peculiar thing for any human being, how much more so for him whose life has consisted of beautiful plans and nearly everything but realized hopes! Longfellow must have had excellent reasons for saying: "Tell me not in mournful numbers, life is but an empty dream." Have I ever experienced a similarity? Well, no doubt I have.

Oh, you dear little birds, give me your lovely notes that they may gladden the heart of one! Oh, dear forest, give me but one of your thousand sunbeams that I may be happy! Oh, dearest Alice, give me but a kiss and I will forget my sorrows! My darling, I am not at all a poetical thinker. Wild violets flower by the river side and tell me no tale of modesty. Fishes flaunt and dash the water into ripples, but this does not promote dreaming and yet in those days when a kiss from your sweet lips was a question of a few hours I never thought that it once would become a question of time. Alice, you are a very dear woman; I love you, and as I might consider myself a big school boy, yet it does seem so feeble only to say that I kissed you. Ah, really time tinged with roseleaves and bright moonlight! I remember your lovely figure in a light dress early one summer evening as well as though I had seen it but a night previous. Do you recollect how I saw you afterwards, my dear, almost too good to think about. That dear room, only to have had a look at it while I was in New York. When I shall see you again my modesty shall be turned into sweet sincerity. A clock will not be forgotten that love may love on time. It will be angelic time. How I long for it you can but faintly imagine, dearest. To think about any time passed in New York and the time I might have passed to a period rather indefinite throws me into a state of extasy every time. If I did know how long I expected to stay, why did I not call to see you oftener and earlier? It is characteristic of me that I have almost come to allow professional matters to mar my pleasures to some extent.

But what can not a graceful figure and a face equally lovely as yours conquer at sight? Dear, you really do not know how often I left the hospital naturally feeling as though I ought to consult some of the different authors as to my cases on hand, and when in your delightful company all was divine. How happy I felt. The touch of your hand was enough to make me forget all that and think only about the lovely woman I was with. I never will forget your first kiss. It was angelic, indeed, a most happy recollection. I do not think an evening has passed nor a morning come since I pressed my by by upon your lips in New York that I have not passed away several minutes of my time thinking of you. You have become to my wandering thoughts my wandering love. Thus I wish I were an angel this afternoon. Darling Alice! In the letter prior to this you have undoubtedly observed that I failed with my initiatory address to you. It happened under peculiar circumstances. In a letter to me you signed yourself, "Yours religiously, Alice." Now, I wanted to address you as "my religious Alice," but became somewhat averse to it, though I thought I would consider it in the course of my writing and come to a conclusion at the close. Well, I had almost finished when an accident case came in (cut with a circular saw). I finished in a hurry, sealed the letter and handed it to my brother to mail. In the evening about 9 o'clock, while reading of Dr. R.'s expedition, I said to myself of a sudden: "Confound my head, I forgot that heading anyway," and felt like going to Hades. I assure you, my dear, I did not like it a bit. It just happened with a letter the contents of which were rather unpleasant. This made me feel as if I wanted to add to its unfinished tone—Do destroy that epistle, please, Alice.

In one of your letters, dear, you remarked that you were convinced of my being good. Well, I hope so, and that you have been for some time, although you expressed your doubts to me several times. You are wrong, darling. 'Tis strange but true regarding our St. Louis experience I think you acted very wise, i. e., I will now say that you have changed me, dearest; but let us not go to the devil, let's go to a base ball match. I remember that you were so interested in the national game. How nice of you to send me those papers. From them I have learned to throw a new ball called the jump ball. I can throw it quite successfully and will try it to-morrow when we play the Morris Club. I'll think of you and win. To think of base ball now and the time we little kids played turn-ball, the remotest ancestor of base ball, makes me smile at the nice old fun we had. There were about a dozen of us to start a game of ball. This was our fun in town, more base and less science. We would make our bats from old fence boards and buy a hard rubber ball. There was none of the foppishness of polished bats and comic opera costumes in those days. Turn-ball required a uniform, and the uniform generally bare feet, and the costumes were various. We had no grand stand, but the school fence answered the purpose well. We played with a bat like a paddle, and the striker ran around four bases, while the outsider fired the ball between him and the bases he was running towards. Thus we were crossed out on one count—or hit with the ball if the thrower was a good marksman, and the harder he was hit the more fun. First base was out, and so over the fence he would go. The umpire was a thing unknown, and points were settled by thrashing the other side. A decision thus arrived at was always satisfactory and there never was an appeal. My boyhood's sunny days—gone. Alice, dearest, this morning I received the present you spoke to me about at the Southern. I was wondering and accusing myself of several wrongs. Why you took the cup back to New York with you I cannot think. It is a magnificent piece of china, and to me it shall be a cup—id's quiver. Now I must row home after hooking and baiting my lines. I am catching fish in great style, having what the little boy calls lots of fun—two and three on one line, and they do pull. Well, homeward bound. By by, darling. Take the very best care of yourself.

With a kiss (oh, any amount of them) and an embrace from

Leon.

Oct. 11th.

My darling Alice:—

That deah boy o' yours received that dear letter. It took an October breeze to waft it thither all the way from the mountains. I am so glad it came. Say, Alice, I think you cruel—weren't a-going to write to me any more. Now, I like that. If you stop writing, I'll continue. There's a little park, not far from my office, and this little park is to me a thermometer. It just tells me how the woods now look, and I fancy that I can about judge how the woods which surround Alice look. The trees are nearly all stripped of their leaves—they looked naked. The nuts are ripe, the squirrels are gay. I haven't been home for so long I do not know how matters are out that way. My friend S—— was telling me the other day that he saw more of me while I was in New York. That's nice. Alice, dear, the U. S. do not consider me a citizen. I can't vote, the officials won't register me. This is rough! Twice registered—once in St. Louis and once in New York, and still no citizen! I am a Republican. Yesterday I was told by a gentleman that I had an honest face. I told him that I was a Republican. He thought so, too. I like the present President, don't object to him at all, but then, you know, if the ostrich—stork I mean to say—would drop a baby in the White House—if only Mrs. Frances Folsom Cleveland would get a baby—it looks so bad. Oh, he can't stay there any longer. I regret that I cannot swell the Republican majority by one. I could go back to New York and vote. At one time I did think seriously of doing so. Had I visited you on the 1st of this month I would feel pretty bad to-day again. You only allowed me ten days, you know. From your letter I judge that you are still building. Why are you enlarging your house there? I am now certain that you will remain a mountain sylph. At one time I was hoping that you again might wend your way to the city gayeties, etc. That part of your letter I would endorse most heartily—"you are still thinking and dreaming of me." Well, I am so glad. Such compliments I can always fully reciprocate with my warmest cordiality. An hour of all the happy hours to-day. Yes, right now would be my sunshine this dull day. To-day two years ago I left Philadelphia for New York. It was there where I passed such pleasant hours. Oh, such happiness! Let me close with a kiss and loving embrace for you

From, very truly,

Leon.

ONE YEAR LATER.

February 28th.

My dear friend Alice:—

Why such a silence? The echo of your last word to me has almost disappeared—so long has it been. My last note to you was from Ft. Worth, Texas. Upon my return to St. Louis (almost a week later) I was in hopes that I might find a cheering note from you. Why is it thus, Alice? What have I done? In your last letter you spoke to me of "forgive and forget." I am always very willing to forgive, but how can I ever forget? That would be almost out of the question, my dear. That you are still in the mountains I am not so very confident, nevertheless I will address this message there, to your mountain home. It happened to me some weeks ago that I dreamed you married a very wealthy business man of N. Y.—?

Such dreams do not come often to me. But dear, why do you not write to me any more? It worries me, for I do not know what to make of it. Do please, Alice, if you have changed your address and this should reach you, send it to me. I will always be glad to drop you a few lines if the intervals are a little lengthened. I expect to change my address soon. As to where I am still in the dark.

With a kiss, I remain,

Yours most sincerely,

Leon.

March 7th.

You know
There are moments when silence prolonged and unbroken,
More expressive may be than all words ever spoken;
It is when the heart has an instinct of what
In the heart of another is passing.

Dear Mrs. Hutton:—

Your long looked for letter came to my hands last night at 11 clock; at that time I had returned from a dinner and chess tournament at Dr. B.'s. It proved to be a harbinger. I am still provoked about that dream of mine. On the succeeding day I told T. of the same and in return he told me in broad smiles that he thought my dream would come true. I told him I wished it could. His smile now assumed larger dimensions, and I became emphatic, insisting upon an explanation for all such "grinning." Now, didn't he have easy smiling and lots of fun at my expense? Why did you do that, my dear friend? It seems to me that T. received the "news" about the same time I mailed my letter to you. He then of course told me all about it, after having kept me in a state of most anxious delay for over half an hour. So my very dear friend will join in wedlock soon? I was somewhat surprised at the news and felt again those indescribable sensations creep over me that robbed me of all my manliness when I bade my dear Alice adieu.

Why should I be surprised? I knew that such a long silence must be indicative of something. It gladdens me to know that you have chosen. Your taste I have always admired. Such charming women as you, my dear friend, do not remain unassociated very long. I hope you will be happy, very happy, and that nature will bestow upon you his precious gifts. His happiness will again bring you back to the city. Oh, New York, the place of my happiest hours spent. How I do love that city. It will not surprise you if I tell you that I might be back soon. I am determined to make that city my home, and shall as soon as I am able to leave St. Louis. Still I am meeting with considerable disapproval, especially from home. This too is what is preventing me, as I think it unjust to place myself so far away from a most dear circle under the present circumstances. I have reference to my dear father, who has not been enjoying very good health for some time past.

My friend, I am handicapped in almost all of my undertakings; something always seems to undermine my most valuable opportunities, coming to the surface at the least expected time. I am an unfortunate chap. I see it more and more every day, and the sooner I leave this city the better.

Have my very best wishes for your future, my very dear friend, and believe me to always be

A most sincere acquaintance,

Leon.

May 19th.

Mrs. Alice Hutton.

My very dear and esteemed friend:—

Several stray sunbeams peeping in through my car window found me wide awake this A.M. I say stray simply because the heavens were hanging full of heavy dark clouds, and the earth showed signs of having been visited by rain. Before I arrived in St. L., heavy rain drops began to fall, ceasing, however, within an hour. I came very near failing to reach the Y. depot in time last night owing to a delay immediately at the approach of the swing bridge. My springing tactics assisted me in getting there as the train was rolling out. Alighting on the last sleeper, I found my way into the chair car where I took up my abode for the night. Disposing of my shoes I fell back in a comfortable position and soon became enveloped in happy and unhappy thoughts. My sleep was disturbed at short intervals, so much so that I envied the party immediately in the rear of me who had been carried away in deep slumbers shortly after the train left Chicago. Thus I dozed and thought and grieved till I left the car at B. S. in St. L., when familiar objects and surroundings assisted me in crowding out some of my thoughts that seemed to have been chiseled into my brain. I am now back again, having once more filled my soul with a happiness that only Alice can arouse, and will probably start for home this evening where I shall finish all my necessaries preparatory to my departure at the end of this (next) week.

You will occasionally hear from me, my dear friend Alice; changing of your name will not prevent me from sending to you a line or two. After my arrival in St. L. I again longed for Chicago and thought to myself, why not stay one day longer—Sunday? But then—such feelings are always in possession of me. I had to go, another day would probably have again found me like a ship upon a high sea—with its rudder lost. I myself could feel that the time that has passed between our meetings has not found any change in me. My fondness—my esteem, may I say love? for you is the very same as it has been since I first had the pleasure of an introduction that unforgotten evening.

I have handed your letter to T. He seemed very much pleased and will write to you. T. has been very inquisitive, and I answered all of his questions as well as I could, and he of course says, as he always does when a point is not made quite clear to him—that he could have done better.

I will now excuse myself, and with my most cordial wishes for the best, remain a
    Very true friend,
          Leon.

         June 13th.
Mrs. Alice Hutton.
My very dear friend:—

This will be addressed to the mountains—to me but a mountain echo. I presume you will by this time have finished, and successfully, too, I hope, your business matters that called and detained you in Chicago. It, too, shall sail under the name by which I have so very pleasantly known you, though by this time I fear it is changed. Well, my dear friend, these are some of the ways of life, and I must forget those that have weighed upon me most heavily. My visit to Chicago has impressed me more than I thought or hoped it would, and although business consideration overcame the impulse, it remained but a question of time when they would pass off and leave me at the mercy of thoughts excited by a friend, the charm of whose grace and character, the nobility and loveliness of whose life, is enshrined in my heart and hallowed in my memory. During our acquaintance, which I dare say was not any too long when "circumstances" found it their duty to call me back whence I had come, you have been to me the synonym of goodness. I was once more a happy man when I could catch your expressive eye, and place my hand in yours with the words: I am indeed very glad to see you, my very dear friend, Mrs. Hutton.

If such a pleasure were only granted to me oftener! Let heavy sighs speak for themselves. I am stationed at B—, Cal., where I have my central office. From this point I am out on the lines of the B. R., in accordance with my profession, almost daily, going North, South, East and West. I am indeed very well pleased with the "fast" business. This city of B—— has some ten thousand inhabitants, is a most fashionable place both day and night and awfully independent. Nearly all of the society belles have had smiles for the stranger, but the stranger has not yet found himself inclined to return such compliments. This of course gives a somewhat "freshly" (excuse the slang, Alice) appearance to the town, not to say anything of the impression it makes. Amongst the faces there are some as pretty as a picture, or more naturally speaking, as a peach. In some respects the conduct of these fair ones can be excused, for I really think, to use the words of some one else, "they can't help it." It's a great social place, and everybody knows everybody. Half of the time I am away, and that suits me.

You will kindly accept my dearest regards, and believe me to always be

A most sincere friend,

Leon.

M., Sept. 26th.

Mr. Robinson.

My dear Sir:—

With these lines I expect to introduce to you myself, hoping that at some future day I may have the pleasure of meeting you in person. A card bearing your name together with that of Mrs. Alice Hutton, followed by the word "married," reached me some time during the middle of August. I regret that I could not extend to you my congratulations in person. I have had the pleasure of meeting Mrs. Hutton through the kindness of Dr. F. during my stay in New York, and must say that you have chosen a most noble woman for your wife. Some four weeks ago I was called to St. Louis and during my leisure time called on my brother. He procured a photograph from his desk and asked me if I recognized a certain party in the picture. I certainly did. Mr. Robinson, if not asking too much, would you care to present me with a like photograph? At present I could only reciprocate with my best thanks, but I assure you that when hymen bestows his happiness upon me I certainly shall remember you.

Trusting you will appreciate this in the spirit it is written, I remain,

With greatest respects to Mrs. Robinson,

Yours very truly,

Doctor B.

Friday, April 5th.

Mrs. Alice Hutton.

My esteemed friend:—

Please allow me to thank you for the kind notes you have since sent me. I was indeed pleased on receipt of every one, and more so on hearing of your safe arrival at home. Alice, dear, permit me to address you thus regardless of the prefix on your card. I have been thinking about you a good many times since I have had the pleasure of meeting your charming personality, knowing well I ought also to give up all thoughts of you as you remark, but I hope you do not mean it, Alice! I must recall our good bye. Why did you not favor me with a slight intimation before you kissed me? I would have enjoyed the touch of your lips so very much more. It was so sudden, "don't cher know?" but by the way, did not the doctor give you a talking to about it? What did you do it for anyhow? Alice, I am inclined to think that I ought to write to you quite differently, and I am certain my big brother would censure me of assuming this style of address. But I cannot otherwise, so forgive me, please—oh, yes, let me tell you. Last Saturday I took a trip home. I spent Sunday with the doctor and folks. Had a nice time fishing. Regretted very much we could not take Alice with us. Played ball, and the doctor pitched the ball during the game, and he pitched very well, although our side was defeated.

Now, Alice, I shall close as I have some business correspondence to attend to.

With hopes for an early opportunity when we can meet again, and in the mean time I shall trust you will not keep your word and let it be your last letter.

Sincerely,

Theodore.

Dear Alice:—

A pleasant good morning to you.

Here is my likeness. Accept it with my kindest regards. If you will kindly remember me with yours, I shall thank you for it.

I am longing for a glance at good Alice's features again. Your letter made me feel wonderfully good, cannot consider it a "Rip Van Winkle" letter—it counts. May I ask you what impresses you that I do not think very kindly of you? Why, the very idea, as I said before—you're a love. The doctor is in the city. I am writing these few lines to you at my desk and thinking of when I first met you right here. Would write more, but am too busy, Alice. Write to me again. Here is a kiss for you from

Theodore.

May.

Alice dear:—

You are at Chicago—that is very near, and yet so far. Any prospects of your striking St. Louis? I hope so. Am worrying to see you again. The doctor will hug and kiss you for me. Sorry I am so engaged, otherwise I would see you before you leave. However, I wish you all happiness, wish you long life and prosperity in your new venture. May the bird be blessed with a good husband.

Lovingly yours,

Theodore.

May 22d.

Alice, my dear:—

The pleasant news in your little note has made me happy and, believe me, I was so overcome with joy to think that I am to see Alice again that I could not sufficiently concentrate my thoughts to write you until now.

Cheerfully I will spend the time stated with you, regret only that the suspense is so long. How are you? Heard you were not looking as well as usually. I hope you are not worrying yourself. The doctor left for home Monday evening. I took him to the depot.

Well, Alice, I want you to get this to-morrow morning, so I must close with my best wishes to you. Write me again, Alice dear, and tell me when you are coming, the train and hour. The doctor intends leaving us in a few days for California.

Good night, dear,
Theodore.

7/1.

Alice, my dear:—

Got your note this A.M. Was overjoyed to know that you are so near me again. You know I had no idea where you have been for a long time, and now I want you to sit down to-morrow and write me a decent letter, telling me all about how you spent your time East, and where you have been, and where I can see you on the fourth. I intend going home to stay until the fifth. Heard from the doctor on the 23rd. I told him Alice was back, and it surprised him. Said he would be glad to see you again. Alice, dear, I am going to take a two weeks' vacation in August about the middle of the month, and I want you and want you badly to come out and go home with me and stay that long. Will you do it? I am dying to see you again. Am feeling much better than when I last saw you, and have been blaming myself ever since for leaving you to go to that one-horse town, Thomasville. How are you feeling? and are you still worrying? Alice, write to me often, and do not write so big, it takes up too much space and paper.

Yours,
Theodore.

July 15th.

Alice dear:—

Times without number to-day, what thoughts, only you can recall them. What a good woman you are Alice! Indeed a good woman! What wonderful control you possess. I think only me you could treat that way. I cannot forget that laugh of yours—that was the happiest (you recollect it must have been five A.M.) and the most cheerful and the sweetest, right from the very bottom of the heart laugh I ever heard or will hear again, dear! May God bless you! Repeat that laugh when you spend the first night with him, and if he has any tender nerves, he will take you in his arms never to let you go. I have heard from the doctor, and he is O. K., and from the tone of his letter seems content. I am glad he is finally settled and is favored with chances to earn a little money. I sent his letter home to-day. I think he will write to you, Alice, for I know he has some love for you. Remember that you are to send me a photo of yourself and husband. Do not forget, and keep me posted where you are, for I may want to write to you again.

So, good bye, dear, or rather good night, and may God guard you safely to your destination.

I am lovingly yours,

Theodore.

Good luck to you to-day!

Alice, dear! The nice letter you wrote me! I liked it. It pleased me—also had the desired effect. Oh, how sad it makes me to feel that I cannot look into your lovely eyes again. Next week you will be gone—gone where? Perhaps thousands of miles away! Well, you simply are somebody else's, dearie! Sorry I cannot write you in return as sweet a letter, time is too short. One thing, Alice, I want—a remembrance from you, something to keep, something to last as long as I live to remember you—from Alice—for you are too good to forget.

With a kiss I am yours,

Theodore.

P.S.—I shall kiss the baby for you, Sunday. Alice, if you will write to me Sunday (one more letter), I will get it Monday A.M., and believe me I will be looking for a letter.

God be with you!

TWO YEARS LATER.

August 14th.

To my dear Alice:—

Even if it is just a line, I write to you. I must write once in a while. Did you know, Alice, that the doctor is sojourning in Europe to attend Medical Congress in Berlin? I expect he will return next week on the "Werra." Oh, I so wish you could see him. I want him to kiss you "only" for me.

With kindest regards from

Theodore.

February 2d.

My dear Alice:—

It's just too long since I have heard from you, and I have almost forgotten your address. So I address this note to the mountains. Alice, please write to me just as soon as your thoughts drift westward. I will send you those photos sometime. I hope you are well.

Please write soon and tell me all about yourself. Is it cold where you are?

Kiss from

Theodore.

February 4th.

Alice, how are you? O.K., I hope! If you will send me your address I will send you those photos. I mislaid it and don't know whether this will reach you or not, my dear. Let me hear from you.

I am with much love,
    Your friend,
        Theodore.

        Philadelphia.

My dear Mrs. Hutton:—

You never said anything about writing, but I cannot resist writing you a few words to-night. How I wish I could have kept you a little longer and talked more with you. I had such a good time with you and my heart's desire was to be with you and is yet. Will you pardon me for writing you without permission? Don't tell if I tell you, will you? and trust you to be my friend? My engagement is broken off. You told me the truth when we sat on the sofa together. I am sorry to say I won't have one place to go on my vacation. I only have a week now, from the 23d of this month until after New Year. The bridge, the bridge, the beautiful bridge! I learned to think so much of it! Oh, my kind friend, Mrs. Hutton, I won't dare to write any more now until I hear from you. None of the little newspapers saw me on Sunday night last in the storm, but how my heart leaped to be alone with you. I am looking forth to the time when I can see you. I am a poor writer, as you will see, Mrs. Hutton. Don't think I told you any fibs—I thought you did not believe me as I was telling you, but it was all true, and if it is not true I will clear out of the country. Now you are all alone; no one else to think of. Will you give me just one thought?

With much love I close, and good night from your friend   L.

        New York.

Mrs. Hutton.

My dear friend:—

Your kind invitation to dine with you on Sunday

last received. I was very sorry I was not home in time to accept. I would have called Sunday, but I thought you had company. You know, you said I would have to take my chances. You will, I hope, pardon me for not answering your kind letter of Monday, April 2d, sooner. I have been very busy. I have to attend to jury duty this week and that keeps me away from the store the best part of the day.

Hoping this note will find you well and enjoying the best of health, I remain,
Truly your friend,
B.

Chicago, Ill.

My dear Alice:—

Yours from St. Louis was duly received and I was both glad and sorry, too, after reading it—glad because the letter was from you, and sorry because you were unhappy even for one hour.

I want to say right here that in my estimation it was exceedingly unkind in your friend E. to desert you so early in the day, after you had made the long trip especially for his benefit, and any man who permits a running match to interfere with a lady's arrangements under such circumstances should be — — well, he should be condemned to run for the balance of his earthly existence.

I am convinced that your case of the "blues" was produced entirely by your loneliness during the day, and agreeable company would have dispersed them entirely; but I say, Alice, you must have had a terrible attack to have fallen into poetry, and such a poem, too.

The metre was good, and the rhyme pretty, but pardon me for saying that the sentiment was abominable. You certainly wanted to convey to me the idea that you were very wicked, but I will have to know of your being guilty of more terrible crimes than I am aware of now before I will believe you to be even as much of a sinner as the average mortal, and I advise you to put your best foot forward now and not let such precarious reflections interfere with the delicate matter you have now in hand. I would certainly carry it far enough to see if there was going to be a grievous fight from the other side and if they do decide to contest, then it is time to talk of retreating. But remember what I told you—that in the event of your being obliged to drop it, you will be no worse off than before except for the fact that some of your friends are aware of the preparations that you have been making. This, you understand, is the way to brave the matter in case the legal affair is a failure, but I assure you that I sincerely hope to see you win, not that success means another alliance absolutely essential to your happiness, but because I think you deserve to be entirely free to do as you like with your own if you so desire.

Now, my dear, I hope you will keep a stiff upper lip and carry out your plan of campaign to the end or until good policy dictates a retreat, and if you are threatened again with the blues, send out for a couple of dinner plates and try to spin them in the air like the juggler we saw at Hooly's.

We miss you very much here, especially at the table, which seems to have lost its voice since you left.

Hoping that you will soon be able to afford me the pleasure of grasping your hand and looking into your eyes again, I am,

Yours faithfully,
C.

Chicago, Ill.

My dear friend Alice:—

Your two letters from New York came duly to hand, and this morning I received your beautiful roses. I must acknowledge that you are very thoughtful, and the flowers were so unexpected that I was quite overpowered for the time being. I have some of them in a glass dish upon my desk and have received a good many compliments from callers on account of them.

From the programmes you have also sent I infer that you are doing the town, so far as amusements go, and you can believe that nothing would please me more than to help you "do" it. Some philosopher (possibly myself) has remarked that one half the world was created to contribute to the enjoyment of the other half, and I am sure that when association is possible you and myself can demonstrate the truth of the statement to an extent at least.

I am very sorry to hear you are going to stay away from us so long, but also must congratulate you upon feeling sure that you won't have any trouble in your case.

We have had the most abominable weather here for two weeks previous to last Sunday that I ever experienced. Two weeks steady rain every day, and although there were no river dams to break hereabouts, I have heard people a good many times say something that sounded much like dam when referring to the weather. I infer from what you said in your last letter that you do not think consistent my statement that I never kiss other men's wives, but in fact I am quite consistent.

I wish I was talking to you now and it would not take me long to illustrate what my idea is.

There has been no particular change at the house. A—, D—, and myself still constitute the tenants at the table, and we all sincerely wish you were here.

I hope you will have occasion to come out before long. Well, keep me well posted on your movements and condition of mind, and I shall endeavor to do the same with you.

We have got so much business on hand now that I sometimes think my mind is not as clear as it might be.

Yours sincerely,

C.

Chicago, Ill.

My dear friend Alice:—

I am going to take the chances of arousing your husband's ire by addressing you as Alice, and if he objects to it I give you my word that it shall not happen again. But when you tell him, as no doubt you will, what a very high regard I had for you and on the whole am a pretty good sort of a fellow and wish both of you all the happiness in the world, perhaps he may overlook the familiarity.

I received your note written on the train, and also the one from New York informing me of the marriage and was glad to hear that there were no serious miscalculations and everything went off pleasantly. I suppose that on such occasions the most trivial incidents of a disagreeable nature are exaggerated into the most ominous of omens by the interested parties, and consequently it is a matter for congratulation to all concerned that your wedding occurred without any unpleasant incidents.

You would have enjoyed a hearty laugh if you could have heard the boys at the house ("boys" means the male boarders generally) telling me Sunday morning about Mrs. Hutton's marriage in New York last week (this in the way of news, remember,) and, of course, when I feigned ignorance of it, they proceeded to tell me all about it and expressed great sympathy for me on account of your outrageously deceitful treatment. How they heard you were married on Wednesday I do not know, but presume Mrs. W—— may have mentioned it.

I shall await with impatience the picture you promised. Expect to sit for mine to-morrow and hope you won't despair of getting one, because you will if it takes the last cow in the barn.

Yours sincerely,
C.

Brooklyn.

Alice:—

Yes, I received your picture, for which I sincerely thank you, and of which I am very proud. I thought of sending through Mrs. W—— my acceptance, but hesitated because I was not quite sure you would be pleased with my taking the liberty of using your friend. One, in circumstances like ours, is quite at a loss to know what to do and especially so when one has a disposition not to displease. However, believe me that your remembrance of me and elegant present gave the new year a kindly assurance which without it would have been quite to the contrary—blue, indeed.

Many thanks.   E.

Boston.

Dear Alice:—

I received your likenesses yesterday. They reached here Saturday. Thank you very much for remembering me. You look well, not as good looking as you once did. If you have no objection I will have the one without the hat, crayoned life size. I always thought you were in a particular way very queer, the evidence that you are yet that way is apparent in your note. Why should I wish to return your likenesses? Why should I not be glad to keep them?

Truly yours,
F.

Dear Mrs. Hutton:—

Would you like to go to the Eden Musee this evening? If so, I will call for you at eight o'clock.

Hoping you will accept my invitation, I remain,

Yours sincerely,
Edgar.

Dear Mrs. Hutton:—

I am quite surprised that after showing so much bravado you should now be afraid of me.

You spoke one time of me being afraid of you, saying you would not hurt me. You were not dangerous. Do you think I am now? Or am I altogether too forward? I hope you do not think so and that you wish I was a little more forward—than I am. Next time I see you (which I hope will be soon) I will tell you how your name happened to be mentioned to your friend.

Let me know what evening you will be at home. I have engagements for Wednesday, Thursday and Saturday evenings of this week. Although I should like to spend one evening in your delightful company by the light of the grate fire with you. Write soon.

Yours sincerely,
Edgar.

New York, January 13th.

My dear Alice:—

Excuse brevity. Will you be at home Saturday evening? If not, then Sunday. I want to win those stamps. I hope I will be fortunate enough to find you at home Saturday evening and without company. You see I am selfish and want you all to myself.

Yours sincerely,
Edgar.

Tuesday, February 1st.

My dear Alice:—

If you will be at home to-morrow evening, Wednesday, I will call. I do not consider that I made a call Sunday. I hope you will look at it in the same light as I do. Had I called alone, then it might have been counted as such. I thought surely I would not find you alone, therefore I invited my cousin to call with me, which I was sorry for and deeply regretted afterwards.

Please write and let me know about Wednesday.

Yours,
Edgar.

New York, February 4th.

My dear Alice:—

Yours received. You ask me if I would have called if you had let me know that you were home alone? You know well enough what my answer would be to that question. Send me word sometime when you are alone, and I will give you my answer.

Hoping that I will see you Sunday evening, I remain,

Yours sincerely,

Edgar.

New York, April 14th.

My dear Mrs. Hutton:—

I have just returned from the country after making a long stay and having a jolly good time. Many thanks for your pretty picture. You must have thought me very impolite not to have acknowledged your pretty gift, but I did not receive it until to-day.

Hoping that you are well and that I may have the pleasure of seeing you soon, I remain, as ever,

Your true friend,

Edgar.

New York, April 18th.

My dear Mrs. Hutton:—

I will call in to-morrow evening. Hope you will be at home. No, I am not married. We will talk about the chess game when I see you.

Yours truly,

Edgar.

New York, Sept. 13th.

My dear Alice:—

I have been out of town for a few days, hence my delay in answering your last letter. The one, telling me that you are leaving the mountains to-morrow, has just been received. You did not say where you were going from there, but I take it for granted that you intend returning to your city house, and so I will address this letter there. Answer immediately and let me know where you are.

I am yours ever,

Edgar.

New York, Sept. 25th.

My dear Alice:—

I shall use every endeavor to join you at tea tomorrow (Monday) evening, and as things look now I believe I shall be successful. I guess you can expect me at 6.30 o'clock, and I am sure we will have a very pleasant time.

Believe me, as ever, yours,

Edgar.

New York, Oct. 25th.

Dear Alice:—

Yours received. Much better, thank you. Will call Sunday, if the weather is good.

Edgar.

New York, Oct. 27th.

Dear Alice:—

Your kind invitation received. Will accept with thanks. I am still under the doctor's care.

With love,

Edgar.

New York, Nov. 4th.

Dear, dear Alice:—

Yours received. You know very well I do not tire reading your letters. I love to receive them, and the longer the better. Did Doc say anything to you about chess? I think he has about enough of it. My dear, I would much rather you would be as you are than like Lena Despard, for she was altogether too familiar with Jack, don't you know?

Darling, will you be at home Sunday? I hope so, and alone.

Your
Edgar.

Sept. 10th.

My dear friend Alice:—

Are you still in the mountains, and when are you going back to the city? I have been in Lexington since July 9th. We intend returning to the city this coming Monday, it being the 18th. I have spent a very pleasant summer and hope you have done the same. I want to see you looking as well this fall as you did last. We are going down by boat Monday. Hope to meet you on it if you intend going down about that time. I suppose you have had a jolly time. I know I have. It has been very lively here, but quite dull now, and the place looks forsaken. At the end of the month I may go down to W. P. for a week. Don't you want to go down? Write and let me know. Write so I will get it before Monday.

Your
Edgar.

New York, Sept. 27th.

Dear Alice:—

Reached home safely. I am awfully sorry you are not going to spend your winter in the city. Why is it you have made up your mind to stay away? I should think you would miss going to the theatre and all that sort of thing. Do not be surprised if you see me pop in upon you some day. I suppose A. is with you. Yes, Alice, you must let me know when you are to be in the city. I have spent pleasant evenings in your company and wish for more.

Write and tell me all about yourself.

Yours with love,
Edgar.

New York, Oct. 15th.

Dear Alice:—

In your last letter you ask if the young lady that had my watch and ring was at Lexington last summer. No, she was not; and then again you ask: Is my sister to be married this fall? To this I will say no, but they hope to be some time. Have you finished building? I suppose you have quite a place now, with your large open fireplace and all that. Dear Alice, you ask me who will take your place? What shall I say? I will try and live in the past and think of you.

Well, do I remember the fireplace in New York. Can I ever forget it, and the sitting room? Alice, do you think you will come to New York this winter? I hope you will. You will let me know, won't you? Don't you miss the theatres?

Trusting you will write soon again, I remain,
Your true friend,
Edgar.

New York, Nov. 20th.

Darling Alice:—

I have not heard from you in a long, long time. I hope my last letter did not offend you in any way. If so I am very, very sorry for it and hope you will forgive me. Won't you, dear? Write and let me know. I hope you are well and enjoying good health. Are you coming to the city?
Your
Edgar.

New York, Jan. 13th.

Dear Alice:—

Yours of the eleventh received with the enclosed proofs. Hope you accepted the one smiling. If so, you must give me one. I hope you are having a good time; in fact, I know you will have as you will be away from me. I also hope you will not stay away long and will soon return.

Write and let me know when you are to be at home, for I would like to show you how to play backgammon.

Yours with love,
Edgar.

New York, Jan. 26th.

My dear Alice:—

Home again. Will call to-morrow, Friday. Hope you will be at home, dear. Will give all the news when I see you.

Yours with love,
Edgar.

New York, Feb. 5th.

Dear Alice:—

I hope you are quite well again. Let me know.

Your
Edgar.

New York, Feb. 10th.

Dear Alice:—

I will not be able to see you in some little time on account of my little brother having scarlet fever. I can hear you say, "I am so glad, for one reason: It will keep him away from me. Just what I want."

I hope, dear, he will soon be over it, for his sake and for mine; for the sooner he recovers the earlier I will see you, dear.

With love,
Edgar.

New York, Feb. 13th.

Dear Alice:—

Yours of the 12th received. There are three of our family who have not had scarlet fever. One of us is away from home. As for myself I am not much afraid, it being chiefly a child's desease; but things will happen, we can't always sometimes tell.

My brother is a little better to-day. I thank you, dear, for your good wishes.

Darling, I should imagine from what you say about the proverb that you still would like to have me call. I am so glad. Tell me, dear, why do you tell me to keep away and think otherwise? Tell me, you want to have me call and call soon.

Yours with love,

Edgar.

New York, March 4th.

My dear, dear Alice:—

Been looking for a letter. Why don't you write? Hope you are coming to the city soon. I am delighted with that picture, dear, you sent me. I look at it about forty times a day and wish that you were near me, so that I might show you how much I love you. I am wedded to that picture—I will never part with it.

Yours with love,

Edgar.

April 4th.

Dear Alice:—

Why don't you write to me? Are you angry? Are you coming to the city this month?

Your

Edgar.

New York, April 23d.

Dear Alice:—

Are you to be in the city next week? If you are, call and see me.

Yours,

Edgar.

July 5th.

My dear Alice:—

I am glad to hear from you. I wrote you several times and wondered why you did not answer. Now I know. I am glad you have not forgotten me and think sometimes of me. You ask me if I am engaged, and if I think of you. How could I forget you, dear? I wish you were by my side asking those different questions. How much better it would be than a thousand miles away. My mother is quite ill, so ill in fact that we will not be able to leave the city on the 10th of July, as we expected. We intend going again to Lexington. We are going to stop at the —— House. Of course, you know where it is, in the Catskills. I will try and get over to see you in your pretty home, dear. B. T. and I are going down on Long Island to-morrow afternoon. We may land in W. P., it depends. We are to remain away about one week. Old man Bonton, I understand, is very feeble; I don't think he will live much longer, poor old man! The photo you sent me I would not part with. I think a great deal of it, and look very often at it. How I wish I could see the original. Write to me, dear. Send your letters to the house and I will receive them.

Yours with love,

Edgar.

———

New York, July 30th.

Dear Alice:—

I will be at Lexington on the eighth of August. Mother is better, and we will be able to leave the city on that date. Why did you not write again? You know I like to hear from you. Did you see the doctor while on your Western trip? Ted. H. is now at Lexington with his family. They do not intend to remain all summer, probably a week or two longer. If all is well I will try and get over to see you. I can almost hear you say: "If you will be real good, you may come." You will promise me a kiss and many of them, won't you, dear? I wish you would come over my way during the summer. Is A. to be with you? I suppose he is quite a tennis player by this time.

I told you I thought of going to Good Ground or W. Well, we went to W. and had a very good time. Old man Bonton is not expected to live. The cancer, which I suppose you know he has, is now eating his face. It has reached the eye, of which he has lost the sight. Poor old fellow! he is very weak and his time is short. I called on the T's while at W. P. Played tennis about every afternoon with them; they have a beautiful place. Saw an old chum of yours. Write as soon as you receive this—you know I love to hear from you, dear.

With much love,

I am your

Edgar.

New York, October 6th.

Dear Alice:—

Received your announcement cards yesterday. Was greatly surprised. Could not believe my eyes, at first, until it gradually dawned upon me that you were married. I hope you will be happy. I congratulate him, as he has one that will make him so.

I have been in the mountains since July 20th; returned yesterday. Hope to hear from you.

Regards to Mr. Robinson, and see me when you are in the city and I will do likewise.

Always your friend,

Edgar.

The mountains, 20th Dec.

Dear Mrs. Hutton:—

I saw our friend Sam Harris to-day, and he will deliver you one cord of twenty-six inch wood on Saturday and two more cords next week. You ought to see our pie to-night—something grand, I assure you—and John is in good spirits, too, yet it seems lonesome to me. It must be the coal stove has spoiled me. For, what else? We shall try our best to finish this survey by Xmas, then I can hang up my stocking in peace. I just received a card saying a box would leave New York on Friday for me. I wonder what can be in it. Something good, I trust, and hope it may be a "surprise."

Did Smithy leave at five this morning? I'm sure I didn't, for when I reached "home" (pro tem.) I found Harrison warming the fire, and we had a friendly cigar till long after one, and you may be sure five came all too soon. To-night our friend is going to sleep in a hammock in the sitting-room. Alas! his room was cold and he had no dog.

I wonder if you got your cutter? But enough of that wondering, for this was to have been a short strictly business note. So, pray, forgive my erring pen and believe me,

Very sincerely,
Winfred.

The mountains, 18th Jan.

Dear Mrs. Hutton:—

I thank you very much for the trouble you have taken with my accident statement. Believe me,

Sincerely,
Winfred.

The mountains, 25th Jan.

Dear Mrs. Hutton:—

I can't stand it any longer. I'm nearly sick. It grows more terrible every day. How could I have done such a thing! Oh, can you, won't you, forgive me? I can't, no, I cannot stand before you, but won't you send me one word? This silence is horrible. And Miss Smith—Oh, I am thoroughly disgraced.

Winfred.

The mountains, 28th Feb.

Dear Mrs. Hutton:—

An hour since you spoke to me—the first time I have heard your voice in many days. But, perhaps, you'll think I should not write to you. Yet there is that within me that urges me to do it. Deeply do I regret my hasty actions of so many days ago. I did you great wrong and could not hope to offer an apology.

I called on you to receive my dismissal, and had you scorned me it would have been my just deserts. But you were kind to me, yes, so kind that although it stung worse than rebuke, yet left me with some hope.

Mrs. Hutton, I am sorry for acting as I did. Yes, from the bottom of my heart I am, and if it is possible to make any reparation, I beg you to tell me.

Believe me,
Very truly,
Winfred.

In the mountains, Dec. 22d.

My dear Mrs. Hutton:—

I regret very much my inability to dine with you on Xmas day. It was kind of you to ask me, and I know what pleasure I miss when I refuse such an invitation—but I go home to-morrow—trusting to hang my stocking on the family mantel.

Remembering the pleasure of a former Xmas day and wishing you, indeed, all the happiness of this happy season, believe me,
Very truly yours,
Winfred.

New York, April 25th.

Dear friend:—

Pardon me for this forwardness, but as I have heard from you through Mary I cannot help but write, if for nothing else but for the sake of "Auld Lang Syne."

I have seen your picture, and I congratulate you on your preservation during the last ten years.

I was very glad to hear from you, and hope it may be my good fortune to some day meet you.

Your old friend,

Paul.

New York, May 2d.

Dear friend Alice:—

Thanks. I will be pleased to go with you to-morrow night. You will have to excuse me, however, from tea this time. I would like to see you first. I will be at your house in time to take you.

Your

Paul.

Dear Alice:—

When I wrote you this afternoon my mind must have been wandering. I find at this time of year, when we are so very busy, it will be impossible for me to go home and get dinner and reach your house in time. So if you can wait until 6.30 before you dine I would be most happy to have the pleasure, etc.

I just arrived this morning from New Rochelle, where I have been since Saturday. Found all the folks well. If you cannot wait until 6.30, please telegraph me. I brought up some dogs with me this morning for the show at Madison Garden.

Your friend,

Paul.

Friend Alice:—

I hope this will find you getting along all right. Now, don't be surprised. I know all about it, and as I felt sorry for sister so do I for you. Such things, unfortunately, have to be done for those most interested, but it must be, as it ought to be, a consolation for you to know that those butchers (the doctors) are doing something to some fellow every day. What do they care, as long as they fill their coffers (I mean pockets)? As there is always a bright side to everything, I hope you will see some of it after your recovery.

When you are able to talk and laugh I will come up and see you. Until then adieu. I don't expect you to write me—no—no.

Again hoping you are all right and that your recovery and rising will soon come to pass without the aid of Gabriel's horn.

Paul.

Friend Alice (in bed):—

I have just received your telegram. I am very glad to hear you are getting along so well. With your constitution and jolly disposition all the doctors in New York can not keep you quiet. Brace up and have some style about you. What will you do with the bonnet and gloves now?

I will come over Sunday evening after tea. If you are not well enough, don't see me.

Paul.

New York, Jan. 14th.

My dear Alice:—

While visiting some friends at Morristown, N. J., last summer I went with them to call on their nearest neighbor. While there I picked up an album, and in it came across your picture. I was surprised. I was more surprised when they told me they knew me well—at least knew of me well. I have seen them many times since and, of course, heard of your marriage from them.

Your card received this morning, therefore, no surprise to me. Now that you have gone and done it, and belong to a very lucky man, it is not fitting that I should say more than to congratulate you and to wish you and yours a bright and happy future,

> Let memory sometimes bear you back
>   To pleasant scenes almost forgot.
> And when you think of other friends,
>   Who loved you well, forget me not.

Good bye,

Paul.

Feb. 25th.

My darling Alice:—

Thank you cordially. Accept my inmost feelings unexpressed. You know my desires, my thoughts; at the same time you must remember my regard and respect for your position. Trust me, I entreat you. I shall and must be careful. In this you will have faith in me. I wish I knew you were alone! Yes, I was just where you supposed when you wrote to me. I spoke of you, and others spoke of you also. My heart would fairly jump at any mention of you. So much love is there in my heart for you. They told me you had been at the Academy, and I was grieved to think that I was absent. But remember what I think and wish for you. I shall always do as you bid. Write when you can and as often as you can. I am dying to see you. Do not forget to advise me if you will see me. I hardly know how to write and what to write. But my love is for you, and you know it well.

Seth.

New York, August 18th.

Dear Mrs. Hutton:—

I know you will be delighted in glancing over the inanimate lines of my chirography.

I arrived in New York tired and thirsty, but as soon as I could get into my uniform I proceeded to quench the thirst as speedily as possible. I am quite good looking under any circumstances, but words cannot describe the glory and splendor of my appearance in full dress uniform.

In fact, I was in great danger of being stolen by some of the young girls, scores of whom followed me for squares.

I found upon my arrival in Baltimore that the cause of my summons was the extreme illness of the captain, and so I was ordered to take command until his recovery, which is indefinite. His sickness will prevent our sailing until spring. I wish you were here to enjoy the sailing and driving. I have a crack horse and a sloop that has never been beaten, so I could make it quite pleasant for you. Alice, I will be able, in all probability, to make short trips to New York. I should be delighted to call if you will kindly grant permission. Please, give my regards to Miss Brown and keep twelve-tenths for yourself. Write as soon as possible.

Believe me ever your friend,

Neville.

28th Feb.

Dear Alice:—

Oh, do you remember, sweet Alice, Ben Bolt? Yes; if Ben doesn't I do, and pleasant are those remembrances. I send a Decanter replenisher, gentle lady, and on Monday I will fill it for you, i. e., if your thirst or another's —perish the thought—has not done the act ere I am with you again.

Remember your oyster supper, Monday, and until then, believe me, your indicative mood and present tense.

George.

Monday evening.

Sweet friend Alice:—

And how are you this evening? I hope quite well. I expect to go off on a long tramp to-morrow, Tuesday, and will not (possibly) be back until late; so, as you first suggested, will say Friday, and then I shall meet you at the house at, say, six. Purcell's, did you say? Very well, ma chère; you can reckon with your host this time.

Yours,
George.

April 10th.

My dear friend:—

What a mockery! You seem to have enough of the milk of human kindness, and, with an alloy of affection, address me as above. I shall do no less.

So I am a nameless, homeless nonentity—a myth. That being the case I shall not be obliged to contribute to charity or serve on jury duty—blissful! Wrapt in the solitude of my own consciousness I can draw the drapery of my couch around me and lie down to sweet dreams.

What an exalted opinion you will have of your own ability to measure humanity when you know more than you do. I shall not deny or affirm anything until I see you face to face.

I will call Wednesday evening, and if you are the noble woman I took you to be, you will welcome G——, and as I shall make you judge and I am major domo of our social affairs, I shall expect justice from one so fair.

Do not fail me (if directories do), and believe me your admiring friend

George.

P.S.—Wednesday evening, 6 P.M., we will dine together.

September 26th.

Mrs. Hutton:—

My dearest friend on earth! I cannot help writing you at this time. As I crossed the lonely bridge at twelve o'clock last night I felt like throwing myself over to end my misery—and what shall I do? Shall I write these words to you? I must come to the point, for I am heavy at heart. I always thought of the difference in our circumstances, so I never dared ask you to be mine. I never was really in love but once, and that is with you, as I told you yesterday. Could I but fly to you now I would love and cherish you all my days and would fly to the end of the earth with you. After I am married it will be too late. Will you answer this note? I pray God I am doing no harm—I shall never forget you—I love you and cannot forget. Your charming face I long to see. I can claim you as a friend if you will not marry me. I will try and do what is right if you answer me "No." I pray you answer this at once, for every moment counts to me. I will await an answer, dearest. Write, if only once, will you, my dear friend? All is true, I told you, after knowing all. If you will have no mercy on me I hope in after years you will have one kind thought for him who loves you well.

      Sincerely,

            Jack.

           June 29th.

My dear Alice:—

  Your kind letter was duly received by me and has been read and re-read several times. It was nice of you to answer so promptly and to allow me the privilege of corresponding with you. It is now the only consolation remaining to me until I shall again see you face to face—for that time I long.

  I have not as yet received that photo. I want you to send me a photograph of yourself—I want a photograph, especially of your face,—that is to me of great interest. I want something in the absence of the original that I can look at and fancy that it looks at me in return, not to remind me of you, for that is unnecessary, for I shall never forget you. I wish that it was in my power to impress into you something of the spirit of my feelings towards you. It is infinitely charming to read in your note to me that you miss me, and as we do not miss those we do not like the natural inference is very patent. My darling, the last Sunday that I enjoyed your companionship opened up to me a really new experience. I thought I was familiar with ladies, and, in fact, I have passed quite a little of my time in their society, but you are to me a revelation. Ah! I can close my eyes now and almost fancy myself by your side again; but I open my eyes and it is all a fancy. Let me relate to you a little incident that befell me last evening. I had an engagement to spend the evening with some lady friends, two graduates of the seminary at Rye, N. Y. They came on to attend the commencement exercises and are now making a short visit at the house of a lady friend here in town. I went up to my room to dress, and as I was early, I lay down on the lounge with the newspaper and a cigar, but the first thing I knew I didn't know anything, as I was asleep. What brought you to my mind I do not know, but I dreamed I was again with you somewhere, I cannot now recognize the surroundings, although I think it must have been at your house in New York. We were in evening dress, and had just returned from some entertainment. It was nearly 9 o'clock when I awoke. I rushed through my toilet and reached the house where my friends were, in a scarcely awakened condition, and it was really late in the evening before I fully recovered my mental equilibrium. To-morrow night, two weeks from the time I was at your house in New York (I date almost everything from then), I am going to Boston to spend Sunday. I expect to take one of the young ladies referred to with me as far as Hartford. She is a very nice girl; she spent quite a while abroad, and I judge papa is in somewhat comfortable circumstances; they reside in New York. Now, I am going to propose to you (not marriage) that I come up to the mountains to see you some Saturday, and remain over Sunday at a hotel, not at your house; what say you? I leave it to your judgment and discretion, and should you decide favorably, you shall name the date. Alice, make it when you have not got a house full of guests and admirers immediately at hand, and perhaps it would be best when Miss Thompson is with you.

Now, don't say "come" if you do not mean it, or if you think it not best and do not feel that you must have me for a guest, because I shall stop at a hotel, provided I go at all.

But do not, for heaven's sake, lose sight of the engagement you have to visit Boston next winter, and mind, your visit is to be a week anyway.

Since fate has been unkind in not permitting me to meet you before, and to see as much of you as I should have done had I known you years ago, I live in the hope that the future will redeem the past.

Now, do not let me wait too long for an answer, and should you think me verging too strongly on the sentimental, I will try and suppress it from my letters—although my feelings will remain the same. I think I could go on writing you for some time yet, but there is, unfortunately, an end to almost everything, and lest you should be wearied I will cease. You ask if we shall ever meet again and express the hope that we may—I assure you if it rests with me we shall.

To think that I should never meet you face to face again would be for me a deprivation unbearable. Heaven grant that you may have something of the same feeling for me, even in a lesser degree. Of myself, I am sure; of you, not so sure. I cannot kiss you good-bye on paper, nor can I fold you in my arms to take one long, lingering look into your eyes, but my desire to do so is just as strong as though it were possible.

Believe me to be to you an affectionate and lasting friend.   Yours,

Lemont.

July 18.

My Dear Alice:—

Your photo received. It is splendid, and no mistake, and my sentiments cannot justly be committed to paper, but must be whispered into your ear with no one but your own sweet self for an audience. You shall have a photo of myself, but it cannot possess the charms that yours does, because the subject is lacking and the photographic art cannot supply the want. I have not got your last letter with me, but will try and answer it from memory. I shall take you to task for misconstruing my last letter to you. Whether intentionally or not I do not know, but I did not request you for an invitation to the mountains this summer, but simply asked if I should come; if it would be agreeable for you to see me as an occasional caller at your house.

I submit to your decision, however, and shall patiently await any opportunity for seeing you at any time you may see fit.

God knows it is hard lines to wait until next winter before seeing you again. Again I assure you I am not at all desirous of working Miss Thompson into any scheme, nor have I any scheme in view with which she is connected.

As far as my being in love with Bella is concerned, I answer you no—and even were such the case I should not be desirous of seeing you two together, as it would be altogether an affair between you and me, as far as I should be allowed to make it, which would make it unpleasant for the third party.

Presume the story of my calling upon her three times a week emanated from the young brother, whom I have since heard is with you. I have seen her twice since we were so charmingly entertained by you at your New York house.

No, my dear, you are wrong in your suppositions. I am in love with a half dozen or so young ladies to a greater or less degree, but that does not count, as that is with me perfectly natural.

I should feel lonesome if it were not possible for me to seek consolation of some one while you are so far away—How's that? Rather unkind of you to repeat and hold up for his amusement the effusions of a young man when writing to an object of adoration. But if you enjoy it, all right. Proceed, I am satisfied. What I refer to is the copying of several passages of my letter to you, but I am glad you agree with me, and it is good of you to say so.

I am always asking favors of my friends, and I shall of you. Here is one: Please explain to me in your next letter (which I hope may soon be forthcoming) the meaning of your saying—You are a strange fellow.

I am interested, you see. You speak of seeing me once more, and "hope we shall meet again, if only for once," etc., etc. Why not for more than once? Should Providence be generous to me I hope to live a year or two more anyway, perhaps longer. I certainly am not intending marriage, and unless you are the doubtful one, why not, I say, for more than once? When I do see you again it will not be for the only time, if I am allowed a word with regard to it. D—— me if I don't think you must have something in the wind yourself—going abroad, going to marry the doctor, social suicide, or some other God forsaken object.—Give it up; it's a bad plan.

I am an excellent person to give advice, and my advice is always good. I do not mean, of course, to advise you in matters with regard to which you are the best judge, as your own judgment is better than mine. You comprehend. Now, while you two girls are there together, please for my sake do not exchange letters from me. It would be unpleasant for me should I discover it, and I might.

Dame Rumor always gets in her little work where the opportunity presents itself, and I have recently been her victim. Nothing alarming, only amusing—as follows: There is at a cottage in Newton a young lady whom I once met here in town about two years ago, and have not seen since.

At a hop the other evening I was again introduced to her, and danced several times with her, accompanying her home when the affair was over.

The next day a gentleman friend informed me that it was current talk among half a dozen or so young people that the above mentioned young lady had once been to me the object of my profound admiration; so much so that I assiduously courted her family, proposed, and then, think of it! was rejected.

I have not had anything amuse me quite as much in some time, considering that I had seen her but once previously.

Have not seen her since; when I do, am going to spring it on her and see what she will have to say regarding it.

Now, my dear, I must shut off before it runs any more, as I have to go and spend the evening with one of the "half dozen" who leave next week for Martha's Vineyard.

The separation will be unbearable almost, but we shall have to submit.

Oh, let me, etc., that is for you.

Now, with all the kisses that I would bestow upon you in person, I leave you to imagine them as enclosed between these sheets, and with nothing but my pleasant thoughts of you for company, I say good-bye until we meet again. Your admiring

Lemont.

July 31.

My Own Dear Alice:—

Yes—you are my own, at least in my estimation; some one may have a prior claim, but that shall not preclude me.

I am glad you should take the trouble to explain your reasons for your apparent veto of my intended visit. You see, my dear, I am such a prosaic individual that I always (or almost always) take everything in a serious light—sometimes more seriously than is intended.

What do you suppose it would matter to me if your house were not in order, or if there were no sitting-room to occupy. As long as I should have you the whole face of nature would be brightened and changed and any thing or place enlivened by your presence would be to me as the Palace of Aladdin.

Enough.

I did not mean to hurt Belle's sensibilities in any way, shape or manner. I am as well aware of the fact of her having a lingering feeling of regard for me as are you. But she is young and will outgrow it. I simply told you the truth, viz., that she and I are the best of good friends; further than that it is unnecessary for either of us to go.

You have, I think, gotten the story of myself and a young lady, told you by Harriet, somewhat mixed.

The only episode of the kind that I think of to which Harriet could refer (do not imagine their name is legion) is one of a young lady from New York who visited Boston about two years ago, and with whom I became very well acquainted. I may have done her an injustice, but at the time I was quite positive it was an even thing on both sides.

She was not a friend of Harriet's; quite the contrary: indeed, I think Miss I. was quite pleased when she returned to the metropolis.

I had an engagement with them both one evening, and as Boston was the nearest of the two, I went there first, and then took her with me to call upon Miss T.—a thing, of course, which I ought not to have done. That was the only time they ever met, and what Belle knows about our friendship I told her.

The New Yorker wanted a husband, and I did not want a wife, and each of us tried to see which would come out ahead. Pardon my conceit if I think I did.

We corresponded for a while, and she came to Boston again, and I called on her, but the affair then dropped.

No, Alice, on my honor as a gentleman, I have not as yet overcome any lady's good resolutions. Having tired of her, I quietly laid her on the shelf and sought fresh fields among pastures new—I told you so when at your house in New York.

And I think if you try you will recollect my views on the subject.

Yes, my dear, I will meet you in New York, not only once, but as many times as you will vouchsafe, and consider myself as one of the most fortunate of mortals to have the opportunity.

I am, as you probably know, twice down to business, and should I come to the mountains this summer, it will have to be at some time during the week in August, from the 18th to the 25th. If that will not do, I am fearful that I shall have to pass it for the present.

When I see you I will tell you the whole story of myself and the young lady whose case you mentioned as a reason for you being on your guard as far as I am concerned.

The absurdity of that amuses me. Why, I would not harm a hair of your head, and you know it. Talk about your wishing for me during the lovely moonlight evenings we have been having recently! Those are exactly my feelings with regard to yourself. Some of the evenings at the shore have been perfect. There are a number of girls who are quite bright and agreeable; one especially with whom I have put in considerable time.

But there has not been an evening when she has been with me when I have not longed that she might fade into nothingness, if she only might be replaced by your own sweet self.

Did you ever read any of the books, the titles of which I wrote down for you? and if so, how did you like them? I have a novel at my room that I read on my way to Brant Rock, Saturday, by Phillips, author of "As in a Looking Glass," etc.

It is rather interesting, and I will mail it to you as soon as I get time to go up and get it. If you have read it, throw it away.

It is strange that you should have passed the greater

part of your life with gentlemen, and consider them superior to women, and that I should be able to say the same (as regards the last few years of my own life) with regard to ladies.

You are fond of gentlemen—I of ladies. I think it is therefore all right, and the human race at large will thus be well taken care of between us both. How fortunate for the poor things!

By the way, Alice, if you have trouble in reading my letters, let me know and I will take more pains with them; when I write and think at the same time the writing is necessarily slurred, as the thinking occupies my entire faculties. Good-bye until we meet again. Do not forget Boston next winter.

Lemont.

Boston, Sept. 26.

My dear Alice:—

Really, a letter from you seems like a voice from the departed—from the happy past to which I had almost said good-bye. It seemed so long since I had heard from you that I concluded it was my ill fortune to have been gently placed on the shelf along with the many admirers of yourself who had had their little day and then been moved to one side to make way for the new comer. At the end of your letter you say, "I will answer it if you wish." Alice, now, please explain. Do you mean you will answer a letter from me if I wish? If that is it, consider by all means that I wish. I presume you have been occupied and too busy to attend to unnecessary correspondence. You are, I think, described in a book I read recently, which spoke of a most charming creature over whom the men raved, but she, with all her many graces, seemed not to comprehend the depth of the affection lavished upon her, and treated her many "ravers" with about as much consideration as would have been their due had they been in reality raving.

Such women are frequently worshiped by men; in fact, by all men with whom they come in contact, but they are apparently incapable of understanding the wealth of such regard.

So you want me to come up and cheer you up a trifle during the bleak November days. Such a prospect is to me delightful in the extreme, the only objection being the distance.

You remember (or have you forgotten?) we agreed to meet in New York for the theatre this winter. Perhaps you are merely intending this as an additional treat for me; anyway, I accept so far as I can now tell. I may have to take a trip out to Western New York about Thanksgiving time; if I do, I will see you either on my way out or coming back. And should I not go then, I do not see but that I can go to the mountains for over Sunday. We will hold the matter open, and I think you will see me then—as to time, can be arranged later.

Let me see—you favored me with a one-sheet letter, but one sheet will not hold all I have to say, so I will go on.

I have seen Belle twice, I think, since her return from your house. She reported a most enjoyable time and numerous conquests. No summer would be complete for a young lady without the self-satisfaction obtainable from having a few young men at her feet—metaphorically speaking. For my own part, it has been my good fortune to be at places where the gentlemen have been (except on special occasions) in the minority, and as a consequence—the world has been mine. I went off on a yachting trip for a week as far as New London with a couple of other fellows, and we had fun, and lots of it.

For mental and physical relaxation give me a good yacht, a jolly crowd and decent weather, and I will agree to enjoy myself, of course the accessories of good "grub" (a nautical term) and plenty to drink are expected to accompany the necessaries. We had them all.

If you do go to New York this winter, let me know by all means; we can take in the theatre, and I can bask for a while in the sunshine of your smiles. But the more I think of it I am sure it would be delightful to be with you in your mountain home, away from the outside world, with a person, for whose society, a man once knowing her, will always crave.

Thus it is with me. I have really seen so little of you for so long; it has all been appointments, and they have been made and broken—all have fallen through. I want one appointment made that will not fall through. If you want any reading matter, let me know and I will send you a few novels to while away the time.

Now, don't keep me in suspense too long this time before you send me an answer. The only way I have recently been able to get news of you has been through Belle. That, you know, is second hand, and such things are always pleasanter direct. She mentioned several gentlemen apparently complimentary for the honor of doing you homage.

Now, be careful, my dear; don't be frivolous. Girls ought, you know, to be careful in choosing their male admirers. I really might be jealous. I think the above sage piece of advice will warrant my closing and again reassuring my state of expectancy until another letter arrives.

I am now and always
Your loving friend,

Lemont.

Boston, Oct. 7th.

My dear Alice (accent on the dear):—

Someone has said, in order to be a successful letter writer it is necessary to answer letters received as well as to write simply upon matters of interest to both correspondents.

I can easily believe from the tone of your letter to me that you were fully as "blue" as you say. I sincerely hope, by this time, that the least remnants of any such feelings have gone away to stay.

I have always declared, when asked concerning it, that I never have the blues and do not really think I do.

The reason being because my thoughts are occupied most of the time and I do not have the time to indulge(?) in any such unpleasant pastime. I can easily believe that if time hangs at all heavily on your hands the receipt of letters, such as you describe, must sometimes incline you to wish yourself again in New York where there is so much with which to divert oneself. But if you are dissatisfied with your present arrangements, as you have no one but yourself to consult, why not return to the city again?

Pardon me if I seem to take the liberty of advising you without an invitation so to do. I have read "As in a Looking Glass!" but not the other work you mention; will get it and read it.

Do I think they are happy? Give it up, my dear. Is any one happy? What is happiness? We, most of us, enjoy for greater or lesser periods in our lives what we call happiness. I think almost every one is occasionally happy. If it were not so, if there were no sunny days and life consisted entirely of rainy and cloudy days, it would be unbearable. I take it you do not have enough to occupy your mind. The reaction from city life to a retired country life is something to which you are unaccustomed, and mayhap, when the newness wears off, you will like it fully as well as the other.

In my own case I am of so nervous a disposition that I like to have something on foot continually; if not, then I do something myself, which resource is open to most of us—more, perhaps, to men than to women.

As I remember my visits to your house I do not think you had any occasion for jealousy. My thoughts were so much occupied with you and by you that I remember having said hardly a "yes" or "no" to Belle while there, excepting perhaps at the table. At any rate she declared, after her return to Boston when I called on her, that she had never been so snubbed in her life, and when I went anywhere again **where she was I would be very apt to know it.**

Well, all right; not my fault, all yours. You should not be so attractive. As you say, next time we will be alone. That meeting will, I hope, constitute one of the happy days which are referred to earlier in this letter.

Have you read "Eden," by Edgar Saltus, or "The Truth about Tristem Varick," by the same author—new publications, the scenes of which are laid in New York? If not, let me send them. They are, either of them, interesting enough to make one finish them after once beginning.

To-morrow night I have to act as usher at the wedding of a friend of mine. He evidently sides with the affirmative side of the question as to whether the marriage contract is a failure or no.

I wish him joy, but am in no great haste to imitate his example. He is somewhat older than I. Perhaps when I arrive at that age I may think as he does. Till then it will be enough blessedness for me, and when I do pick her out (can I say among the many?) I'll ask your advice on the subject. That is fair; isn't it?

I quote from your letter: "Well, now I must close this letter and go to bed—I am all alone this evening up here so far away." I'm sorry, but can't help it, my love. I am hundreds of miles away at present, but if fortune smiles in November I hope to be by your side—and then—ah, me! Yes, I can read your letters without difficulty. If I can read my own, I am sure I can anybody else's.

I have not seen Belle for quite a little time, not since her new mother came to live with her. I have been intending to call there for quite a while back, but have not quite reached it. Shall do so this week. I wonder how she and Hudson are progressing. You have doubtless heard her speak of him. I gathered from what she confided to me on my last visit that he was becoming very attentive. It would be curious if they should finally make a match of it.

I have known of him for years, although not acquainted with him, and should judge he is quite a nice fellow and would make her a good husband. But either she would have to tone down somewhat or he would have to liven up, for he is a very quiet and reserved fellow.

Let me know the route you take from New York, and I will write to New York for a time table.

If time really does hang heavily on your hands you ought to be able to write a large number of letters and I shall hope for a speedy answer.

My photo will be forthcoming. How about yours for me?

Yours as always,
Lemont.

ERS OF MY SECOND WIDOW-HOOD.

My second husband and myself
Alice

LETTERS OF MY SECOND WIDOW-
HOOD.

LAST NIGHT.

Last night the nightingale woke me.
  Last night, when all was still,
It sang in the golden moon-light,
  From out the woodland hill,
I open'd my window so gentle,
  I look'd on the dreaming dew,
And oh! the bird, my darling,
  Was singing, was singing of you.

I think of you in the day-time,
  I dream of you by night;
I wake and would you were here, love,
  And tears are blinding my sight,
I hear a low breath in the lime-tree,
  The wind is floating thro',
And oh! the night, my darling,
  Is sighing, is sighing for you.

Oh! think not I can forget you,
  I could not, tho' I would,
I see you in all around me—
  The stream, the night, the wood,
The flowers that slumber so gently,
  The stars above the blue,
Oh! heaven, itself, my darling,
  Is praying, is praying for you.

New York, Dec. 28th.

Dear Alice:—

Last night, just about dark and just about the time of day, I was ushered into this vale of tears and woe. So many, many years ago! The mountain box arrived at my house containing the beautiful Afghan and the pleasant little note from you accompanying it. You may rest assured that I shall throw the Afghan over me when those afternoon naps are taken, and sometimes in the evening, and that I shall not be likely to forget the giver.

There's a lot of work in this gift and of your own hands, and this gives a special value to it to me.

I thank you for it and for your good wishes.

Your friend,
Robert.

7/18.

Mrs. Robinson.

Dear Alice:—

Although in a very great hurry I can not leave this good old city without dropping a line to a dear friend. I arrived here this 9 A.M., and shall leave on the "Werra" for Germany to-morrow, Saturday, at 8 A.M., to be gone about five weeks. Expect to return on the "Ems" and arrive here about August 18th. I feel so natural in this city that I hate to leave the good old place.

With kindest regards, I remain,
Sincerely,
Leon.

California, June 22d.

Dear Mrs. Robinson:—

I wish to thank you for the beautiful flowers you sent me, considering they were in a lovely state of preservation. To me they were very much. I sometimes wish you had not sent them at all. I suffered with the thoughts they awakened, and in my present existence I am hardly in a condition to allow such thoughts to enter my mind. I wish that providential angel of mine could very suddenly drop me in front of you. I have so much to tell you and wish to look upon your kind face again. Ever since I left New York my life has been to me a disappointment. I came very near being numbered amongst the dead. Appendicitis was the cause of it all. Subjecting myself to an operation, which was to me a joy at the time, an operation that in itself may cause death at any time, I was one of the fortunates that passed by it. My illness caused a rapid falling in the health of my good mother, who died soon after I returned from California whence I had gone in search of health. Good woman! She died too soon. But "her boy" feels as though he was the cause of a great deal. A month before I was stricken down with this dreadful disease I became engaged, at least I thought so; but when the young lady convinced herself that there was no hope for my recovery, after several weeks of despondency, cheered up and married the other fellow. I fear I have grown somewhat indifferent in my profession, although I considered several offers to go before the footlights. With all this I have not lost any of my hopes of soon entering into private practice. I am still in the C. B. service, and am very well pleased. My only drawbacks are my heavy social expenses, and they must be cut down. How are you anyway, my dear friend? Have you a family? It has been very hot to-day. If it keeps on I shall arrange for my vacation—probably at the sea shore—and I shall think of you.

My kindest regards to you,
Very sincerely,
Leon.

March 20th.

My dear Alice:—

How much I longed to be at your side those last few days, my dear. Those are sad hours, unpleasant reminders; still we must bear them. Time, the great and only wound healer, must come to our rescue. Oh, I wish I could have been with you to console, comfort and cheer you up. Poor, dear Alice! I trust you are well. Please address me when you feel well enough.

Love and kiss from
Your affectionate
Theodore.

Southern Hotel, June 1st.

My dear Alice:—

Much rather I should like to speak to you to-night, but here I must sit down to a table and pen these lines to you. Don't the stationery seem familiar? Please, glance at the heading, and place your fair hand near my heart. It's some days since I received your letter, and, I assure you, my joys were unbounded, for it was one of those I used to, "used to," get from you in days gone by, Alice. Dear Alice, I am so glad you are in such good health. That is one consolation. Isn't it? And a great one. I believe I could write seventy-five of these sheets to you, but I must not. How long since I have written to you! Oh, my! By the way, you have asked me how the doctor was? Something has told you. The poor boy has been stricken with a terrible affliction and has been hovering between life and death since March. In the prime of life, the picture of health, spirits and joy six weeks ago—to-day helpless and almost reduced to a skeleton. Alice, please, never complain when you enjoy good health.

My most unfortunate brother's illness was of such a serious nature that it necessitated the opening of the abdominal cavity, which occurred at the hospital in this city, and he has been so low since that his death was expected hourly. I am happy to say he has since improved slightly and his recovery is now more hopeful. Oh, Alice! I tell you this is a sad blow, and I hope you sympathize with me.

Pray that he may again enjoy good health. A queer circumstance is that brother wrote a book on abdominal treatments, intestines, etc, and he becomes afflicted with it and almost dies.

Brother was still associated with the C. B., and was working on medical briefs, etc., to be presented at the next international meeting of doctors at Rome next September, where he expected to be present.

Alice, I fear I am tiring you; so, to something else. You said you spent the winter alone. Why did you do it? Here nearly everything is as of yore. I have not changed any, only I am not as big a goose as I was (confound it). I never permit my thoughts to run in that direction, for it would surely drive me crazy. You are such a good, kind woman, Alice—and I shall love you eternally for that.

When are you going to the World's Fair, dear? Do you not soon anticipate a trip West? You remember, I tried to see you East—do you remember? Refresh your memory, Alice! But you cut me, oh, a cut that reached my heart to the very bottom. It surely must have reached the bottom, for it aches still occasionally. Adding to that, two weeks before I intended starting East I was laid up with typhoid fever for three months. I do not think I ever told you. Alice, I hope this letter will find you in a more contented frame of mind and happy and in good health and spirits, for that is the wish of your love in the West.

Write me soon and, please, send me one of your latest photographs. I'll return the favor.

Good night,

Theodore.

June 10th.

Alice, my dear:—

I received your esteemed note some days ago. It made me feel sad, happy and God knows how, Alice. Brother is getting along very nicely now, and I am so glad. I went out home to see him last Sunday and found him much improved.

You know, I took him home ten days ago. He could not remain at the hospital on account of the beastly heat and exceedingly poor food.

Received a letter from home this morning saying

he is able to be around some. The poor fellow has had a terrible siege of it, but, thank the Lord, he is getting over it. He sends his kindest greetings to you.

Alice, I am sorry you did not think of going to the World's Fair. What detains you? If nothing prevents me I shall hope to go about the middle of July. Will we meet? Where is your telegraph station?

Good night, Alice! Fare thee well, the wish of
Your love in the West,
Theodore.

Oct. 3d.

My dear Alice:—

It always cheers me to hear from you, Alice. We have been treated miserably of late. We had the great misfortune to lose our dear mother, and we have nearly all been sick with grief ever since. It was a terrible shock and to me the hardest blow of my life.

Alice, sympathize with me. Brother has recovered and returned to California to resume his duties. He asks me to remember him to you. Alice, I feel sorry for any one who has sickness in the family.

Write to me again.
Theodore.

May 18th.

Alice, my dear:—

I received those pretty violets. Did you pick them for me? I was just thinking of you, leaning on my arm, strolling through rocks and cliffs, picking sweet violets. How much sweeter they would be. But right here is what I feel sad at, one of your remarks—one that you no doubt entertained on a rainy, cloudy day (not see each other's faces again and not gaze into your mild eyes anymore). Why, the very idea, Alice—absurd, perfectly. Do you remember what you thought the day I met you at the station in St. Louis, and what you said to me? No doubt, poor thing; you have had your troubles, and they will tell on one. But, Alice, a few peaceful months, plenty of fresh air and rest are productive of great changes, you know, and are bound to overcome and put away all that you seem alarmed about.

Then, Alice, you are such an athletic woman! Why, such never grow old. Bah! Cheer up! Don't talk about old any more, please; it makes me tired. What may you be doing now? You have returned to the mountains. Who is with you? Alice, dear! As you see I am writing to you from the Jonah place, the Southern, where you would not love me a little bit, nor be loved. I have been thinking and come to a thinking conclusion that you did not treat me right at all. Alice, strawberries are in again, but we are not together. Oh, by the way, did the doctor send you one of his photographs—of himself? We speak of you so often. Have you made up your mind where you are going this summer?

Now, if I could only invite and have you here to dine with me this evening—I would feel better than I do with more than a thousand miles between us. May this find you well and in happier spirits,

So, farewell, dear Alice.

Theodore.

Nov. 21st.

Oh! you Honolulu:—

Well for the land of the living! Who'd think it? Alice, God bless you, dear!

You are well and happy—how good that makes me feel! Do you know I have been thinking about you? Your very welcome letter was received with open arms, and I've been feeling "out of sight," so to say, all day. Post mark says "Honolulu, Oct. 31st—San Francisco, Nov. 17th,—and St. Louis, 21st."

Seems impossible to me that I love you with that distance between us, but I do.

Why did you not tell me more about yourself? You never even remarked how the weather was and, by the way, who was traveling with you? Oh, I do not care, you would not ask me along anyhow. You are mean.

When are you coming back? Please, don't stay away for good; neither of us could die without coming face to face—yes, lips to lips, I dare say, on this puzzling earth again.

I am well—same young chap. Brother the same, surgeon for the C. B., and every body alive of our family and fairly well.

Alice, I happened to drop into Tony Faust's yesterday and spied a tray of strawberries, and I exclaimed "Halloo!" Alice, dear, they came from Florida. I wrote to you before you left the U. S. Promise never to slight me thus again. Yes, I know you will promise. Ada Rehan plays in town this week. Wish I could get tickets for two. I think I would be living then. I am awfully glad you met somebody like me. You won't forget your innocent love altogether. Oh, yes; the girls! Oh, pshaw! I never loved one head over heels yet. If I ever find one like you I will say good bye! And, Alice, if I should ever get married, will you still love me? You are a good woman—Alice, think of that night, you angel. I fear I will make this letter so long that it will never reach you and I should like to stop, for the thought of you sets me nervous and I must try and forget you between now and bed time, or else I should feel sleepy to-morrow morning.

So, farewell to you, dear, and God bless you, is the wish of

Your love in the West,
Theodore.

Alice dear:—

I wish you a bright, cheerful and happy new year.

Theodore.

March.

Alice dear:—

May be you ain't a birdie! Melbourne Feb. 8th! Will you stop off?

A letter for the doctor, how nice! He will be greatly pleased—I am sure—I know it.

He said to me that he wondered why Alice never thinks of him any more.

Will this reach our "Alice?" Doubt it, but I must address you and I hope you feel it this very minute.

I hope you got my letter at New Zealand.

Thanks, thanks twice for that sweet likeness of yours. It made the bottom side of my heart flutter. I treasure a photo of Alice, taken in Zululand, highly. Thanks, you little rascal; are you coming home via Africa? God bless you (while you are gone) and help you to land safely again on U. S. soil in strawberry time.

Farewell, darling angel; write to me, Alice.

Your loving boy,

Theodore.

4/8.

Alice dear:—

Too bad you didn't put yourself right in the centre of that pretty bouquet and come along to St. Louis. I am sure you would not have been out of place peeping out of a bunch of roses. Nevertheless I was greatly pleased as it was.

Thanks, Alice!

I am just recovering from a severe attack of La Grippe—been down several weeks with it.

Think I'll migrate to California or some other warm climate sometime, or I will surely die soon here.

How would an invitation to the Grand Opera (Abbey and Grau) strike you to-night or any night this week?

Wish I could have escorted you to "Romeo et Juliette" Monday eve, Mme. Melba and the two De Reskes.

Write me a letter soon, Alice, please. Kisses for roses.

Sincerely and lovingly,

Theodore,

My dear Alice:—

Why so quiet? I hope you are not ill. Strawberries are ripe again. The sight of them means pleasant remembrances. I am better again and hope you are more so. Nothing new here.

Write soon, please.

Yours as always,

Theodore.

My dear Alice:—

Photo received; it's pretty. Impressed me with a desire to see you again and give you a good hug.

I placed you on my dresser and see you every morning. You know, I live with sister way out in the West end. My younger sister is also there and going to school. She is very sweet and cute now. Golden hair and pale face, blue eyes and pug nose. Sister H. had a little girl, and after we all learned to love it, it died. It was nearly two years old. My younger brother is also a doctor. He is a six footer. L. is at California. He was with us on Sunday last and I handed him your photo. He seemed delighted to be face to face with Alice. Pa is still at our country home killing time, hunting and fishing and keeping hunting dogs. We all go to see him occasionally. More later on. Alice, I don't seem to understand the real estate transaction you refer to in your last letter. How are you fixed? Can I come up to see you sometime when I have a chance, which I expect may be some time this fall? You had better post me so I won't drop in on you, for, when I drop, I generally stay awhile.

I may spend the winter in California. I am getting tired of Grippe every year; still I don't know what I'll do. Where do you think you will move to? Don't forget to let me know, dear Alice.

With much love, your affectionate.

Theodore.

A kiss for your photo. Please excuse penmanship. Must be 200 in the shade—4.30 P.M.

Alice dear:—

Do you know that I have been real angry with you (don't cher know) for not writing to me?

I thought to myself, Ah, ha! It's summer again; sweet Alice is playing summer girl and doesn't want me to drop in.

Your cute little letter from London made me feel "better." But say, my fair rover, may be you ain't a daisy. You are much too far away for me to think about you. And how can I picture that sweet Alice's Southern laugh with miles of salt water between us? Somehow I do not want the picture—I want the real one, don't you forget it?

Alice, my health has greatly improved lately, although I only weigh one hundred and forty pounds and carry not an ounce of superfluous flesh, although I would look well with some.

I wish I could have crossed the ocean with you— bet sixteen to one I could add thirty pounds in a very short while.

I ride my wheel a great deal, and that keeps me in good shape.

By the way, you don't ride, Alice? If you and I could do London on a wheel, wouldn't that be gay and nice? Then I fish, and next month shooting season opens, and that will get all my spare time for sixty days.

Fare thee well, Alice, and God be with thee.

Theodore.

Alice! Money is getting very close here. Too much politics cannot buy gold. So look out and do not let yourself get separated from your bank account.

T.

Newark, N. J., 3/23.

My beloved friend:—

I heard only to-day of your loss by the death of your beloved husband. I am truly sorry to hear of it and extend to you my heartfelt sympathy. I hope you remember who I am. I feel sure you do and I sincerely hope to hear from you very soon. I want to extend to you now, in time of your affliction, the hand of friendship and of love. I am poor at consolation, but what I try to do is most faithfully sincere and true.

I am not in Trenton now, nor at Philadelphia. The above is my business address where all letters will reach me. I sincerely hope and trust one will come here from you very, very soon.

I have thought of you many times of late, and I have wondered where you were and how I could reach you. Please, be kind enough to write to me and tell me when I can see you and where I can write to you.

Very faithfully and sincerely,

Yours always,

Seth.

New York, June 15th.

I have before me a letter dated "Wednesday 18—," written by one I thought much of, who at that time was a guest at the Gedney House. I have treasured that letter these years, because it was the first and only one I ever received from her. In it she tells me, as I look at it, "write to me care of Gedney House, and I will call for it soon; write only once until you hear again from me. With much love, etc., etc." I have not heard since. Having waited a reasonably long time, I take the opportunity of writing to the address given me by one of her friends, and endeavor to reopen our long closed correspondence and friendship.

Will you not kindly write to one in confidence, who is your ardent admirer and who has always remembered you kindly and with love?

I shall be glad to hear from you and, perhaps, we can arrange to see one another some day when we can say face to face what had better not be written.

Please write and tell me that you remember
                Yours as ever,
                          Seth.

New York, October.

My dear Alice:—

I got a letter from Mrs. B—— on the 1st, in which she says that the horses, dogs, cat and chickens are all doing well and that James is well and was graveling the carriage road and was taking good care of everything so far. This letter was in reply to one I wrote, asking for news. No answer to your letter reached the Vendome, and I thought it best to see how things stood. I duly received your several cards written in the cars on your way across the continent, and the final one, written on the day of your departure from San Francisco, and was very glad to know that so far at least all had gone well. It is to me wonderful how quickly and entirely your hurt foot recovered, and I only hope that there may have been no relapse. I am looking for a letter from you within a few days from Honolulu and shall then know how you found things on board ship. I trust your state room was a pleasant one and that the passengers were agreeable and that your room mate—if you had one—was not of the fussy or sea-sick variety. Your Honolulu letter will no doubt tell me about these things. How time flies! You are due in Auckland to-morrow, no, to-day, and have very likely already been met by the brother you have so long been separated from. The telegram to L——, sent a few days after you sailed, contained just four words, the address made 5 more, and the charge was $13.68—$1.52 a word—so you perceive writing is somewhat more economical; but if the dispatch reached him all right and he was in Auckland to receive you, it was money well spent. I have heard nothing from the G's as yet, nor have I seen Mrs. A. The latter instance is not a very strange one, inasmuch as the only chance of seeing her would be an accidental meeting on the street. I have been very well. Heard Melba sing Sunday night and Plancon. They both did splendidly. You recollect Melba gets her stage name from Melbourne, where she came from. If New Zealand can send along a singer equal to her, let her come. There is plenty of room for all such artists in this region, and there are but very few in the world equal to her. We had a general election all over the country yesterday. The Tammany ring in this city was routed—horse, foot and artillery, and the Republicans made immense gains everywhere. We are even going to have a Republican Board of Aldermen in this city, a thing that has not occurred before within my memory. I shall send you by this mail yesterday's and to-day's papers, containing particulars of the results of the fight. The very latest news is that there is some doubt as to the Board of Aldermen—three districts being in dispute.

It has rained here half the time lately, and in Massachusetts a heavy snowstorm occurred the other day, and they had to get their snow plough out in Hanover to clear the roads.

Sothern, Hopper and the "Milk White Flag" are still flourishing. Sothern is the only one of the three that I have seen, since you saw them with me. Lillian Russell has just brought out her new English success, "The Queen of Brilliants." The papers do not agree in their criticisms of it. I shall have to take it in and judge for myself. There are some other new things, which, if you were here, I would take you to see; but I trust you are going to have so good a time in New Zealand that you will not miss the New York theatres.

You must write and tell me how things out there strike you.

I do hope you will get a saddle to ride on that suits you and a horse equal to Billy.

Most of your money here has been invested, leaving you about enough to buy five bonds more, which no doubt will be done before I write again.

Matters here are moving along quietly. There is nothing of a personal nature to communicate that is at all startling.

I shall expect that Honolulu letter of yours to bring me good news of you up to that date, and the first one from New Zealand to be of the same kind, and the succeeding ones ditto.

With best wishes,

Your Friend.

New York, December.

My dear Alice:—

Since last writing I have your two letters, posted in Honolulu and Samoa, and was delighted to hear that up to that stage of your long journey everything had gone so well and that you had had so agreeable a trip. It was strange that you should meet with people that knew Mrs. T——, and had been to the mountains and remembered your house.

Samoa is the home of the novelist Stevenson, who went there to live in consequence of having consumption, and, from what you say, he must have made a wise selection for his home. I saw in the Herald the arrival of the "Monowai" at Auckland on the 18th, so I hope the rest of the voyage was as pleasant as the first half and that your brother was at Auckland to meet you.

The G——'s arrived on the 15th, and Mr. G—— called to see me next day. He was looking in splendid health, in fact, so rugged that I did not know him. His wife had a hard time coming over, being sea-sick.

They were going out of town for a few weeks; but I think they have returned to town, as he called again a few days ago, but I was out. I was in hopes he might come in again ere this, so that I might give you the latest news of them. L——'s wife has presented him with a little girl. You remember, perhaps, that they have a boy, some seven or eight years old. J—— seems pleased with the new comer, but says he is not getting as sound a sleep as before. The natural antics of infants are among the penalties of having them, however, and must be borne with good grace.

The horse show was a great affair—crowded every night. It might, perhaps, be better called a fashionable woman's show, for the 400 filled the boxes in the giddiest, gayest attire. They are now doing the same thing at the opera, but have less on; more of themselves is now to be seen. Melba, whom you heard and remember, is singing beautifully and acting better than last season. One American prima donna, Emma Eames, made her first appearance for the winter the other night, and so did Nordica, another American. It is curious that out of the three leading prima donnas now here two are American and the other Australian—not one of them Italian, and of the leading male singers two are Poles and two French. The Italians now-a-days seem to be taking second place.

I send you a Harper's Weekly, showing some of the Horse Show scenes, and hope it gets to Kamo safe.

Do you remember, in De Wolf Hopper's operetta, Dr. Syntax, where one of the girls leads a little dog on the stage and says she calls him "Chauncey Depew," because he speaks for his supper? Well, I was there one night, when the real Chauncey Depew sat right behind me and seemed to enjoy the joke very much, but a young lady, who was with him, took it very seriously and seemed to think it necessary to be very severe and dignified for the remainder of the performance. By the time she has doubled her age she will very likely have halved that dignity of hers. I notice that many people mellow with age.

I have not heard a word from the mountains since last writing and take it for granted everything is going on right, but shall write up again shortly to Mrs. B—— and find out.

I have been very well since you left. I was sorry to hear that leather bag had turned out so poorly, but the sea air did it I guess. The one you bought for your sister, being packed away, will, I think, open up all right.

It was luck, was it not, that you happened to strike the best boat of the line? I am wondering if you will return in her. I see she leaves Auckland on the 20th. Your life in New Zealand must be something of a novelty, but yet, I imagine, you fall into it quite readily, being in good health and entirely at home on a horse's back.

I am thinking you are enjoying things there very much with your brother and sister and nieces. I am sure they will all like you.

By New Year's a letter from Kamo should reach me from you, which I hope to get and find it filled with good news of you.

       With love,

           Your Friend

The mountains.

Dear Madame:—

Please excuse the liberty I take in writing you. I would like very much to become acquainted with you, if agreeable.

I met you twice last week and was very much impressed with your appearance. Any correspondence between us will be sacred and strictly confidential, for my intentions are perfectly honorable.

If you should decide not to answer, please destroy this note or return it to —— ——.

Very truly yours,
F.

April 18th.

Dear Mrs. Robinson:—

My brother Winfred has just returned from the West and after all these years given up the fight for life. He is in a very precarious condition, and we cannot tell how long he may be with us. It is his special request that I write you his message of farewell. He says he cannot go without saying good bye to one who has afforded him so many pleasant and comfortable hours when he was most in need of a cheering companion. Any message or letter you may care to entrust to me I will be most happy to deliver for you.

With kindest regards,
Yours,
Winfred's Brother.

Dear Mrs. Robinson:—

In consultation with Winfred last night he says he would very much like to see you, but does not know that he will be able to, even if you should take the trouble to come over. If you are willing to take the chances, why, come ahead. He is with mother at No. ——. It is really very doubtful whether you will be able to see him should you come.

If you are likely to be in New York or Brooklyn any evening I would take great pleasure in calling on you and will deliver some messages that are entrusted to me, but of which I shall not write pending your possible opportunity of seeing Winfred in person.

Meantime regard me as your friend and confidant in all matters pertaining to Winfred.

With kindest regards and hoping soon to meet again, I am,

Yours,

Winfred's Brother.

If you request it I will make an evening out to you at your pleasure.

To Mrs. Alice Robinson.

Dear Mrs. Robinson:—

Your letter was received this morning. The dear boy died last night at eleven.

My kindest regards to you and let me come and see you sometime.

The funeral will be private.

Yours,

Winfred's Brother.

Dear Mrs. Robinson:—

In your last letter to Winfred, directed in my care, you made request for one of his photos. I doubt if I could find an extra copy of his last picture and, perhaps, it is just as well, for it does not show him as you knew him. It is the picture of an invalid and, I think, you would much prefer the likeness I enclose. This shows him as I saw him when I visited him last summer to get what I thought would be my last talk with him, and in reality it was our last talk, for after his home coming he was changed—changed so that there was none of his immense show of pluck and ambition left in him. He came home to end his days with his old mother, and he knew how short the time would be.

I hope you will like his picture. It is not one of New York's city refinement, but shows him in his rugged Western simplicity and is altogether an excellent likeness.

He spoke much of you during his last days and left some few messages for you.

I shall expect to see you some day and talk to you more fully of the dear boy.

With kindest regards, I remain,
    Yours,
      Winfred's Brother.

      March 29th.

My dear Mrs. Robinson:—

I beg to acknowledge receipt of picture, which will find a pleasant place among my friends and it will always serve as a reminder of our meeting and the delightful trip down the Hudson.

Hope you have fully rested from your long journey and are again surrounded by your many friends.

I will send you some views when taken in the early spring.

With pleasant wishes, believe me,

          Very truly.

          New York.

Dear Mrs. Robinson:—

You don't know how pleased I was to receive your letter. Mr. E—— and myself have often spoken of you and the very pleasant time we had for so short an acquaintance.

It is great pleasure for me to recall instances of this kind.

Have been here in the city most of the time.

Often have I thought of you while alone at dinner. How much nicer one could relish it in the company of a nice and agreeable lady to share it with. I can say the same of the theatre. Were you here in the city and saw fit to accept of these two pleasures I could have assured you a good time. Have had but little else to do to other than enjoy myself. I accidentally came across our other mutual friend, Mrs. R——. You remember her? She looked very charming and asked if I had seen you.

Your friend, the Gold Plum Pudding, I do not think very generous or else he would have given it to you as a souvenir and he, why, he would have never missed it, judging from the way he spoke of his interest in mines, etc. But, you know, sometimes talk is very cheap.

I can fully appreciate the state of your feelings up there, in among the snow banks, after coming from such a delightful climate.

Am planning a trip to Colorado and expect to leave next Tuesday or Wednesday. If anything should happen, then I don't go. If you will let me know when and where you are to be in the city you can rest assured that I will call on you.

Will be in Poughkeepsie next Monday and Tuesday, c./o. —— Hotel. Will be delighted to hear from you there and in case the letter fails to reach you in time, my address for the next four weeks will be c./o. —— Hotel, Denver, Colo. Will not be there all of the time, but anything sent there will be forwarded to me on a day's notice. Have been out walking, and my hand is so unsteady that I can scarcely write.

To-night I go to see "Trilby"; last night Mr. and Mrs. Kendal; the night before the Casino; one before that, Koster and Bial's, and previous to that Bellew and Mrs. Potter, so you see I keep on the move.

Hope you can read this letter without being exhausted.

I will be pleased to have the pleasure of a letter at Poughkeepsie and, if agreeable, when I come on the first of September, I will be pleased to renew our acquaintance.

          Your friend,

                           B. B.

                          Chicago, Ill.

My dear Mrs. Robinson:—

Your interesting letter of the 19th received, and pleased me very much. You see, I am on my way to

Denver. Expect to leave here Sunday noon and dine in Denver Monday evening at 7 P.M. Will try and locate our Gold Plum Pudding. Saw Mr. E—— and gave him your message. The meeting of Mrs. R—— was purely chance and I mentioned it as a singular coincidence. Three minutes before I had passed the Hotel Marlborough and she popped into my mind, and on the next block you can imagine my surprise at meeting her. Well, our short acquaintance proved very pleasant or, at least, was so to me and, judging from your note, you were sufficiently so as not to forget me. I do enjoy nice company so much when it is a nice, agreeable lady. You must not think by this that I enjoy the society of all ladies. That is not so, because I am very fastidious and like to select my company. You can see from this letter that you come in under the head of those that I admire.

How perfectly stupid my trip has been from Poughkeepsie here—no one to talk to. There was only one nice young lady in my car. She acted as if she would like some one to cheer her up; but dear old mamma was with her, so that was spoiled. My journey seemed one of a week. How I wished our little party of four were going to accompany one to Denver. Wouldn't we have a jolly time? I see, you as well as myself, while in New York, got around some. Don't know why you should underscore "not" in regard to the bronze models. In comparison to some of the others they were decidedly modest, and for the life of me I cannot see why they have made such a fuss over them. I don't take much stock in these straight-laced people.

You mention your large open fire-place—that reminds me of my boyhood days; we had just such an old fire-place. When you talk about comfort I think one finds it there on a cold, stormy night. Hickory nuts, cider and apples—how I wish I could have them now. I would have enjoyed meeting you in New York; I believe I could have given you a pleasant time. I see you are fond of the theatre, after theatre means a nice little supper; you are then in a condition to enjoy a nice little chat. I said to Mr. E—— that upon short acquaintance you proved a very nice and interesting person, and the more we saw of you the better we liked you. I sincerely hope, when I come on in the fall, I may have the pleasure of renewing our friendship. How nice in you to remember that poor man. I hope, for your sake, he will be kind to the poor animal. You must derive lots of pleasure from those cobs and your saddle horse. It will only be a few days now when the country will look the most lovely. The foliage is coming out so fast and the flowers so beautiful and sweet. I wonder after this scrawl if you can find time to write me while in Colorado. My headquarters will be —— Hotel. I can get my mail from there every twenty-four hours in any part of the State. Will try and write you some time when I am not in so much of a hurry. But I am afraid, if I don't write now, I will not have another opportunity until after I reach Denver. Take good care of the dogs and horses. When out airing them, occasionally, think of me, and by all means cure that cold.

Trusting this will find you well and happy, believe me, Your friend, B. B.

Auckland, New Zealand, Nov. 17th.

Mrs. Robinson.

My dearest friend:—

    I received your kind and most welcome letter yesterday morning and hasten to answer it, as the mail leaves at 10.30 P.M. I cannot tell you the pleasure it gave me to receive a letter from one so dear to me and to know that, although we are absent from each other, you do not forget me. I felt awfully lonely that night on the wharf after the steamer left. I felt as though I had parted from the best and only friend I had in the world. It is strange that such a feeling should spring up in such a short acquaintance with both of us. I say both of us, because I believe the feeling to be mutual. By the way you express yourself in your letter I hope you were not offended at the way I spoke that evening in the hotel parlor. I could not help it. I was sincere in all I said, and I am still. My feelings towards you now are just the same, and it lies with you whether we are to part forever or not. I know I have been wild, but I am over that now. My health is on the mend, which I know you will be very glad to hear. I will leave here for Sydney this week. As soon as I make a move I will write and let you know.

    In your letter you say that you do not know what I will think of you, because you wished I was with you. Well, I can only think one thing and that is that your thoughts were the same as mine. I would give anything to be with you all the time. You need not think that I kept my put-off engagement with those young ladies, because I did not. I have not felt like visiting since you left—why? you can tell yourself.

So, now my dear friend, I must close. Hoping you are enjoying yourself and trusting that you will not be offended when I say, with best love,

I remain sincerely yours,

Leonard.

P.S.—Kindly write at once, as I will anxiously await an answer.   L.

Auckland, New Zealand, Nov. 22d.

My dear Mrs. Robinson.

My dearest friend:—

I have just received your kind and most welcome letter this morning and now hasten to answer it, as the mail leaves this afternoon. You had not received my letter when you wrote this last one, but I hope you got it soon after. If I have said anything in it offensive to you I hope you will forgive me, but whatever I said was sincere and I could not help it; I had to write the promptings of my heart. If the memory of that evening is fresh in your memory you can imagine how it is in mine, and, oh, don't I wish for it again. But you say it can never be. That remains with you. Your will is mine in this matter and by you I will be guided. But I would like to see you just once more. Oh, for another happy hour, but I am afraid it will never be. I cannot write sentiment, but I can write sense. Now, my dear friend, I must tell you the news. I leave here on the 28th, at 5 P.M., for Sydney. My health is improving all the time but slowly. I will write again before I leave, and give you all particulars. We are having miserable weather, raining and blowing all the time, and I have not been out much lately. I hope you will answer this at once. If you do, I will get it before I leave. I should like to know for certain when you intend to go to Sydney, as I am going to do my best to see you again, if possible, unless you object; any letters you write address them here and they will deliver them to me as soon as they can. I will send you my photo as soon as taken, and that will be as soon as possible. And I do earnestly hope I get yours before I leave. You say you will stay at the Australia in Sydney. Let me know that I may not make a mistake. Let me know where you will be at Christmas and you may depend on a letter from me.

So, now I must close. Trusting this will find you well in health, and living in the hope of seeing you once more before you return home, believe me, with best love,

   Yours most sincerely,

       Leonard.

I have lots more to say, but I dare not say it; your letter forbids me. Good bye! Think of me sometimes.   L.

   Auckland, New Zealand, Nov. 23d.
 Mrs. Robinson.

My dearest friend:—

Your kind and welcome letter of last Monday has just arrived, and as the "Wellington" sails for Whangarei very soon I take the first opportunity of answering it. This is the third letter I have sent you, and I hope you have got them all right. I made a mistake in my first letter when I told you my steamer left on Wednesday; she leaves here on the 28th for Sydney. I will send you a letter on my arrival at Sydney, and hope to have a letter from you telling me when you intend going to Sydney. I do not know of any place where you could board in private apartments, but I will try and find you a nice place, while I am there, and I will let you know before you leave. I have made up my mind to see you again if it is at all possible, and spend another happy evening or even hour with you before we part, perhaps, forever, as you say. You advise me to remain here, and you say I may find some young lady with lots of money. I hope you don't think I could fall in love with any young lady because she has lots of money. Money is a very nice thing to have, but if I did not care for the person I would not marry her if she was loaded with money. You say I have a girl in Sydney. Well, I have lots of fair friends there, but there is not one among them that is anything more to me than another. I could not lead any girl to think I cared for her, when I did not. It is strongly against my principles. I like them all as friends, and they seem to like me, but no more. I spoke to you on that subject, because I really care for you and love you. But you reject me on principles of your own and I cannot help but admire you and sincerely trust that our friendship will always continue. I am having a very quiet time here. When you go home to New York I hope you will think of me sometimes and write me a letter. I cannot tell you the pleasure it will give me to receive and answer a letter from the dearest friend I have in the world. I can't reconcile myself to the fact that I will never see you again. The memory of that evening is so fresh in my mind that it is not easy to forget it. I sometimes wish that I could and then again I would not forget it for anything. A pleasant hour like we spent ought not to be forgotten, as it is a bright light in many a dark hour. It will be to me.

Now, my dearest, I must close, hoping to have one more letter before I sail and another one when I arrive.

With best love and wishes for your future welfare, believe me to remain,

Yours most sincerely,
Leonard.

Auckland, New Zealand, Nov. 17th.

Mrs. Robinson.

My dearest friend:—

I received your telegram yesterday morning and now hasten to answer it. My steamer is in, and I have just been down on board, and I sail to-morrow evening at 5 P.M. Your letter will be here on Thursday morning; letters will be kept for me. My health is so far improved now that I think by the time I get through my trip I will be well. I will see if I can find you a nice place to stay in in Sydney. I will be there about the middle of January, and I hope to see you then. If I should not see you then I am afraid I will not see you again. We are having beastly weather here—raining all the time. I hope you are getting better weather in Kamo, if not, I am afraid you won't enjoy yourself much. Did you feel the earthquake last Sunday morning? We felt it pretty bad. It woke me up; the house was going from side to side like a ship at sea. Well, dear friend, my holiday is over now, and I am to return to work. I suppose we cannot always have a holiday. I will be in Hobart Christmas day. I have no friends there, so don't suppose I shall enjoy it much. I will send you a letter to reach you as near Christmas as I possibly can.

Although we may never see each other again we need not forget each other, and a letter occasionally from you will be very acceptable, I can assure you, and to answer it will be a great pleasure to me, and if ever I land anywhere near New York you may depend I will come and see you.

So now, my dearest friend, I must close, with fondest and best wishes for your future, and, living in the hope of seeing you again some day, believe me to be

Your most sincere friend

Leonard.

Sydney, Dec. 11th.

Mrs. Robinson.

My dearest friend:—

I arrived here to-day. I received your two letters and also the proof of your photo, which I think is a very good one. I cannot tell you the pleasure it gave me to receive and read your letters and to know that you don't forget me. The last letter was very short. I hope I have not offended you at all—or were you too tired, to write a long letter? I think that was the reason.

for if I had offended you, you would have told me. I received a telegram from you the day I sailed and would have answered it, but it was from Whangarei and I did not know where to send it. I thought you had perhaps left Kamo and were on your way to Auckland. But the answers that you asked for you found in my letter. I wrote you about the sailing and arriving of the steamers and when to write. I am very sorry you are not comfortable at Kamo; but cheer up. The time will soon pass and then we must see each other once again before we part, perhaps, forever, to kiss good bye. It is a hard thing to say good bye forever to those who are near and dear to us. But circumstances will not always allow us to do what we would like to. My dear friend, you tell me, if ever I marry to marry a girl I love. Well, I hope you don't think I would marry any one whom I did not love. But I am afraid the day is very far distant, when I get married. I do hope to see you soon. I cannot find suitable apartments for you. Will try again.

Now, my dearest friend, I hope these lines will find you in the best of health and spirits, living in the dear hope of seeing you once again. So with best love and a kiss, I remain

Your most sincere friend,

Leonard.

Sydney, 17/2.

Mrs. Robinson.

My dearest friend:—

Just a few lines which I hope will reach you about Christmas, wishing you a very merry Christmas and a happy and prosperous New Year, which, I can assure you, is the heartfelt wish of your friend. I would have written before, but I have been so busy and often too tired for anything. We had a passenger who committed suicide by jumping overboard the night we sailed. The boat was out one hour, but no trace of him could be seen, and the night after a baby died on board. I hope you got my letter. I was awfully busy and I am sure you will excuse the black lead. I often look at your photo and think of that happy evening at the hotel and the hurry down to the wharf—and then the boat sailing and leaving me on the wharf alone. I felt very lonely. I wonder will we ever meet again. I hope so sincerely. But although we may never meet again I am sure we will never forget each other. I am sending you my photo along with this. I hope you get it all right and let me know whether you like it or not. I wish I was where I could spend my Xmas with you; wouldn't we have a happy time? Be sure and not disappoint me. I will look forward with great pleasure to receiving a letter from you, and will be very much disappointed if I do not get it.

My dearest friend, I must close. With best love and a merry Christmas to you from

Yours sincerely,

Leonard.

Melbourne, June 12th.

Mrs. Alice Robinson.

My dear friend:—

Just a few lines to let you know that I am still in the land of the living and that I am well, and I sincerely hope that you are the same. You will be surprised to receive a letter from me, but I cannot forget an old friend like you. I do not know whether you will be pleased to hear from me or not, but I think and hope that you will be. I hope you enjoyed your trip home and that you found everything right when you arrived. I am sure you would be glad to get home again. I wish you lived in San Francisco so that I might sometime see you. I often think of you and of the confidential little chats we used to have together, and of that evening in the Albert Hotel and at the Domain. I have that ring that you gave me, and I prize it very much. Everybody admires it. I wonder if I will ever see you again. I hope so. If ever I land in New York again I will come and see you. I missed you a great deal after you left. You made me promise to write and tell you if ever I got married. Well, I will do so if ever that day dawns on me; but I have not found the girl yet, so I guess it is a long way off. Besides, I can't afford to get married yet. Dey told me that he received a letter from you from New York, and I was rather disappointed and I think a little jealous, because I did not get one. But I hope you will answer this and let me know how you are. If you are still writing to Dey, do not tell him that I have written to you. I don't wish him to know. So now, my dear Mrs. Robinson, I must close. With love from,

Yours very sincerely,
Leonard.

San Francisco.

My dear Mrs. Robinson:—

Your long, kind and welcome letter just to hand, and am glad to hear that you are well in health. We sail this afternoon at 2 o'clock, so I have no time to write a long letter. I am very sorry you cannot help me in my little difficulty, but I know that everything is dull now, most everything. I sincerely hope your book is a great success, but expect to hear on our arrival, if we come back. No time to say more at present. Will write from Samoa. So now, my dear friend, I must close. With kindest regards and best wishes, believe me to remain,

Yours sincerely,

Leonard.

Good bye and good luck. Excuse scrawl; am in a terrible hurry. I guess the air will be blue on the dock this afternoon. L.

At sea.

My dear friend, Mrs. Robinson:—

I now take the extreme pleasure of answering your letter, which I only received the day we sailed. I was rather surprised to hear of your writing a book. I sincerely trust it is a great success. If it is you must let me know. I am glad you are pleased with my picture. I think it is very good myself. I am sorry it cannot speak to you as you wish—I would make it do so if I could. Yes, L—— has struck luck, at last. But he has another trouble now; his hair is all coming out in patches and his moustache also, and it is making him wild. I think he is afraid his girl won't have him with bald patches on his head. Good luck to him, I say. I would not mind having one thousand of his cash. It would come in handy just now. I do not know just what will become of me. I want to give this up anyhow, and what I will get into then, God only knows. But I guess I will pull out of it all right in time. I am not a fellow that gives in very easily. Those were indeed happy days we passed together, and I am glad that you look back to them as golden days. I do. I wonder will we ever meet again. Would you care to see me if I came to New York at any time, in not quite such comfortable circumstances as I am now in? I hope I never do; but a fellow like me never knows where he may fetch up. I think I would be ashamed to come and see you, although it might not be my fault, but my misfortune. I saw Mrs. A—— the day I got your letter, but it was before I received it. I got the letter about half an hour after she went away. She and E—— came down to the ship. I did think of you the day we sailed, but I had no occasion to make the air blue— everything went pretty smoothly. I will get you a photo of the Cemetery Bridge if I possibly can. I will try in Auckland. We did have a lovely time that evening. Do you remember the night the "Wellington" sailed, and me on the dock holloaing out that I would see you in New York? I did not expect to see you again anyhow, but strange things turn up in this world.

It is now 9 o'clock on Thursday night, and we will be in Samoa about midnight and sail to-morrow morning for Sydney. I am quite well. Many thanks for the kind inquiry. There is some talk of the ship not returning to Frisco, but we will know for certain in Sydney. I will write and let you know if we should not come back. I hope she does go back. I hope there is one of your new photos for me. I will expect one when we arrive back on the 10th of December and will expect a letter on arrival with the good news that your book is a grand success. If we do not come back the letter will be forwarded to New Zealand. Everything is pretty much the same on board. There are more here than I care to remember you to. I am awfully greedy, ain't I? So now, my dear friend, I must close.

With every good wish and a fond kiss, believe me
       Ever your sincere friend,
                          Leonard.

Think of me sometimes.

                                At sea.

My dear Mrs. Robinson:—

At last I have received an answer to my last letter, which I thought I was never going to get. You posted the letter on the 3d of December to Frisco and I received it in Honolulu on April 4th, so this is the first chance I have had of answering it.

We arrive in Samoa to-morrow, Sunday, on our way to Sydney, and this will come up by the "Monowai." I do not know where the letter has been, but I am very glad I have got it at last. I really had begun to think that I had said something to offend you in my last letter, but I am very thankful such is not the case.

Well, about L——. I do not know whether you know, but his marriage is off. I will hang on here, but am properly sick of it. I wish to goodness I could get something to do ashore in the United States. So Mrs. T—— wants you to come to California to join her. Well, what do you think of it? Are you going to do it? So you really would be glad to see me again, and wouldn't I be glad to see you? Gosh, didn't we enjoy our little selves the few opportunities we had of doing so? Well, I live in hopes of seeing you some day. I am keeping well, but nearly got killed. One day lately had a fall, but am all right now. All thought I was killed—it was a close call.

I do not see the C——'s now. I do not know how they are. I am sorry your photos were a failure, but I hope the next ones will be better and that there will be one of them for me. Well, now, my dear friend, I must close, hoping to have a long letter from you on my arrival in Frisco and trusting you are in the best of health.

With fondest love and best wishes from
    Yours sincerely,
              Leonard.

I cannot tell you how glad I was when I received your letter. I really thought I had offended you. I was always wondering what was the matter and was going to write and ask you, but thank goodness, everything is all right. You do not know how much I value your friendship.

        Good bye,
                  L.

San Francisco.

Mrs. Robinson.

My dear friend:—

I received your kind and most welcome letter the other day and I now hasten to answer it. I would have done so sooner, but I have been awfully busy. I received news of the death of my young brother and I have had so much to do arranging things for my mother and sisters that I have had not a minute's time to spare. This will be a short note, as we sail in an hour, but I will write you a more lengthy one from Honolulu. I am very well in health, but low in spirits; he was my favorite brother and I feel his death very much—but I must shake myself up or I will get melancholy.

Well, my dear friend, good bye for the present, and you will get another letter in about three weeks or a month after this.

Trusting you are quite well and hoping you will enjoy your holiday, believe me to remain ever

Your sincere friend,

Leonard.

I know you will excuse this short note under the circumstances.

L.

On the Blue Pacific.

Mrs. Robinson.

My dear friend:—

I now take the pleasure of writing to you, as I promised in my short note from San Francisco. We are sailing away on the old Pacific and expect to arrive in Honolulu at 8.30 to-morrow, and we will leave the same day for Samoa. So you are quite alone now.

You must feel lonely. I wish I were there to keep you company. We would have a good time. Don't you think you had better employ me as caretaker of the house—then I could look after you and you after me? So you are thinking of coming to see me next winter if we are in Frisco. I hope we are. Won't I be glad to see you? It seems an age since I bade you good bye on the Sydney wharf. I have not seen any of the C.'s lately. The eldest girl is married about three months back to young Mr. T——. I guess you saw him at the house once or twice. He is a fine young fellow, and I think they will make a happy couple. Yes, it did serve L—— right the way he got treated. As you say, he has given a lot of girls the go by, and he has got it himself now. The "Arawa" was sold to the Spanish government to run to Cuba. But she is lost now about five months back. So you think I could not settle ashore. Now, well, that is a great mistake. I only wish I had the chance. Mrs. A—— was down this trip and she looks very well, very charming. I tried to get a photo of the Cemetery Bridge, but could not get it. I will try again this time. Will you ever forget that day? The Bridge and the Domain! Oh, Lord! I would live it all over again—but I am afraid I never will. We will be back in Frisco on the 10th of July, and I will expect a letter from you on arrival.

I hope your horses are better now. You seem to think a great deal of them. I suppose you look upon them as companions. Well, now, my dear friend, I must close. With love and best wishes from

Your sincere friend,
Leonard.

San Francisco.

Mrs. Robinson.

My dear friend:—

We have again arrived back in dear old America, and no letter waiting for me from you. You surely have not forgotten me. No, I guess not. You are enjoying yourself and forgot to write. Well, I have got a picture of the Cemetery Bridge, which I will send along with this, and I guess it will bring lots of pleasant recollections back to you. It does to me. I do not think I will ever forget that day. I wonder will it ever come again. I do sincerely hope so. They were red-letter days in my life—the few days you and I were together. Suppose this will find you at some summer resort enjoying yourself to your heart's content. Well, I hope you are enjoying yourself. I guess it is pretty hot back East. We are having lovely weather in California. Gosh, don't I wish you were living here instead of New York; then I would be happy. I wonder will I ever see you again. I have met many women since I met you, but none that I cared for as well as you. I saw Mr. and Mrs. S—— in Auckland; they wish to be kindly remembered to you. I have not seen any of the C——'s for some time, but I hear they are quite well. L—— has gone to England in one of the home boats. I do not know what he intends doing, nor do I care, and I guess you don't either. Everything is pretty much the same here. Business is pretty dull in California, owing to the election, so there is not much chance of getting anything to do just yet. I must hang on where I am.

Well, my dear friend, I guess I must close, trusting this will find you quite well. So, with best love and wishes, believe me,

Ever yours sincerely,
Leonard.

Hoping to hear from you very soon.

Feb. 17th.

Mrs. Robinson.

My very dear friend:—

I send you this short note hoping that it may find you quite well. I would have liked very much to hear from you before you left for home, but I suppose you did not know where to write; so, will excuse you. I, by chance, discovered your address the other day, and I came very near going to see you off. I wished I had been going with you; but I thought, perhaps, you would not like it, so I changed my mind. I expect you will sail by the "Mariposa." I have written to you at home. You will see by that letter how I have suffered for you. My heart is broken. Please, write me a kind letter when you get the time. I am walking in to post my letter, and I will write every month to you and will walk in in hopes of getting one from you. I will come to the States to see you if you wish it. I have been very bad about you—how much I love you, you will never know. My dear, kind friend and well wisher, how can I thank you sufficiently for sending me that beautiful present? If you had asked me what I would like I could not have told you, but you sent me the very thing in that beautiful flute. I never saw one like it. I thank you again. God bless you and take care of you till we meet again. But if you get married I wish you good luck, whoever he may be. I wish it was me. But I would not care so much for myself if only you were happy and that I could see you sometimes.

You tell me on your card to remember and think of you sometimes. Why, you are never out of my thoughts—morning, noon and night I am looking into your pretty eyes. I love you with an undying love. I am leaving this camp to get away from drink, and when I get strong again no power will ever make me drink again.

Yours in love until death,
Basil.

Kamo, Feb. 5th.

PREFACE.

My very dear friend:—

That you will receive this letter in the best of health is my prayer night and morning. I am not quite as well as I should be; but I am recovering slowly but surely, I hope. I lost seven pounds in weight since Christmas. How it happened I will leave you to guess. To commence—how can I ever thank you for the happiest Christmas and jolliest New Year I ever passed in my life? I cannot do it; the gratitude of my heart is too great to put into words. They are so tame.

Mrs. Robinson.

My dear lady:—

Do you remember how we went down to the river? How you did flirt with me! I was half in love with you then, and when we went down to the race course in the evening I began to admire your beautiful eyes and I thought them very dangerous, and I asked you if you took delight in breaking men's hearts, and you answered so truly, with tears in your voice, "no, no." I did believe you and thought I was quite safe with you. But, oh, how much I was mistaken, my dear! My heart had left me, but I did not know it then. I think Cupid shot his dart into my heart when we were introduced, but gone it was into thy keeping and gone forever.

You are the only lady that I have seen for twenty years whom I could admire and adore. My dear love! Well, we had a jolly time while it lasted—but I was not prepared for such a good time. After you left us every one seemed dull. I will tell you what a time I had. Now I am just going to ask you how I could help loving you. One day I asked Miss Jones where you were, and she told me in your room, and told me to go there and see. I went and found you sleeping. Then I vanished to dream about you—to think of you. After a while I came back to talk to you, more in love than ever; but I did not even then know how much I loved you. I often think of the day Clara and yourself came to where I was to see what I was doing, and I was quietly sitting on the door step, and you gave me such a pleasant smile that I never will forget. It did my heart good. God bless you! One more time, when you were coming out of the store, you gave me that pleasant smile and a gift. I can never forget it while my memory lasts. Do you think I can forget the old tree, where Mrs. F., Miss

J., you and I sat, and where we passed such pleasant moments? No, never shall I forget them—they are the only pleasant thoughts I have at present. Sometimes I take out my keepsakes and look at them to cheer my heart. I will tell you what they are, but you must not tell any one. A picture of a lady, a small handkerchief with a letter in one corner, two little flowers and a small black-headed pin and, last but not least, a cap that just fits my head—and it just fits you, too. You have a good-sized head for a lady, and I know there is plenty of good in it.

Well, the morning that you left me at the store I did intend going up the road with you, but you bade me good bye in those beautiful words that froze my heart and I felt powerless to move. And when you started I saw a tear in your eye and I felt so badly, and again, when you waved your hand, I started off to the cottage and for hours I cried for you. I would have followed you, but I thought it best not, for it would have looked so bad just then. Well, I had a drink after a time and went home to Mac, and we talked of you all the evening. Now came the time I found out how dear you were to me and how much I loved you. I went to the store the next morning, and on my way back I sat down on the small tree by the small river, where we had all four sat one Saturday afternoon. I was thinking about you, when all at once a voice seemed to shout in my ear: "She is gone, for ever—for ever—for ever"—when I fell off the tree on to the ground unconscious. It was then about 10.30 A.M. when that happened. How long I lay there I do not know, but Miss Jones came along on horse back and she asked me what was the matter. I sung out to her I had lost my best friend, and the way I said it frightened her horse and away she went. Still the voice kept repeating, "For ever—for ever" in my ear. How long I lay there I do not know. It rained and I got home wet through. It was night when I got there, and I never lifted my head from my pillow for three days, and I never slept for nine nights and days, thinking all the time about you. I thought to kill myself, but thought it might give you pain. So I resolved to try and see you once again.

I cannot eat, it seems to choke me. I cannot sleep for thinking about you. I cannot work, for I seem to be looking into your eyes all the time, and I carry a heart in my breast like lead. Sometimes I cheer up for a few moments, and then all seems to fall back again. You must see me again, if only for five minutes, if you care the least for your own Basil—and you will find very few like me. I will give up drinking forever. Ask me to come and see you, when you are at home, if only for a day. I will write again and let you know what I intend doing. I will try to get to England by the end of May, then I can be home in July and I can soon run across to you.

I thank you again for the flute—it is the best present I ever received in my life. You could not have thought of a better thing—when I thought you had forgotten me, then to get just what I wished so many times for. I do not know how to return such a gift.

I fear you will marry—but if you do before I see you again I hope you will be happy. I would like to be the happy man. But let me come to where I can see you sometimes, for I am broken-hearted. You will think this a selfish letter. I hope you enjoyed your trip to Sydney and other places. I will talk more about it in my next. Please write soon and let me know how you are.

With my best love to you,

Your
Basil.

Pinau, April 10th.

My dear Alice:—

I received your kind and welcome letter four days ago and was very pleased to hear you were quite well and enjoying yourself, and that you enjoyed your trip to Melbourne (how I should have liked to be with you!) and hope you will arrive safely at home. I suppose you will be glad when you get there to take a rest after all your wanderings. I am glad you got my Auckland letter, for your reply to it cheered me very much. I am better in health and I hope you are well, too. You say I must not fret about you. Well, I do not fret quite so much now, but I think of you all the time. You say, let the past be a fond memory! Dear Alice, it could be nothing else, it could not be otherwise, and it is the fondest and brightest I have to think of you, and I shall always love you so long as I live.

> Thy voice is near me in my dreams,
>   In accents sweet and low,
> Telling of happiness and love
>   In days long, long ago;

Word after word methinks I hear,
  But strange it seems to me
That though I listen to thy voice,
  Thy face I never see.

From night to night my weary heart
  Dwells on the treasured past,
And every day it seems to say
  You come to me at last;
I kneel—I work—I watch and pray
  As time runs slowly on,
But yet I only have but thee,
  The best, the dearest one.

You will excuse me writing my little song, but that is the one I sing mostly now. My voice is in grand tune just now, and I have two engagements for May— one is the opening of a large hall and the other is in support of a free library at Aponga. If it had not been for your present I could not have sung half as well as I do. You would like to have my likeness? I will send it as soon as I can get it taken. If I can get it taken in time will send it with this letter, but I would rather send it in my next. I will then tell you why I was so pleased that you asked me for my likeness. There was to have been another or more races here, but there were no horses entered—at least not enough—only five in all, and so they declared the races off. How different from the last time.

I have not been over since I wrote you the last time, but intend, before I leave forever, to have a look at the old place.

Dave brought me your letter out from Kamo four

days before I intended going in to see whether you had written me. I told him you sent your regards to him, and he asked me to remember him to you. I said I would do so if I wrote, because I have no faith in any one. Mac is in the old camp, and quite well again. You told Patsy to look after me when you left, and he did so right royally, too. He is a good sort. I will stay here until next March. Then I shall go to England, and, perhaps, I may have a last chance of seeing you. Now, I do not want you to be alarmed at anything I say, for I would not do a thing without your consent and all I ask for my great love for you is that you will remember me sometimes and write me a letter letting me know how you are getting along. I could write for a week about ourselves, but you would think it all nonsense. But, if ever you are in need of a friend, send me a line and I will go through anything to get to you. I remain yours until death.

You say you are growing stouter every day. Well, that's all right; never mind stopping yet. My sister is a fine looking woman, about as tall as yourself, and weighs two hundred and six pounds. Laugh and grow fat, is an old saying.

So, I conclude, you must have been enjoying yourself very much down here. I am glad you enjoyed my poor company.

If you go to Europe next year I should like to know, for I might meet you there if you do not get married in the meantime. There will be plenty of fine fellows in the States wanting to marry you, and why not? You are young yet. I just wish I could have had the courage to have asked you. I will have to stop. I could go on writing for ever to you.

I remain yours until death. Bless you!
Basil.

Ever of thee fondly I am dreaming. I have just been looking at your likeness—I will get a frame for it.
B.

Kamo, Sept.

My dear Alice:—

I send you this short note to let you know that I am quite well, hoping you are the same.

I am writing a letter to you, but I want to send my likeness with it. I went to the photographer three weeks ago and he promised to let me have them in three days, and I have been or sent twice a week, and I have not got them yet. I expect them to-morrow, but I must let you know why you did not get your letter sooner. I will not say much now. Hope you will forgive me for what I cannot help.

With many thanks for your kind and loving letter, I remain,

Your own till death,
Basil.

P.S.—I will send my letter next week whether I get my photos or not. I would have gone to town if I had thought the fellow would have been so long over them.
B.

Kamo, Sept.

My dear Alice:—

I received your welcome letter and was glad to hear you were quite well as this leaves me at present.

I went into Whangarei to have my likeness taken as soon as I got your letter, and he promised to have them done in a week's time. I called for them, but they were not done, and he put me off another week. I wanted them very much as I thought you might change your address before you got one. I felt sorry you could not let your estate, but do not let it trouble you overmuch, because they are making it more valuable by making good roads, and it will all come right in a little while. I would like to be with you this month to have a walk among the trees and view the beautiful bay. I have seen it many times and would like to see it again. You will have a fine time this month—the great boat race coming off. How I would like to be there! I wonder what sort of a Christmas you will have this year? It will be very cold where you are at present, nothing like last year, I believe, but you will have New York to fall back upon. I do not think I will ever have another Christmas like it as long as I live. I was very happy on that day. I had to leave the place where the old tree lay, for it used to make my heart sore whenever I saw it, thinking of the happy moments that we had passed there together. I wonder who you have got to tie your shoe strings now? There are plenty would like to do it. I have moved camp to six miles off Kamo, and I could have a very good time. I am right among the settlers and they make a great deal of me. They have parties and dances—singing all the time and flirting in galore. I could be married a dozen times over if I wanted to, but only think of you all the more. I have had some very broad hints from the girls themselves, but they cannot make me out. They have a splendid hall here, where I sang once, and I thought they would bring the house down when I sang for them. I sang the "Anchor's weighed" and "Afton Water" with two encores, and I got a great name. I will send you one of the encores. I was singing it to you, although I was looking at them.

LATER.

I have got your likenesses. I am glad, so that I can send you one with this letter. I sent you a short note for fear you might think I was neglecting you, but I hope you will never think that. You say you are getting thin; why, that is only good health after your sea voyage. You must leave all worry alone and be cheerful, and you will soon look well again, and if you get your likeness taken you must be sure to send your little chippy one. It will please him more than anything you could send him. My pictures are very common things. I do not like them, but what can you expect from Whangarei? I will go into town at Christmas and have some good ones taken and send you one.

THIS IS ONE OF MY ENCORE SONGS.

In the gloaming, oh my darling,
    When our lives are fading fast
Time will sooth the aching anguish,
    Each sad memory of the past;
May your life be bright and happy,
    Golden as the sunbeam's ray,
We may, dear, yes, meet together
    In that land far, far away.

I will send you another encore song in my next— It is a very pretty one. I have just heard that the "Defender" won the race and claims the second on a foul. I saw J—— the other day. He does not look over well; business is very dull with him.

You must send me a line before Christmas. I shall very likely go to Melbourne, but if I do I will let you know. Mind you take care of yourself this winter, and if ever I can do anything for your happiness, command me.

   I remain yours till death,
               Basil.

               Kamo.

My dear Alice:—

No doubt you will think it strange that I did not write before now; but, as you know of old how great my friendship is for you, I know you will forgive me. I did not want to send you any bad news.

I heard that Mr. and Mrs. J—— were very sick and not expected to live, that is some time ago, but they are quite well again. (A—— was down to a ball here. I was to play and sing there, but I had another engagement, so I sent my friend to fill my place—he plays the violin). She was attended by her French governess. She looks well and behaves nicely. Old Charlie is in the store—he who married us in the kitchen—you remember?

I would like to see you now, dressed for the opera—but you will always look well to me, no matter what dress you are in. I would like to live in New York just so I could see you now and again; it would be nice. I am glad you liked your trip down here—it is something to think about. That niece of mine, whose photos I sent you, has gone to sing in London, and

I believe she will be a success. You might have kept all the photos if you liked. I will not send you any of these. I will send you some fresh ones by and bye. My brother and sister wish me to go home to England very much. I have got some money now, and I think I will take a trip up to the Thames gold fields, and then I will have a look at Melbourne. Should I not stay at either places I will go home (via Frisco). I am leaving here next week. I thank you for the picture of the two cats you sent me, and I also thank you very much for the songs that you propose sending me; but I shall have no address for some time now, and I think you have done plenty when you sent me that flute. I play it every day and think of you.

The people here are very sorry I am leaving. I am at parties every week and thank you in the flute. I will send you a photo from Auckland. All the people that you knew at J—— have left and gone I do not know where.

Your
Basil.

> When other lips and other hearts
>   Their tales of love shall tell,
> In language whose excess imparts
>   The power they feel so well,
> There may perhaps in such a scene
>   Some recollections be
> Of days that have as happy been
>   And you'll remember me,
>   And you'll remember me.

Ever thine,
Basil.

St. Louis, Mo.

Mrs. A. Robinson.

My dear Madam:—

Found your card at the Bank yesterday—my first appearance down town for some days. Was anxious to see who could have called upon me at the bank and for some time did not recognize the name. If it had read "Hutton," would at once have known who it was.

Our friend C—— is married to a young lady with some $100,000 in her own right and appears to be happy and as usual contented. Should you at any time visit St. Louis in the future, kindly let me hear from you in advance and I would be most happy to try and make your visit pleasant. I am very sorry that it was impossible to see you during your short visit. I am,

Sincerely yours,

L. L.

St. Louis, Mo.

Dear Mrs. Robinson:—

Your kind letter of April 12th came duly to hand and read with pleasure. Should judge you are getting to be like myself—a traveller; but after a while it becomes quite tiresome. Sorry, indeed, your desire to see me did not enter your head before you reached St. Louis, as I am sure your short visit here would have been made more pleasant. Yes, C—— was lucky, but some people always fall into good things. From your charming picture of C—— am convinced you had quite a preference for him while you were here; but we often, all of us, had a good time and think of the past at times and wish it was possible to be younger by a few years. The hotel is the same, but all new people, some pleasant and some otherwise. But, you know, we can always make ourselves at home in any place.

Sorry you find it so lonely—wish I was there for a few days. At times I feel lonesome, but it only lasts for a few hours.

Sincerely hope your cold is much improved if not entirely well.

Thanks, I am all right. It was something curious to me; but, you know, we all are born curious but hope I won't be troubled that way any more.

Hoping your spare time is passing more pleasantly, and that you are happy in all things, I am, as ever,

Your friend,

L. L.

Liverpool, August 6th.

My darling Alice:—

Words fail me to express my feelings towards you, my girl, for it was lovely to see you this A.M. and get a farewell kiss, to say nothing of the splendid letter, which I found at the hotel.

We left at 8 o'clock and are now waiting for the crowd to come off, and then we shall get away. You need not be the least anxious about me this trip, for the thoughts of my last passage are still uppermost in my mind and I am not quite such a scamp as you may think. Your combs will arrive, I hope, as soon as this letter, but the straps I can bring you on my return. This is only intended for a note to let you know that I am going to keep my promise and send you a letter at the last minute, before we sail, when I shall be able to have a little more leisure time.

Cheer up, dear, and enjoy yourself all you can, and believe me,

Yours sincerely,
Bob.

Liverpool, August 6th,
11 o'clock.

My darling Alice:—

You will see by the above time we are now soon to sail, and your humble servant is sitting in his cabin to do his writing. Already my troubles have commenced as the people are all more or less dissatisfied, and some of them seem to think I arrange their seats in the saloon. Mr. P—— has just been up with his letters and showed me the lovely present you sent him. I need hardly say he is delighted, but I console myself that this boy is the best off. Your letter in itself is enough to make any fellow happy let alone your extreme kindness to me, which I shall never forget. Be sure you write me, girl, and send the letter to Pier —. There does not seem to be any of the A. R. style among the crowd, and doubt very much if I shall ever meet another like you, girl, for, somehow, you were too good for an old salt. But, however, we will not dwell on the subject, for, as I said in my note of to-day, words fail to express my feelings. So, must leave you to imagine all the nice things you can do for yourself.

Enclosed is a list of the crowd. You may look out

for a wire directly I reach Liverpool, and remember I will be in London the following day. So long!

Yours sincerely,
Bob.

November 20th.

My dear Alice:—

Your letter came as a surprise to me, and I don't think you need have been so hasty to return, as nobody could say a word about your being down here. But, however, I shall hope to see you the day we get in, next voyage, when none will be any the wiser. I have not enjoyed myself a bit here this time, but then there is not any more of the A. R. type. I hope you will have a jolly time on the P——, and you must tell me all about the trip on my return. We had a fairly decent run out, but lots of bad weather and bad luck at Polish Bank, which T—— had a share of. Thanks for the time tables. No doubt, I shall be able to find my way out to the mansion, where I hope to be the star boarder. I have got some one to address this letter to you, as my handwriting is so well known on your ship. It would be useless for me to attempt to convey my feelings towards you after all your kindness to me, for certain it is, old lady, I have never met anybody to equal you, my girl, and I sincerely hope some day to be able to repay you for all you have done for me.

I shall hope to see your boat at sea, as we do sometimes see her.

Accept my love and believe me,

Yours devotedly,
Bob.

Liverpool, Jan. 14th.

My darling Alice:—

Your loving letter was duly handed me on my arrival yesterday, and I cannot begin to express how much I feel indebted to you for such unbounded kindness to me. Of course, I am very sorry that you will not be with us on the passage out, but perhaps, as you say it may be for the best. And another thing—the ship is full, so that there would not have been much chance of us seeing much of each other, at any rate not half as much as this boy would like. I am anxious to learn how you fared on the P——, and who fell in love with you; but this you can tell me when I see you, my love. Your description of the men at No. —— is very amusing, and I cannot imagine a fellow making such a fool of himself without any encouragement. But then, you girls delight to tease us, I know. I have carefully preserved my time tables for —— and will wire you the moment I get anchored, so that you will know when to expect me. Just don't I wish you were near enough to collect a good hug and kiss.

Please excuse this letter being short, as I have to pay the crew off. F—— is going to write you. Cheer up, old lady, and get the place good and warm by the 20th, as I am in hopes you will have a boarder that day.

With fondest love and unlimited kisses, believe me,

Ever yours,

Bob.

Sandy Hook.

My darling Alice:—

How can I begin to express myself after all your kindness to me? It really is too good, my love, the way which you have treated this old sailor. I only wish it were possible for me to repay you, old pet; but at present I can only hope for the future and trust some day fortune may smile on me again. After running like a two-year old I caught my train and went to sleep till we reached Jersey City. But, oh my, it was very difficult to get out of bed this morning; even now I shall be glad to get rid of the pilot, so as to get into my nest.

Mr. P—— desires me to convey his kindest regards to you and hopes to be able to come over and see you next time. Please, write me a letter to Liverpool, my love, for I am already longing to see you, my queen, and I have made up my mind to fix my days better on the next trip, for —— has done too much traveling in the few days he has been here. It is beyond me to express how happy I feel always with you, and can safely say, darling, that you are never out of my thoughts, and whatever happens, darling, you may always remember your boy retains the warmest feelings of affection for his little woman with the mansion at ——. It may not surprise you to hear that I am feeling very tired and that it will take me all this passage to rest and get myself once more. The cigarrettes will be duly conveyed on my next trip, also the cigars, as they slipped my memory before we left the docks. L—— has just been here and he seems very upset about his stay in New York. He asked me how you were, but I told him I had only seen you once, and upon my showing him my lovely silk scarf he wanted to know where it came from, so I said a girl in Brooklyn sent it to me and thereupon the gentleman said, "You ought to go and see that girl, sir!"

This letter will not reach you till Tuesday, my sweetheart, but you will have time to write me by Wednesday's mail. So don't forget, as I shall be hungry for your letter.

So long, dearest; try and think kindly of this boy and accept heaps of love and a ten-minutes' kiss.

Believe me, darling,

    Your loving sweetheart,

                  Bob.

                Milton, Dec. 14th.

Dear Mrs. Robinson:—

I was so glad to get a letter from you the other day and the photo, which was a splendid one. I will send you mine when I have them finished, though I don't like them much. I am so sorry to hear that you are not enjoying yourself though. It must be very far away and lonely. I don't think, however, that you can be more miserable and wretched than I am. My God! I think sometimes I shall go mad. Shut up all day in an office, cut off from the glorious sunshine, the trees and the flowers, which are my very heart's blood, I can only see it glimmer through the windows and hear the birds singing outside, and I pine and pine so for freedom. Oh, you don't know what I suffer. This morning, when a stockman rode past gaily on his horse, swinging his whip, a lump rose in my throat till

I thought I would choke and, old as I am, I had hard work to keep from bursting into tears. I would sell my coat for one moment of true, glorious sunshine of the Islands and a horse to ride again, and what's more, I'm going to obtain them. I have written to a fellow in the Islands to ask him to get me a job, and if I get a favorable reply off I'll go. Perhaps I'll be going over by the "Mariposa," though most likely by the next steamer, as I won't have received a reply before then and I havn't got enough money to play about Honolulu. In fact, I don't know how I'm going to get over. But, perhaps, I can scrape up enough money for a steerage passage, and if not I must try and work my way over. I really believe, so great is my longing to get away, that if I was playing poker with you again I wouldn't feel any compunction in getting twenty or thirty pounds from you. So you see how I've fallen.

I envy you so being able and free to get away from the place you don't like. Anyway, if it is slow, you are in the open air and can do what you like. I do hope I'll see you again before you go over; though I don't think I'll be able to play you a game as I'm saving every shilling. Wouldn't it be jolly if we could go over together? But then you would be an "'igh" and "'aughty" saloon passenger, while I'd be an "'umble" steerage one. Anyway, if we do not see each other again, I hope you will write to me sometimes, and if you send me your address I'll write to you. If I ever manage to have a home in the Islands I hope you will come over and make it yours for however long you choose to stay, but I am afraid that is a very remote pleasure as I have no money to buy any land for many a long day if ever,

I wish I had some rich aunt or somebody who would adopt me or die conveniently and leave me her money; then I would come over and see you and play you poker to your heart's content. But I have never had any luck in my life. Well, well, I won't give you any more of my croakings. I know you will think of me when you are having a jolly time of it on the "Mariposa" and wish me luck, I am sure. I am just living on in hope now, and if I am disappointed—my God! I can't think of it— I have broken the bridge of my guitar, so my last consolation is cut off and the thought of having to enter that office to-morrow is awful. 'T is a very pretty place and the fellows are nice, but it's a number of miles from Dunedin and we seldom get in. I was a week with my parents in Christ-church, and they welcomed me back like the prodigal son and I had a lovely time. I wonder when I shall see them again.

I have nothing to tell you, though, by the way, I have seen Mr. Thomas. In fact, I saw Mr. and Mrs. Terry and that other young fellow that played poker with the doctor and mail agent yesterday; they were all well. I did not have much chance of speaking to them. I hope you will write soon to me and send me your address. You forgot it last time, and so I had to make it out from the postage stamp. I hope sincerely that I will see you again and wish you lots and lots of happiness. And now, with "Aloha nui pau ole," I remain,

Your affectionate friend,
Nap.

Milton, Jan. 21st.

Dear Mrs. Robinson:—

    I am so glad to hear from you to-day. I was wondering where you were and if my letter had ever reached you. I am so sorry to hear you are not coming here. I would like to see you so much again, as I don't suppose I will ever see you any more. Couldn't you manage to change your mind and come on from Melbourne? I'm sure you would like it and you could catch your steamer here. I will not probably be going in her, as I have not got any reply yet to the letter I wrote to see whether I could get a billet in the island and I have not managed to save up the necessary money yet, nor ever will I expect, as I'm too extravagant and can never save. So, I suppose, I'll have to endure this for a bit till I can manage to get on to a station hereabouts. But I'll get back some day, you bet. I wish you had told me the name of your noble adorer; I am quite interested in him and admire his good taste. I hope he will be successful in getting his money, and when you are Lady Somebody you must promise to visit me.

    Thank you from the bottom of my heart for the kind and generous offer you made me in case the happy event should come off. But I would not take advantage of it, as I am sure ladies always want lots of money and haven't any to spare. But the offer is typical of your kind hearted self and I appreciate it deeply. It's not likely, unluckily, that a rich aunt will die and leave me any money for the simple reason that I haven't got such a thing, but I guess I'll scrape along all right somehow. We have had a couple of dances while I've been here, very jolly, and I've often been into the theatre, and, taking it all round, we have lots of fun. But it does not make me like this place any the better. Nothing will satisfy me but the fresh air.

If you see Mrs. Grey in Honolulu, give her my best love; tell her to be good and not to forget me. I hope you will write to me occasionally. I would be ever so pleased to hear from you at any time and will always look forward to seeing you again some time or other.

Well, I must say good bye now, and I hope to hear from you soon. And now with "Aloha nui pau ole," I remain,
   Your affectionate friend,
            Nap.

           La Perouse.
Dear Mrs. Robinson:—

I am very sorry to have fallen out with you, especially as your stay here is so short, and finding pretty well the other night what kind of an opinion you had of me I did not like to go down to see you again. However, this is to wish you a safe journey across to Melbourne and a pleasant passage home to New York.

Hoping you have enjoyed a happy Christmas, I am
   Yours sincerely,
            Dave.

           La Perouse.
Dear Mrs. Robinson:—

Thank you very much for your kind letter in reply to my note. Have also received your second note requesting my name for your birthday book. If the name on enclosed slip is too large, please let me know and I will send another smaller. On Thursday, the 3rd inst., I landed in Sydney, ten minutes after you had left for Melbourne, with Mr. Dugan. I would very willingly have gone down there to see you, but thought you might not like it; so I stopped where I was. Am surprised you have not yet left for Melbourne, but I suppose you will be starting shortly, perhaps before this reaches you. My face is still aching like the very mischief so you may guess I am not in particularly good humor. I never had such a wretched miserable Christmas in my life. Nobody came near me and I was not asked out anywhere, which is the result, I conclude, of being poor. Add to this that my tooth took fine care to keep up a perpetual pain the whole day, together with the misery of falling out with you, and you have a pretty fair photo of my Christmas 18—. If you get this epistle before leaving for Melbourne, please drop me a line to say which boat you are going by and I will be looking out for her arrival at the other side.

In the mean time I hope you will enjoy yourself down there and better again in Auckland.

Well, good bye, Mrs. Robinson. Trust you are quite well. I am,
     Yours sincerely,
         Dave.

———

        La Perouse.
Dear Mrs. Robinson:—

I received your kind letter with the photo and thank you very much for them both. It will be nice to look at your pretty face occasionally, when you are far away in America. Am not at all well to-day, although my toothache is a good deal better; so I will only send just a short note to say that I hope you have enjoyed your trip to Napier and Gisborne and to wish you a safe journey to New York.

I saw your old friend Basil the other day and he told me he intended going to see you off. I will send my love to you by him, but I expect he will make a mistake and give you his own instead.

There is nothing in the way of news here that would interest you, and as I really feel too ill to write any more to-night, I must conclude.

I wish you a safe passage home and every possible happiness. Any chance of getting a letter after you are settled in New York?

I am,
Yours sincerely,
Dave.

La Perouse.

My dear Mrs. Robinson:—

You may depend I was both pleased and surprised to get your kind letter of the 9th of August. I often wondered whether you would write to me from America. Of course, Basil told me every time he heard from you. In fact, I knew before he did, as I generally got his letters for him or else received them when they arrived here. I have not been well lately and am terribly shaky to-night, so please do not expect anything better than a disconnected scrawl.

As far as news is concerned there is very little to tell you. I have only been to M. once, I think, since you were there. Miss J. and Mrs. F. have gone, and there is a new governess recently arrived from Paris, although she is English. M. has also left these camps and is now living at Ruataugata, a place you pass through about six miles this side of Kamo on your way to Mangakahi. I have left Aponga, where you and the others came on a visit that day. I rarely ever see Mrs. T. now, as I do not stay at that hotel, but will deliver your message when I do see her. I notice that you send your love to her; you didn't send me any. I suppose I am outside the pale of your affections altogether. Do you know that although we fell out I can't help liking you? It's a case of "With all your faults I love you still," and I was very sorry that I missed seeing you once again. Do you remember Mrs. G——? Well, she and her husband have parted. He is still here. She is in Auckland, keeping a little shop and doing dress making, etc. That cowboy gentleman called Willie something or other has gone gum digging. I am sorry you lost your beautiful dog, as I suppose he was a great favorite. Tell me, if you ever write again, how the rug turned out.

Now, I am too ill to-night to write a pleasant letter or even a readable one, but if I ever receive another one from you I may then, perhaps, be better able to answer it.

In the meantime trusting you are quite well and wishing you every happiness, I am, dear Mrs. Robinson,

Yours sincerely,
Dave.

La Perouse, January.

Dear Mrs. Robinson:—

I received your kind letter of December 3rd all right. How very good of you to write to me again and such a nice letter, too. You write in such a natural way that it is almost like speaking to you or rather like having you speak. What a pity we could not get close enough for that—isn't it?

You were quite right in saying our summer would be well on by the time your note got here. It is fearfully hot now and the driest season we have had for years. I am sorry to hear that they did not fix up Leo's skin entirely to your satisfaction, but still it must be nice as it is.

What about that "little bit of a dog" you have—isn't he a whole one? You ask if my toothache is right again. It is better, thank you, but in other ways I am not very well and think I ought to have a change.

If I ever get enough money together I would like to go over to America—just to see New York and Mrs. Robinson. I lived in San Francisco for about two years a long time ago, but never had a chance of going East, and at the rate I am traveling now, never will. That's the worst of being poor. What a lot we miss by it! Ever since your letter came I have been praying for that artist who spoiled your photos, as I was so very disappointed at not getting one. You never sent me a kiss either. Will you next time? And be sure to enclose some little thing or other for keepsake—a piece of your hair will do nicely. If I can't get another photo, of course, I keep the one you sent me from Auckland put away safely.

By the way, I have seen two or three different photos of you, but none as nice as you are yourself. If I ever get any news that would interest you I will write again, and in the meantime I will be looking forward for another letter from America.

Well, good bye, Mrs. Robinson. Trusting you are quite well and will soon write again, I am,

Yours sincerely,
Dave.

Chère A.:—

I have waited to see you—but, alas! vainly, for I have just learned the painful intelligence that you have gone ashore with your friends (whom Heaven confound), and you did not leave a message for me.

I enclose you this atrocity which I committed last night and which you said you admired. If, however, it has the effect of affording you a laugh now and then it will serve the purpose for which it was written, namely —of keeping in your remembrance in however slight a degree,

Your very sincere friend
Will.

January 25th.

Monowai, Jan. 24th, 18—.

A DAY DREAM.

Fresh comes the breeze above
  King cup and daisy,
The woodlands are rich with the hyacinth blue,
Dreaming a dream of love,
  Lying so lazy,
Dreaming a dream that can never come true.

Can buried blisses rise?
  Past time return again?
Nay, save in memory, the past is no more;
Yet, as I shut my eyes,
  I can forget my pain,
My heart is linked in thine close as of yore.

Draw my face near to thine,
  Yea! and those lips, so sweet,
Set me a-trembling like reeds by the stream,
Sweeter than Jessamine,
  That the south wind doth greet,
Kiss me again, love, 'tis only a dream.

Good bye to Alice.

Auckland, New Zealand.

Dear Mrs. Robinson:—

I received your letter on the 4th, and was very pleased to get it. It was very good of you to remember me and to write, especially as you had your favorites to entertain.

I am pleased you liked my sister. Brothers should not have favorite sisters but, perhaps, I have a special conceit about Lillie. How did you like Mrs. B——? You can tell me on your return.

I saw by the papers that you had a rough passage to the other side from the Bluff, but I suppose you felt no bad effects from it. How are you now? I hope well. Have you gained another stone in weight since you said good bye on the "Monowai"?

I will be glad to see you back again even though it will be only for a short time. I have had your picture framed and it looks very nice. That is the next best thing to having yourself to admire.

Are you coming back on the "Monowai"? I must try to find out when she is expected here, for I should like to meet you—that is if you have no one better, and if you will allow me.

I see by the end of your letter that I have not yet convinced you that I have no girl. Perhaps I shall be able, too, when you come back. At any rate I have had no nice walks since you have been away.

Now, my dear Mrs. Robinson, I must stop right here—not because I have no news, but because it is nearly twelve o'clock.

So, with kind regards and hoping you are having a pleasant time I will say good bye and believe me,

Your sincere friend,
Harold.

Auckland, New Zealand.

Dear Mrs. Robinson:—

I am very sorry for what has happened. It is not my fault I can assure you. I have no enemies, Mrs. Robinson, and I have no wish to be bad friends with you now, on the eve of your departure for your home in America. We have been very good friends so far. I feel very sorry indeed that my sister did not refrain from writing me when you asked her. All this might have then been avoided. Now, Mrs. Robinson, will you see me? If it is only to say good-bye and part good friends, for it is possible that we may never meet here again, but I trust and pray that we may meet in that everlasting Kingdom that our Heavenly Father, God, has prepared for all who love Him in sincerity and truth. If you will see me, will you kindly send word by this young man? I shall be free from one until two to-morrow (Friday) for lunch, or to-morrow evening. I remain still, your sincere friend,

Harold.

Auckland, New Zealand, Nov.

Dear Mrs. Robinson:—

I daresay you have ere this given up the idea of ever hearing from me again, though it is just twelve months since you left in the S.S. "Mariposa." You have not been altogether out of mind, though you have been out of sight. I have often wondered how you have been getting along since. You remember you were to let me know of your safe arrival when you got to either Honolulu or New York; but as I did not receive a letter from you all this time (and I really did expect one) I thought, perhaps, you would not be very angry if I wrote you just a short one to let you know that I am still alive and have a desire to be retained on your list as a friend. Of course, Mrs. Robinson, our friendship was somewhat marred towards the close of your stay here, but I think you thoroughly understood that I was not to blame. Now, dear Mrs. Robinson, I wish you could forget all that passed then. Just try to let us think of each other as though those things had never been. That is the way I want to think of it. Don't you think that would be the best way too? Just let us be now what we were during the short time I had the pleasure of being in your company while in Auckland —"The best of friends." Shall it be so?

I often see the people who lived at the Caithness while you were there. I remember all walks and talks we had together during those few weeks. You may think that I am only saying this for the sake of filling up paper—but it is not so. I really do look back with pleasure to those evenings. I have been chaffed about you once or twice since you have been away. I suppose that is because you were to church with me. But I can stand to be chaffed about you.

I was disappointed when the first mail arrived after you got home, when I got no letter and no photo. I have not forgotten my promise to you to send you mine. The one you had taken when here is still in Hanna's show studio.

I would like to send you by next mail a small present, just to remind you of Maori Land and also as a seal to our friendship. I suppose you will get it about Christmas.

And now, Mrs. Robinson, I shall have to ask your forgiveness for something I have done since you left. It is about that diamond scarf pin that you so kindly and generously gave me. I gave it away. But when I tell you the circumstances you will see why I did it. After what happened between you and my mother I could not wear it, because she was so angry with me that I went to see you at the hotel and also because I went to the steamer to see you off. Then, when they saw I was not wearing it (because I kept it for a long time hardly knowing what to do with) both my mother and sister asked me to give it to them; but after the way you were treated by my mother I did not see what pleasure she would have in it—so I would not give it to her. I had it made into a brooch and gave it to a friend of mine, the lady that I was to have brought round that night to meet you. I do not like to hide anything that I do, so I thought I would tell you about it. It was not because I did not prize it, but because it was spoken of in a rather nasty way as belonging to you or rather coming from you. I thought, for the sake of peace, and to put it out of their way, I would send it to Mr. T——, and for the sum of £2 I had a gold bar and the stone in the centre. You will remember that night at the hotel I asked you what I would do with it. I hope you understand the position I was placed in and how I felt about it.

If ever I get anything given to me again it will be my game not to say who gave it to me, then I shall not be troubled about it.

I took your photo out of the frame in the drawing room as you desired. I have it now in the drawer of my desk at the store.

Now, Mrs. Robinson, I must ask you to pardon me for the liberty I have taken in writing you. Trusting that you are well and that I will hear from you soon, with my kindest regards, believe me as ever,

Your sincere friend,
Harold.

Friday, 11/15.

New Zealand.

Dear Mrs. Robinson:—

You will be wondering if I am dead or as bad, I suppose, when I have been so long in replying to your kind and welcome letter under date of December 23d.

I am sending this to the mountains, for I suppose you will be back there by now. Has the chief left the ship or does he still go to sea? I have not seen the C——'s since you left, only Mr. C. once. The Misses C—— are very nice girls, so also is their mother—what a nice little woman she is! Do you remember the way she used to hold your hands and ask you questions? I have a very clear recollection of you getting your hat hung up in the tree. Then you, buying the plums, and you and I eating them coming along Princes street by the Albert Park. I do remember the windy drive to Onehunga and Otahuhu. It was a pity it was so very windy you had to put your hat straight on several times besides having your hair blown into your eyes. However, the next time we go out driving together we will have a hooded buggy to protect us from the wind. I fear that is a pleasure that is not in store for me any more. I wish I could have made your stay here in Auckland more pleasant than I did. I hope you will get the photo with this letter. The reason you have not heard from me is just that I had no new ones taken. I like to fulfill my promises. You may return the one you have to me.

By the way I saw a photo of yourself in Hanna's in Queen street. You are dressed in white. Do you know it? I came on it one day as I was looking around. It was a sight for my eyes—it was so unexpected.

Now I am going to have some fun with you, Mrs. Robinson (on paper). There was a lady at our house the other day who saw your likeness and said she was sure she saw you at the Lake in January of this year.

You might tell old friends when you make flying visits to New Zealand.

I assured her she was wholly mistaken, for I said you were in New York City on December 3rd.

I made a discovery when I went to the Post-office to send that parcel to you. There is no parcel post between New Zealand and America, so it is going through the New Zealand Express Co. by the way of London. You will get it some day over there in the mountains. It is a glove box made from New Zealand woods (inlaid). I hope you are quite well now.

I am very well myself, and still at the same place. I must close now or I will not have anything to say next mail.

With my best wishes, believe me as ever,

Your sincere friend,

Harold.

New Zealand.

My dear friend Alice:—

I hope you will not think me "cheeky" when I address you thus. I received your welcome letter on the day you expected I would, on the 21st of May. Thank you very much for the photo of yourself which you sent me with the other. It was very good of you to send it down to me without me asking you, but then you are always very good. But I had better stop trying to make pretty speeches or you will be scolding me next time you write. The "Ruapeha" arrived in London about the 29th of May, so you should have got that parcel about the 7th of June. I could only pay the carriage on it as far as New York, so I want you to tell me when you answer this what further charges you had to pay on it.

So it is all up between the chief and the young lady. So far as I am concerned I would say let them go. I could not go to Symond street the night you set, because I had some people at the house. I have been down past the Caithness on more than one occasion. I looked up to the corner of the veranda and remembered the place where we used to sit. It brought back very pleasant memories, but it also brought up sad memories—sad, because those times will not return.

I hope you will not feel lonely keeping house by yourself. You will be able to take short trips as you say, and that will be very enjoyable. By the way, that was rather a pretty idea putting the photo on the silk ribbon. Did you cut it out? I would like to get a New York paper occasionally from you. Thank you very much. Did you get the Graphic, which I sent you? I will await the arrival of the photo of your horses with interest. They are good horses, I know. I sometimes see that Mr. H., who was at the Caithness the same time as you. I still go to the same church where you went with me. It has been painted this winter and looks quite new again. I have smiled sometimes when I think of something you asked me once. You asked me if I was good. Never heard it put that way before. Well, I am still good and attending church and teaching a class of girls in the Sunday school. The "Mariposa" is alongside this morning, so she will take this letter.

Trusting you are in good health and happy, and hoping to hear from you again soon, I remain as ever

    Your very sincere friend,
                              Harold.

                                    Auckland.

My dear Alice:—

I am going to write you a long letter this time. First of all, you did not do as I asked you to do, namely, to tell me how much you had to pay on the parcel. Now, you just tell me the next time you write, please, Mrs. Alice. Your last letter was very welcome, especially as I missed getting one mail. I was rather sorry to hear you were unsettled over there. Have you sold your horses? You will be feeling quite lost without them. I can quite imagine you going to camp meeting, because you favored me with your company when you were here in Auckland by coming to church. I was glad to have you with me, I can assure you. The girls all wondered who you were, I know, and I felt very proud of it that you were a friend of mine. I hope you have enjoyed the meeting very much. I hope you have also from it got a lot of good. I shall be interested to know how you liked it. You know we never have any such meetings out in these parts. Now, dear Alice, there is one thing on my mind which has given me a lot of trouble, and I want to ask your forgiveness. I have never forgiven myself for giving away that lovely present which you gave me—the diamond pin. I explained to you in my first letter why I gave it away. You did not say whether I did right or wrong. I wish you would tell me what you think about it; I shall not mind. It did seem so cruel to give it away after you being so good and kind to me. But, perhaps, you understood my feelings. Things were so miserable for both you and me when you were here that I did not know what to do. You would not hear of taking it back yourself and I would not give it to any one in the family. I have been sorry since for what I have done. I might have kept it for a keepsake. Will you forgive me, and try and feel how it was when I did what I did? If you will do that I shall feel happy and I promise you that I will never willingly offend you any more. Do you believe me? You may, for I am in earnest. You seem to be very dissatisfied with the States just now on account of your friends leaving. Perhaps you will think better of going to London to live. You seem to think that I will be getting married and stepping off some of these days. Well, the truth is, Alice, I have not even got a young lady. Could you help me to get one if I come over to you in the States? I have a dream, you know, that some time I will come over there to see you, but as yet it is only a dream. Perhaps, if my gold mining speculations turn out well I might manage it, but we will see. It would just be lovely to see you once more and have a long chat, face to face, instead of on paper. I was speaking to a young fellow the other day who used to work in a store in Philadelphia. He said he could give me a letter that would get me a place in the same store at about $20 a week, but I think that is hardly good enough. I did not know that the "Arawa" had been lost. It would have been a terrible affair if she had gone down with your precious soul on board. I wonder, too, why you went home so soon when there was no immediate hurry. I was truly sorry to lose you. I often wish I could take your arm now and go for a nice long walk. I wonder if it will ever be my good fortune to do so again. I never thought of "for ever" and "never more" in the way you do until I got your last letter. I know what a long time it is now; it seems that one can scarcely grasp it—it is so long. I am glad that the past has made you think. It is the best thing any one of us can do and, Alice, if you and I should never meet again on God's footstool, shall we meet in that better world where there shall be no more partings, neither sorrow nor crying nor pain and where God will wipe away all tears from their eyes? (Revelation 21 and 4.)

I enjoyed the Heralds very much, thank you. I would like a paper with Talmage's sermons published in it. Do you like the Graphic, or would you like one or some of the other papers—The Star or the Herald?

Now, dear Alice, I must close as it is half past eleven o'clock at night. With love, believe me ever,

Your true friend,
Harold.

New Zealand Post-office Telegraphs.

To Mrs. Alice Robinson, passenger by R.M.S.S. Mariposa, Auckland.

Regret unable to see you again. Wish you pleasant journey. Good bye.

M. Harris,
Wellington.

Port Chalmers, New Zealand, April.

Dear Alice:—

Your letter of February 21st only reached me on April 2d. The envelope bears the post mark of February 21st, and where it has been lying all this time I cannot find out—as I have made inquiries at our office and also at the Post-office but cannot get any satisfaction.

When we left the Auckland wharf I put myself in a position so that you could see me—and I you—and I watched until you seemed to mingle with the crowd and fade away. I then said to myself: There is a good little woman I might never set eyes on again, but shall never forget. I saw Williamson climb over the rail and shake hands with you, and must admit felt rather annoyed, as I thought I was the last, too.

There is no mistake, little woman. I am sure that on our departure from Auckland you felt very miserable. I could see it in your face. And no wonder, considering the long time you had spent on board the ship where you knew everybody and all hands had a good word for you. As regards myself, our acquaintance was not as long as yours with some others, but flatter myself it was long enough for us to understand each other, and I shall always think of you when I hear the word Lake Takapuna mentioned. That was a jolly day for me, and when I take another run over there I shall sit on the stones where we sat together and think of the happy day we spent.

The mussel shell hangs in my cabin, and I intend to keep it, and am glad to hear you have yours safe— also the lake weed.

What a pity there is no telephone from here to the mountains, so as we could have a long talk with each other. I don't know why you should think it would have been better if you had stopped at home and not taken your trip, as I fail to see where you have caused trouble (as you put it in your letter). As for thinking it would have been better if you had thrown yourself overboard the night you nearly fell into my arms, my advice is, put those thoughts out of your head, as I am sure you have something to live for. A woman with your disposition can always make friends wherever you go, and as regards myself having something to live for, I know I have. While reading your letter again to-night I am wondering if you have kept your vow, I mean in reference to speaking to anybody on board the "Mariposa." Now, I hope you did speak to everybody and had a good time; if not, your trip must have been very miserable, as you are a light-hearted woman by nature and fond of company—therefore I hope you had an enjoyable trip. And now, dear girl, I suppose you are home again among your friends and living in your happy home on the Hudson. I wish it were possible for me to just get a peep at you, to see how you look. But God knows if I shall ever have that pleasure.

Well, Alice, I must end this and say good bye, hoping to hear from you sometimes, at the same time wishing you all the happiness it is possible for you to have.

Dey.

If you can think of it, dear Alice, send me a few papers sometimes, and if you would like any New Zealand ones I will send them to you with pleasure.

Once more good bye! I am only sorry that I cannot send you a kiss, but consider the will for the deed.

Dey.

Dunedin, New Zealand, June 11th.

Dear Alice:—

Just a few lines to let you know that I am alive, but I have not been well. I have been in bed for some time with inflammation of the kidneys, and, dear Alice, I have nearly passed in my cheque. I have been three weeks in bed and am anything but strong yet, but hope to be very soon now. I have been in Dunedin since shortly after I last wrote you and was quite busy until I took ill, which was caused through catching cold and not paying attention to it.

You must know, it is very cold here just now, as it is the depth of winter and we have plenty of snow on the ground and hills. I only wish it was warmer, as I should like to take a walk or drive. But the doctor will not let me go out yet, and here I am shut up in the city hotel all day in front of a large fire. In fact, I should not be writing this letter to you, but cannot help sending you a line, as we were such great friends when you were out here—we spent a pleasant time together. Perhaps I am selfish, but I would like very much if you were here now and I had you to help me pass the weary hours away. I have received your letter telling me you were back in your mountain home, and I somehow think you do not seem glad to be there again, but suppose felt as though you could not settle down again after having been so long away. And now, since you have met all your old friends, and dogs and horses, you do not feel inclined to move again.

If I ever get to San Francisco I cannot say; but if I should, I shall not forget to telegraph you as soon as I arrive and if it can be managed will ask you to take rail and meet me half way, as I am longing to see you again, even if you will only let me take your hand. I am afraid you will think there is very little interesting matter in this letter, but you must excuse the scarcity of news and the writing as I am not the man you knew: I have had such a shaking up! But, Alice, don't be afraid of me, as I shall soon be the fat fellow you knew.

Now I shall conclude, hoping to hear that you are settled once again in your mountain house. I also hope the time is not far off when I shall have the pleasure of seeing how your grace is.

With kind love to you, dear, and all the happiness this world can give, is the wish of your old friend

Dey.

Christ-church, New Zealand, August.

Dear Alice:—

By the last mail I received from you a card with a few lines on it complaining that I had not written you, and you address me as dear friend, asking also if I have forgotten you. Well, little woman, I thought you knew me better than that, but since receiving that card I got another communication in the shape of what I call a letter you would write, and when I read it, which I do often, I can see you with your light cloak on, also the white cap you used to wear on board and your lorgnettes that you bought in Christ-church. Everything is as fresh in my memory as if it only occurred yesterday, and I have not the least desire to forget anything that occurred during the short time we were together, as I always look upon that trip we had together as the most pleasant one I have ever had and would give something to have it over again, but suppose that will never be as the chances are you may never come to this part of the world again and God knows when I shall come to America.

Yes, Alice, I have been very ill and all alone here in Christ-church. It is nearly three months now since I was first taken bad and suppose I am greatly to blame myself, because when I got all but well from the first attack I went out and caught cold and, of course, took ill again and was obliged to take to my bed and stop there for two weeks, but, thank goodness, I have cheated the grave digger so far and am feeling something like myself again, also am getting back the fat I lost and reckon in a couple of months I shall be as plump as ever.

By the last outward mail I wrote you, also sent you a weekly paper with a full description of the Sounds; also pictures of them. I know you will be interested as I suppose you have not forgotten Milford Sound. I can see you smiling now on the top of the wheel house, with W. and S. standing beside you, while I had to content myself with that fair-haired girl; but never mind, Alice, you were happy and that was all I wanted. Look out for the letter and paper, as I addressed them to the mountains.

It seems strange, but I have never seen W. or S.

since they left Sydney, and I have been in Sydney and Melbourne since.

Thanks, dear Alice, for the papers you have sent me; they were very interesting to me and everybody wants them here after I have done with them. With this letter you should receive four (4) weekly papers, one of Sydney and three of New Zealand. In one of the N. Z. papers you will see the trial and execution of Mrs. Dean for child murder. She is the first woman hung in New Zealand and I think, as everybody else does, that she got her deserts and feel confident you will think the same when you have read the particulars.

I am surprised to see that you have left your mountain home, as I thought you were so attached to it but suppose you know what is best for you, and sincerely trust you will be happy in your new home. What would I give to be seated with you under the shade trees you write about. Sometime when you are seated under them you might think of one who is so many miles away.

I visited Lake Takapuna last time I was in Auckland. A friend of mine named B—— was passenger to Sydney and, it being such a fine day, we made up our minds to take the ferry to the North Shore and walk the remainder, which we did; also walked back, and you may be sure we were very, very tired after reaching the ship. We arrived at the hotel in time for lunch, and must admit it was a little better than the one you and I got. Then we walked down to the Lake and sat down on the spot where you and I sat. The lake weed was there, also some shells—I did not disturb them, as they were the cause of pleasant thoughts running through my mind. While seated there I was so quiet that my friend said to me: "What are you thinking about, old man"? and I answered, "I would give five years of my life to be seated here just now with the last lady I saw seated here where I am." Then he said: "Well, I am sorry that I cannot be transformed into that lady."

Everything, Alice, seems just the same as when you saw it last—the ducks on the lake, the boats in the water —nothing seemed altered. After we left the lake we went towards the hotel and sat in the room where you and I had our cup of tea. Then I took my friend up the tower to show him the view, after which we had a drink and started for Auckland. I am glad you still have the shells and weed, also the stone from Lyttleton.

I am very sorry to hear that your dog Leo is dead, as I know you were very fond of him. By the way, you used to talk of him to me. Perhaps I may see his skin some day—who knows?

Now, dear Alice, I must draw this letter to an end and hope you are well and happy in your new home; also am glad you have some nice friends living with you. Also trust that God will watch over you, and make your life a happy one to the end. Good bye, dear! With love from

Dey.

P.S.—If convenient send some more of those nice papers, and I shall send some in return.

D.

Christ-church, New Zealand, October.

Dear Alice:—

By the last mail I only got two papers from you—not even a line to say if you were well or anything. What have I done that you have not sent me a few lines lately? I know you have not forgotten me or you would not send me papers; so in the future I shall expect a letter from you, if it be ever so short. I sent you some papers, and one had some views of the Sounds in it, but am sending you one this time, which is named Fiord Land. It gives a good idea of the amount of ice and snow there is in this country, also views of Milford Sound and other interesting places here, and as you have been in Milford Sound and viewed it from the top of the wheel house, perhaps you will recognize the place. Do you remember what a beautiful day that was? I will never forget how nice you looked and how happy you seemed when we steamed up that Sound. Strange to say, I have not been there since, and have no desire to see it again, but if I should happen to be in the ship that calls there when we are steaming up the centre I shall think of you.

Unfortunately I have been ill again, the old complaint—kidneys. I caught cold through my own fault and have been laid up for three weeks, but am glad to say that I am getting well again and will be more careful in the future. What with my first illness and the second one, I have been in Christ-church now just five months and will be jolly glad to get away to sea again, which will be next month, I hope, but do not know what ship I shall be going on.

T——y is ashore just at present, and it is his intention to start for England next month. He wishes to be kindly remembered to you.

Now, Alice dear, you must excuse this short note as I am still very weak and unable to write a long letter, but hope you will not forget to write sometimes, as I always look forward for some news of you every mail and must thank you for the papers that you send me.

Now good bye! Hoping you are well and quite pleased with your new home, with love and kisses,

Dey.

Christ-church, New Zealand, December.

Dear Alice:—

Your letter of the 6th October to hand, and you don't know how glad I was to hear from you. Why I should be so glad to receive letters and papers from you often makes me think, and the more I think the more I get mystified, as I know very little about you except what you have told me and you know about the same of me. Yet, on the arrival of every mail, I look forward for news from you, and I can only put it down to one thing and that is this—I am very fond of you, and very often wish you were not so far away so I could hear your merry laugh and kiss your lips as I would like to. Don't be surprised, little woman, if I should turn up in the States one day and ask you to let me take you in my arms once more. I wonder if you would refuse. I don't think so, as I know what a lovable little woman you are; but if I should never see you again you have impressed me so much that it will be hard to forget you, and by the tone of your letters I think you often give me a thought, and a kind one at that.

I often think of the first time I spoke to you. I seemed so glad after, and we seemed to be friends from the first meeting, and somehow more towards the last, and as far as I am concerned. Still that last night at the Albert is one that I shall often think of; also the last I saw of you as we were leaving the wharf for Sydney. I don't think I saw anybody on that wharf but yourself. I watched until you seemed to fade away, then I thought, "Just my luck."

Yes, dear Alice, send me your photo; it did not arrive by this mail, so don't forget. I am looking forward to its arrival, and when I receive it I shall get the prettiest frame possible for it and keep it hung up where I can always see it, so that I shall be reminded of my love in the States, if it is necessary, but don't think it will be.

I do not remember Mr. H—— of Sydney, and have not seen anything of W——'s, D——e, B——r or S——n; they have all disappeared. It does seem funny where people you have met go to; they say good bye, and perhaps that is the last you see or hear of them.

I get the Metropolitan Magazine you send me, I find the contents very good, especially some of the pictures, and the reading matter is very interesting. I am sending you this time the Auckland weekly paper, and the Xmas number of the Graphic.

T——y is in Dunedin and expects to sail for England soon. I told him you wished to be remembered and he sends his regards.

Now, dear Alice, I must conclude, hoping you are well and enjoying yourself at P——, as I suppose, and hope you got back safely from your drive to the mountains.

As for myself I am as strong as ever and have got entirely over my illness. So, with kind love and kisses, and hoping to hear from you soon, yes, surely by next mail, believe me,

Your love in N. Z.,

Dey.

Dunedin, New Zealand, January.

Dear Alice:—

Your welcome letter of Nov. 30th to hand; also the papers; I was especially glad to receive the letter, and hope you will always send me a few lines as anything in the shape of a letter from you is always welcome. When I am reading your letter I try to make myself believe that I can hear you speaking the words, but cannot persuade myself that you are really speaking as there is something wanting, and that is your old smile, which I cannot forget and have made up my mind if things go well with me for a little longer, I shall hear your voice again and kiss that dear face of yours again and again.

Yes, little woman, in my last I told you that I had been ill again and suppose it serves me right. After the first attack I did not take care of myself and had a relapse, which was worse than the first dose, but I am glad to say that I am nearly myself again but a good deal thinner. The warm weather has done me the world of good, and I have just returned from Auckland where

I have been staying for three weeks with some friends, and when I was in the Albert Hotel I used to think of you, especially of the last evening we spent together. In fact, I thought so much about you and that evening that I was not content until I had a look at the room where we said good bye.

I hope by the next mail to receive your long promised photo, and when I get afloat again will send you one of my ship.

You surprise me about your new home. I thought it was just the place that suited you, and I rather like your idea about settling in California, as I think it would be just the place that would suit you; the climate is so nice, but you do not mention which part you prefer.

Now, dear Alice, I must conclude as I have made a mistake about the closing of the mail and was obliged to hurry up or miss it, and I did not want to do that.

I am sending you three papers which I hope will please you.

So, with fondest love and many kisses, believe me

Yours,

Dey.

Melbourne, Australia, March.

Dear Alice:—

I suppose you are beginning to think I have forgotten you as you have not received a letter from me in some time. But, do not think that, little woman, as your image often occupies my thoughts and, perhaps it may appear strange to you, but when I think about you I can always see you, and as I did that night you put your head through the port and I kissed you for the first time. Of course, you remember it just as well as I do. W———n was there, and also T———y, and my earnest wish is that we might have it all over again but suppose that is impossible, as you often mention in your letters that we might never meet again.

The reason why I did not write last mail is that I missed it. It was on a trip to the Macquarie Islands, which lie to the south of New Zealand. We had a party of sixty people who were going there to inspect the Islands so as to select a position for a lighthouse and were away five weeks. I intended writing before we left, but thought we would be back in time if they had only made a business trip, but they were not bound to time.

I saw the Duke to-day. He tells me he intends going to sea again. I cannot understand a man going to sea with that amount of money. I wish it was mine. If so some of it would be spent on a visit to you, as I should like to see you again very much, even if it were to say good bye again.

Your letter of December 24th I have just read over again, and it is easy for you to write "give all thoughts of me up," but that at present seems impossible. They say time works wonders, and perhaps it may, but I feel sure the time is far distant when I shall forget you, and to show you that I speak the truth I will do anything you wish but cease writing to you—that I shall never do until I have lost all trace of you. I am not the least afraid that you will forbid me writing to you as I think it gives you nearly as much pleasure to hear from me as it gives me to hear from you.

In your letters you express your love for me, and it gives me pleasure to read them. Then, again, I have often thought we could never be anything but friends, as you used to impress on me so often that you would never marry again, in fact, you mentioned that fact the last night we had together at the Albert, and I have often thought you did it out of kindness; but it was too late then. You had made the world seem brighter before that night after our first meeting, which was on the "M———," when you were leaning over the rail. Somehow after that you seemed to fill up a gap, or something that was wanting in my life. So I have considered since that it was fate that brought us together, and if you think it is better to just remain friends only I must try and be content, as I would do anything you wish. Your photo arrived safely, and I often look at it and wonder what you are doing. Perhaps you are looking at mine, and I am very pleased you think the last I sent you a good one. As for yours I think it splendid, and am awfully glad you sent it as I can often look upon it and think of you. I keep it in a prominent position, whether ashore or afloat. At present we are lying at the Melbourne wharf. Do you remember, dear, you were landed there? I do.

As for my health I am quite recovered from my illness and am my old self again, just as you knew me, but not quite so fat, and I sincerely hope you are enjoying good health as you deserve it, dear.

With this letter I am sending you Hobart papers. That will be a change from those I have been sending—

one is the Xmas number and is full of Tasmanian views, including a view of Hobart, which I think you will recognize. You will see the steamers at the wharf that the "Monowai" occupied when you were with us.

Now, dear, I must conclude, or you will think I am never going to end. But, to tell the truth, I feel as if I could go on writing forever, and I am afraid if I do not stop you will get tired reading this letter. So I shall say good bye, but not without a kiss, as I have just kissed the nearest I can get to you, and that is your dear face mounted on silk ribbon.

The "Monowai" is due at Auckland on the 26th of this month, and I expect on my arrival to get a letter and some papers from you; if not, I shall be very disappointed.

I have been wondering if you have made up your mind to live in California or, perhaps, you are there now. If so, I hope you get this letter.

Well, good bye this time, Alice. Wishing you every happiness and good health,

Your sincere friend,
Dey.

Auckland, N. Z., May 11th.

Dear Alice:—

On May 16th, the "Alameda" sails from Auckland, and as she brought your letter dated March 24th, I am writing you by her return.

Your letter was very welcome and I will forgive you for not sending me either paper or letter by the "Monowai," and hope you have forgiven me for not writing by one mail. If I remember correctly I think it must have been at the time I was away at the Macquarie Islands, which, I think, was mentioned in my last.

The Duke is in Dunedin cutting a great dash. I saw him the other night. He was with a clean-shaved fellow, something like himself, and he seemed so taken up with his friend that he hardly noticed me. So I have made up my mind he will be the first to speak when we meet again.

By the heading of your letter I see you are still in the same place and not yet gone to California. Have you given up the idea, or are you still waiting until your mind is made up?

Yes, Alice, I would like very much to be running between London and New York, but that is, I suppose, as you say, out of the question, very few vacancies occurring in those ships; besides I should want very great influence to get one of those appointments.

I shall be in Auckland again in a few days, and suppose will call in at the Albert. If so, I shall think of you as I always do, especially when I see that place.

Yes, my dear, we have had many passengers this season, but they are getting less now as we are just beginning to feel the winter; in fact, you might say they have it in the South, as there is plenty of snow on the hills at present and I am afraid we are in for a severe one this year. Last year was bad enough, but the snow has started very early this winter.

I wonder when I shall get that photo you have promised so long. Well, I will wait patiently, as there is one of you just over the head of my bunk at present, also a shell similar to the one you have.

I am sending you some papers; also a nice little book on the Sounds. The Metropolitan Magazine I like very much. It is a splendid paper.

Now, Alice, good bye again, until you hear from me again. I was going to write "See me," but goodness knows when that will be. I wish it were possible to know as I am longing for it.

So with fond love and kisses, also hoping I come to you in your sleep, I remain,

Yours,

Dey.

Dunedin, New Zealand, July 4th.

Dear Alice:—

To-day the glorious 4th, but little notice is taken of it in this town—they are too Scotch. I have only seen the stars and stripes floating at one place, and that is at the Consul's. They don't seem to understand anything about holidays here, unless it is St. Andrews.' or New Year's day. Now, if I had been in Sydney, I should have gone with some of my American friends to the picnic they hold every year, and you may bet it is a jolly good one. On June 29th I reached Dunedin and found some papers and two letters from you. You do not know how glad I was to get them, as I did not even get a letter or newspapers from you the mail before, and I am sorry now, but I felt so hurt that I did not send you either letter or newspaper by the return mail, so I hope you were not angry when you found the mail had arrived and I had not written.

The swallow's wing came safely, and at present it is fixed near a shell over my bunk, and every time I see it and the shell I always think of somebody who is far away, living in a place called P——. While I think of it I must not forget to let you know that the Duke has left here by the "Kaikawa" for England about a month now, so he might cross the Atlantic and call on you if he knows your address, or, perhaps, you might meet him accidentally. What a lark, if you meet! I should like to see your face, but I must inform you that he looks quite different now, as he is clean shaved, and must admit it is anything but an improvement.

Do you remember Mrs. R——? She was a passenger by the "Monowai" to Gisborne—the trip you travelled to Melbourne—and was in the same cabin as you. She is the wife of one of our captains. Well, I was spending an evening at their house this time when at Dunedin (she is living there now), and she told me she often wondered what had become of you; also said that you seemed to be very much in love with the Duke as you were always talking of him. But I let her know that it was quite different now, and she seemed glad. I do not think the "Monowai" will be running to Frisco much longer as there is a new ship being built for that trade, and if I should be lucky enough to get her and can possibly manage it I shall take a run by rail to New York—if only to get a look at you. I do not say that will satisfy me, but it will be better than not seeing you at all.

Your photo with the feathers around your neck (I mean the one taken at Auckland) is always before me. No matter when I am in my cabin I see you. You always seem to be looking at me. It is a good photo; you have the old smile that I remember so well, and when I am looking at it I often wonder what you are doing—perhaps lying in your hammock under the trees at P—— and thinking of me, I hope.

We are in for a very severe winter this year. At present it is very cold, and goodness knows what it will be like next month.

Now, dear Alice, I must finish, hoping you are keeping well and are as jolly as ever; also hope your horses are all well again, and that the day is not far off when you and I will be seated together behind them, if only for one short drive.

Once more good bye! May you always have everything that this world can give, is the prayer of

Yours sincerely,

Dey.

Dunedin, July 25th.

Dear Alice:—

Your welcome letter dated June 17th reached me yesterday; also the Harper's Weekly, Book of New York views, Hudson River views and Metropolitan, and many thanks for them. If I were only near enough you should have your reward with interest for sending them. As for the book of New York views that I shall most certainly keep; everybody who has seen the book admires it very much. The Harper's Weekly is a good paper, especially the issue you sent. What a time it must have been for those unfortunate people at St. Louis! There is no mistake, when you have a fire, accident or storm, it is a proper one, and by the views I think St. Louis has had its share of tornadoes for some time.

Your letter this time is short (but sweet), and I'm afraid mine is going to be short also, as this country is so dull just now and there is very little news. All you read in the papers now is the inquiry into the failure of the Colonial Bank; it is before the parliament just now and I am afraid some of the directors will get into trouble before the inquiry is finished.

This has been a severe winter so far; in the North they have had rain and gales of wind for the last month. The South is very cold, nothing but wind, rain or snow—they have hardly seen the sun for a month. Everybody seems to have a cold, and no wonder. You want to be web-footed to live here just now.

In my last I wrote that the Duke had gone to London, so I cannot give you any more tidings of him; but as I wrote before, you might meet him in New York one of these days.

I am surprised to hear you are tired of America. I always thought you would live in no other country, but suppose you are like other people who have left the country to which they belong and seen other places —they always have a feeling that they would like to return to the places they have visited. As for you living in Auckland I cannot imagine that, as I am sure it is too slow for anybody, especially people who have lived in or near large cities. If you had said Sydney or Melbourne I could understand, as there is some life there, but nothing would please me more than see you walk down Auckland wharf some fine day and say you have come to stay.

As for myself I have spent the most of my life traveling and often wonder if I could settle down on shore, but suppose it all depends who it is with, as I am sure I should want a companion, and it would be a long-haired one at that—one of my own sex would not suit.

So you have had your photo taken again at last, and I am glad you think it good; also expect a copy of it next mail, if not, look out, as you have promised it for a long time. But I don't think you can improve much on the one taken at Auckland; to my fancy it is very like you, and as I see it many times during the day I often remark to myself, "I wonder what that little woman is doing now, and if ever I shall see her again"?

On my arrival at Sydney this time I expect my mother will have taken a house, as she is there now and at last I have gained my point. I have been trying for the last three years to get her to leave Melbourne and have succeeded at last. Ever since she left Sydney to live in Melbourne she has been ill, so I think Sydney climate suits her best.

Now to conclude. I hope you are well and happy; also that you will write me a longer letter next time, as I am never tired of reading your letters no matter how long they are.

So, good bye for the present, Alice! With much love and kisses from

Dey.

September 2d.

Dear Alice:—

The "Mariposa" has arrived without a letter from you. What is the matter? I hope you are not ill, and I don't think I have offended you with anything I have written. If so I am awfully sorry, as it was not meant. But am glad you did not forget me altogether. The newspaper reached me safely, also the photo; now, that pleased me very much. It is a good one, and I like the costume. The hat is a daisy, and would like so much to be near enough to kiss you under it, but as that is impossible just at present, try and imagine that I have done so. There is no mistake, that is the most stylish photo I have seen for many a day.

I have very little news. You know what a quiet place this is; nothing to break the monotony—they won't even give us an earthquake now; we have not had a shock for some months, and this winter so far has been exceedingly fine—hardly any snow in the South as yet, though everybody at the beginning thought we were in for a severe winter. I do not know what the place is coming to. Were it not for visits we make to Australia I don't know what we should do to amuse ourselves. Certainly there is, when on shore, a little more life in Australia, also variety, but our stay is short, so we can't see everything in the time we are there. There are two American companies there just now—one is playing "Trilby," and the other "A Trip to Chinatown." I have seen both and was very much pleased with them, especially the "Trip to Chinatown." Both companies are doing big business, and I hear there is another company to arrive next mail, so you see the Americans are getting a turn now and I think they will be in demand hereafter.

I am sending you some newspapers. Now, dear, I must conclude, hoping you have written me by the good ship "Monowai," which arrives here next week; if you have not I shall be greatly disappointed. I also hope the letter that I expect will contain good news and that you have not been ill or have had any trouble.

With heaps of love and kisses I remain,

Yours,

Dey.

Christ-church, New Zealand.

Dear Alice:—

Your letter of August 24th has reached me and also has given me a surprise. I little dreamed that you were in London, or had any idea of your going there and I cannot fathom now what took you there; you must have made up your mind very suddenly.

When the "Mariposa" arrived and no letter from you I began to think you were getting tired of writing me, especially as the "Monowai" came in before her, and no letter by her either, so I thought I would give you a chance to drop the correspondence if you wished and did not write you by the last mail. But, at the same time, I did not think you were over the Atlantic in London, and I sincerely hope you had a good time. According to your letter I think you have enjoyed yourself, also still have a fancy for the brass buttons as the captain and the chief officer seem to have been your resort. Well, little woman, there is nothing like enjoying yourself while you can, as they say you are a short time alive but a long time dead. So my advice is—have all the fun you can without injuring other people.

I received the two papers, also your photo. Why, you write and say that perhaps I shall not care for it I cannot understand. Of course, I care for it and think it splendid, and those I have shown it to wanted to know if you were Scotch—that is on account of the plaid dress, I suppose.

As I said before, in one of my letters, you cannot improve on the Auckland one; in that I see the woman I know as Alice, in the Brooklyn one I see a well dressed woman, but somehow the features are altered. Of course I will know it was meant for you, but there is something wanting. No, dear Alice, I don't think you can improve on the Auckland one; there is an expression on your face that is familiar to me in that one.

So you intend to return by the same steamer—quite right. If you had a good time going over, I hope you will have just as good a one going back; but at the same time I must admit that I feel a little jealous when I think of the good time that chief officer and captain will have, because it is quite true that you are good looking and one of the most fascinating women I have ever met, and I am not fool enough to think other people cannot see it, as that is impossible. But as everything about you seems quite natural I suppose you should be more proud of it than sorry, and I trust that you will live many years yet to show off your good looks and fascinations.

As for getting you an opal, that is an easy matter; only let me know about the size, say this—also shape, and say whether it is to be blue or milky. As for the cost, that is an after matter. I have one in my ring now, it is about this size—and oval in shape. Everybody admires it, and if that size should suit I shall get you one. I am rather anxious to hear from you again, just to know if you met the Duke.

Now, dear, it is just midnight; so I must finish up, but somehow I feel as if I could go on writing to you all night. I wonder would it be worth reading if I did. By the time this reaches you, you will be back in America, and I wish it were possible for me to jump out of the envelope when you open it. That would give you a surprise.

Well, dear Alice, good bye for the present, hoping you have had a good time on your return trip. I am going to bed and hope I may dream something pleasant of you. With kind love from

Dey.

Brooklyn.

My dear Mrs. Robinson:—

Yours received with thanks for your kind invitation to join the card party.

I shall be present at your house if I am in the city; but, I am sorry to say I expect to be in Washington on about that date.

With kindest regards I remain,

——, Conn., May 17th.

My dear Mrs. Robinson:—

Are you still on earth? And if so, where? Knowing that you usually spend your summers in the mountains I have or will have this directed there. A friend and myself are intending to take a trip this summer and wish to visit T——e, and while there would like to call on "Alice." Pardon me, but it seemed so natural for me to think of you by that name. Can you? Of course, you can, but will you inform me which is the best hotel for us to stop at P——. Belle is married to a rich young fellow in Germany, or who is stationed there. Mary has been in Germany for three years, but came home last summer. Father and mamma are going touring through Europe this summer. The girls at home are expecting to have a grand time—"Cats away, etc."

If you are not at T——e and this letter should by chance meet your glance, please write and let me know how you are. I have been wanting to see you for such a long time that I think you might at least give me the privilege. In fact, I never claimed the friendship of any one I so much appreciated. Now, laugh! I can hear you laughing and saying: "You foolish boy!"

Kindly write me and say how and where you are. The next time you go to New York, please write me and, with your permission, I will come down and call.

Anxiously awaiting some sort of reply, I remain,

Very truly yours,

Fred.

June 24th.

My dear Mrs. Robinson:—

Your kind invitation and letter were received, and would have been answered before had I not been out of town.

Regret very much that Mr. A—— and myself will be unable to call on the date you mention, as Mr. A—— will be quite busy until after August 1st, and also, concerning myself, will state that my people sail for Europe about that time.

A few years ago you knew me as a sapling and I would call you "Alice," and as my friendship has always remained and you have never been so cruel as to correct me. I am just going to resume my audacity and say Alice. There you are smiling and saying: Well, well, if that fellow isn't still a youth!"

Did I tell you Lemont had married? Well, he has and you must remember to ask about him when I call, for it seems amusing to us all. Tell me how I can find you if I ride down on my wheel some morning, that is, come to New York on the train and then ride over to your place just to say "Hallo, Mrs. Robinson!" Actually, the more I think of you the more I have to tell you; in fact, I feel like a regular old gossip this morning.

With much love,

Fred.

P.S.—Will it be convenient for you to have me call some morning? The reason I have not mentioned any date is that I would most likely come on Sunday when it is pleasant riding.

September.

My dear Mrs. Robinson:—

Many thanks, indeed, for your very kind and thoughtful present. I only received it just as we were leaving the station. I had expected to see you on board. I am told that knives, scissors, etc., "cut" friendship. We must excuse the word somehow or other as I should be very sorry, indeed, if that did. I hope to see you next time, and then next time. Why, you'll be out with us.

With very kind regards, pray, believe me, my dear Mrs. Robinson,
Very cordially yours,
F.

London, Oct.

My dear Alice:—

What an awfully selfish young cad you must think me for not seeing you off, and I have not been able to excuse myself for it. I thought, dear girl, that the other people were going to help you right to the ship, and my going would only make it harder for me to leave you in the end, so I determined not to see you at all that morning. When I was told you had to look after everything yourself to the ship I was really ashamed. But if you come over again you will not have to complain of inattention on my part, I give you my word. Won't you come over again soon? I would give a lot to have you here again. You might have stayed a week or two longer when you were here.

That old fossilized skinflint Bill is still here and worries me considerably. Thank God, he leaves soon.

Mrs. S—— returned from the continent (parlez-vous français?), is still here and is rather a peculiar individual. I've not settled about my Australian trip yet, but should I go I hope you will let me call on you on the way.

Since you left I have been working hard on the eye, trying to forget a pair of nice eyes in P——. No doubt you are having a grand time on the steamer. I hope you are well looked after, which I think goes without saying. The weather is beastly bad here, with rain all the time. How did M—— stand the voyage? Of course, you will tell me all about the trip when you write. It's going to be a rather lonely winter for me here in London. And now, my best girl, write me soon. With my best love,

       Yours,

          D.

         New York.

My dear Mrs. Robinson:—

 No doubt you will be surprised beyond mention when you read this. The fact is I have been trying for six months to get your address and did not succeed until last night when I heard it by accident. As you probably know I am living home again and am getting on first rate with every one. I have a good position at the above address and have bettered myself a hundred per cent. by coming home. None knew of it until I walked in the door. Contrary to my apprehensions I was received favorably and have now become a member of the family again. I was told you had gone to Australia. I suppose it must have been a very pleasant trip. I am going to enter some bicycle races on the 30th of next month and shall have to begin to train in about a week, so you can imagine that between business and training I won't have much spare time; however, if you want me to, I will write to you often. When you answer this, please, address as the above, as there might be some too curious people elsewhere.

I must close as it is dinner time, but will write soon again. Should you move, please, let me know and oblige,

Yours cordially,
Nell.

New York.

My dear Mrs. Robinson:—

It is now some time since I received your letter, but until now have been prevented from writing for the reason that I have been laid up with my arm and leg up in bandages the result of a bad fall while training on my bicycle. I expect to enter the races at Plainfield, N. J., on Decoration day and must work hard to regain what I have lost while in bed. I suppose the people are just beginning to go to the mountains now —are they not? It must be awfully lonely up there for you all alone, is it not? I should think it would become so monotonous that you could hardly bear it stuck up in such a place as T—— is—I want to be where there is some life and variety. I suppose you think an awful lot of your horses and that you are a fine rider. I am a great lover of horses myself. In Florida I used to have a half broke mustang and would go out riding with a country girl. She was just as full of life as could be. She would get on her saddle by herself, and once there used to go flying through the woods at a great rate; but even Florida with all its (supposed) charms was not good enough for me, and I finally came to the only place in God's world, New York.

I must close now. Hoping to hear from you soon, I am,

     Yours, as ever,
           Nell.

           New York.

My dear Mrs. Robinson:—

 Your letter was waiting at the office when I returned from my vacation, a period of one week. I think the change you made was very wise, as it must have been very tiresome stuck up in the mountains with no enjoyments whatever. The family have all gone to L—— for the summer. I remain in the city now. So, you see, I am alone as father goes to L—— nights. I am going in some cycle races at Manhattan Beach next Saturday, but I cannot run as I have not been training and am in poor condition for a race. What train do you take to get to P——, and can I get connections so as to leave the city at 7 P.M. and return at a respectable hour? I am very busy now, so I cannot write, but when I get some time I will write a long letter.

 Hoping this will find you in the best of health and spirits, I am, as ever,

           Nell.

           New York.

My dear Mrs. Robinson:—

 I hope the letter I sent you about a week ago reached you. If it did I have received no answer. I should like very much to call on you next Saturday afternoon. I can catch the 2.20 P.M. train, which will bring me at P—— at 3.40. Will you be in on that day?

I went in some races on Saturday, but the track (Manhattan Field) was so muddy that I could not do better than third in my heat. I hope to do considerably better on the 24th. I suppose the weather at P—— is as disagreeable as in New York at present, isn't it? Do you still possess that large dog you had in the mountains? I always admired that dog, even if he was a little cross at times. What sort of a place is P——, and what do the people do there? Is it a summer resort? I suppose driving and riding are your chief pleasures. Are you not awfully lonely all by yourself, or have you friends with you? Have you learned to ride a bicycle yet? If not, you have missed lots of enjoyment. During my week's vacation I went out for a spin with a young lady every morning at half past six. We went to Fort Hamilton on one of our tours and went all over the grounds on foot and came home in time for dinner. Well, I must close now. Drop me a line on receipt of this, so that I will know if I am to call Saturday or not. Awaiting your reply, I am,

Yours sincerely,
Nell.

New York.

My dear Mrs. Robinson:—

Your note received; was very sorry you were engaged. It's extremely doubtful whether I can call next

Saturday or not. If I can't I will call Sunday morning. I don't suppose I shall find you at church during the A.M. Will I? I shall enter the bicycle race at Manhattan Field on the 20th, provided I can raise the entrance fees. I suppose you often visit New York now, do you? I am disabled now, so cannot write, but merely scribble. This is to let you know that I will probably be out Sunday on a pretty early train. Until then I am,

Yours sincerely,
Nell.

New York.

My dear Mrs. Robinson:—

If you have finally persuaded yourself to go and see me race at Manhattan Field, let me dissuade you from going as the races are going to be held at Manhattan Beach instead. I shall ride but don't expect to win anything, as I shall have to race all the noted class "A" racers. However, if you go to the beach and I see you there, I am sure I can ride ten seconds faster than if you were absent. Don't let any one know, as papa does not want me to race.

I got home in time to dress and be at business last Monday. I shall come out and see you whenever I can. We have not had one row as yet. We were so interested in our little game that we overlooked that. Write soon and if you do go to the races, don't be dignified but yell for all you're worth.

Hoping you are well in good health and spirits,
As ever,
Nell.

New York.

My dear Mrs. Robinson:—

Your note received. I will leave New York on the 1.45 P.M. train to-morrow, which will bring me into P—— in good season. It is compulsory for me to leave Sunday morning on the 9 train. At present am rushed, so cannot write.

Hoping you are well, I am,
Yours sincerely,
Nell.

New York.

My dear Mrs. Robinson:—

It is now quite some time since I last saw or heard from you. I hope you are not ill. I shall try to come out to see you as soon as I can as I am training now for some races to be held at Plainfield, N. J., on Labor Day. If you go you will see some good races. I shall look for you, as I am sure you would prove my mascot. Write and tell me how things are at P—— and whether you have regained any of the money you lost when we last played.

I have not much time now, so will cut this short. Hoping to hear from you before Saturday, I am as ever,
Nell.

P.S.—Let me know if you are going to the races.

New York, Sept. 1st.

My dear Alice:—

Your letter arrived last night, and you have no idea how glad I was to hear from you. However, you did not surprise me much when you told me about the fine time you had on your trip, because a person of your jolly disposition must naturally be the centre of attraction. I am awfully sorry you are not coming home soon. I was beginning to feel as though P—— was a second home for me.

As to my plans I do not know what to say. I cannot obtain a situation that is worth taking and at times feel quite despondent. Here I am, 31, and cannot support myself, much less a wife, so I am going to try my luck at fortune hunting. If you hear of any one who has money and wants to marry a good looking American over there, why let me know. I can give them a good time on their money. I am surprised that you did not make connections in the A. and H. case. How did it turn out?

By the way, I've lost my heart, but what's the use—there is no money in it? She is a peach, though. Occasionally she poses for the Standard.

I guess we'll go Republican all right. Bankers don't seem to feel sorry at all. They are shipping gold into the country instead of out. How I wish I were with you, as that fellow from New Zealand says—if only for a moment.

I am all alone and don't see a soul all day, so you must not blame me for going with actresses, models, etc. The mails take so long to reach from you to me that you should answer at once. I know your handwriting as far as I can see it. Do not break too many hearts.

I will close now; hoping to hear from you in the near future, I am,

>Yours sincererly,
>
>>Nell.

>Sept. 29th.

My dear Alice:—

Your letter arrived this A.M. I was delighted to hear from you. I am glad you like London and hope you are having what you were made for—and that is fun. As for me, I am in the straits. I can't get any work. If I had a position where I could earn my living I would board out. I feel that if there was ever a fellow born to be rich I am he, and still I have not got a sou, and not only that—I got into a scrape that cost me $25 to get out of. I spent that sum instead of getting myself a suit of clothes. When are you coming to New York? I long for the day when I can sit down and talk, eat and play cards the way we used to do. A fellow could forget his troubles and be happy at your house. Do you know I get awfully despondent at times, because I cannot see any future at all ahead for me? What I need is just what you say you need—the almighty dollar. If we had all we wanted, wouldn't we cut ices"? I guess we go "gold" on election day all right, and if I had the wherewith, I would bet fifty to one on it. The general opinion is that there is no doubt about it, so what Mr. R—— said need not bother you. I had a very funny thing happen to me the other day. If you remember I once told you of a girl I used to go to see. Well, she is married now about four or five months. I was surprised to get a letter from her imploring me for God's sake to come and see her at two P.M. Well, I went and was there about ten minutes, when she saw her husband returning from business. She nearly had a fit and she told me she would write; just then he entered the door. I was introduced and after a few words of explanation made my exit. I have never heard from her since.

Please write on receipt of this and I will patiently wait until I get a letter, or better yet, see you. Let me know when you are coming home, on what steamer, etc.

I must close now. Hoping to hear from you at your earliest convenience, I am,

Yours sincerely,
Nell.

Railway Survey Camp.
Parker, New South Wales.

My dear Mrs. Robinson:—

I must apologize for not replying to your note long ere this, but I have been away on survey work almost since my return home, so I feel sure you will forgive. I was pleased indeed to hear of your safe arrival home and trust you are still enjoying good health. I met Miss W—— before she left for the country, and had the promise of a note before she left for London; but, as I have been away from Sydney, I was unable to see her again. We got on well up to the last. I thank you heartily for fulfilling your promise and will keep your letter in remembrance of the very happy time we spent together. I enjoyed my trip from start to finish like yourself, and it was no doubt greatly due to the very agreeable companions I met with on the "Monowai." I hope we may meet again some day.

Our poetical friend returned to Sydney about a fortnight after I did, but I have not seen him since. I wonder has he crossed over to your side of the world? Poor man, he deserves better luck.

I am still single and am afraid likely to remain so for some time, as I have not been able to catch Miss Right's eye yet.

With kindest wishes, I remain,

Yours sincerely,

X.

S.S. H——.

New York, December —, 18—.

My darling Alice:—

This will be a very short note, but I must ask you to accept my fondest love and best wishes, old pet, for all your kindness to me, not only this time, but ever since we met.

To say that I love you does not begin to express my feelings, so you must imagine all sorts of nice things for yourself.

It was delightful to have you down here, and trust you will come again.

With fondest love, believe me,

Yours devotedly,

Bob.

S.S. H——.
At sea, December 31st, 18—.

My darling Alice:—

The weather has been grand since we left, so I have ample time to collect no end of sleep, and am now feeling A 1 after my stay in New York. As this is the last day of the old year I have made up my mind to have a good paper chat with you before midnight comes, as the boys are all coming up then to have a social drink just by way of welcoming the new year in good old-fashioned style. I may mention right here though that it will be my last smile for some time, for I am already feeling quite different by going slowly as I promised you while on board here.

Please accept my warmest wishes, darling, for 18—, and I sincerely trust that it may prove a thoroughly happy year for you in every sense of the word. It would be impossible, my love, to attempt to thank you for all your extreme kindness to me, but I trust you understand me sufficiently well by this time to know that I am thoroughly grateful for all you have done for me.

It was too bad my not writing last voyage as promised, but I will endeavor to make up for it this passage by sending double quantity, so hope you will not have to scold me on that score again.

Our thirty-four passengers are not what you would call lively, and they all go to bed about nine, so you may guess I am at a loss to know how to pass my time; but, considering I have so many letters to answer, I shall have to try and get some of them off my mind, and if all goes well I mean to do all my writing at sea in the future, as one can settle down so much better here than on shore, especially if you are around. Myself and Mr. R—— have often wondered if you folks went straight home or finished the day up in New York.

I was very delighted to see you again, but there were far too many here for my fancy, and I almost felt like killing old E—— when he kissed you; but as long as you will not have him call on you I don't mind. So remember this, little sweetheart.

L—— seemed very pleased with his little self when he left—of course you know who he is. I feel awfully sorry for him, because you could see he is a fellow with brains and a comical sort of genius to boot. Goodness only knows what Mr. and Mrs. M—— must think of me. My note from the Hook was obliged to be short as I had several things to attend to. I wonder if you have managed to do the puzzle yet? The recollections of last week are still to the fore in my thoughts, and I would a thousand times rather be able to pop in on you to-night instead of trying to convey my thoughts by letter. You are a dear old girl to me, Alice, and I can assure you, love, that I would do anything for you, for somehow you seem to understand me and a word from your dear lips has a great weight with me, which I trust to let you see on my return.

There is not the slightest doubt that too much drink is bad for me and thoroughly spoils my pleasures, in addition to making me feel ill as well, so I am just going to commence the New Year on fresh lines; I won't say a total abstainer, but as far as the ship is con-

concerned I am going to leave it alone. Dr. M—— has been doctoring me up, and I hope to get into Southampton looking very fit.

My table is filled with passengers, but they are so frightfully quiet that I am glad when the meals are over.

Poor old R—— is, like myself, writing letters to while away the time, so you see life is none too gay on the H——. James and George will be having a little leisure time now that the —— has taken his departure, although I don't suppose it matters much to them my coming, as I generally manage to get on with them all serene in spite of breaking the cutter. Directly the pilot left I found that I had broken another promise in not sending you a sailing list, but will put one in with this scribble.

If I go on writing much more you will not have the patience to wade through it, so I had better draw to a close for to-night in the hope that before the end of the trip I may be able to scare up something to write about which may interest you.

Good night, love! With every good wish for the New Year, believe me,

Yours lovingly,
Bob.

Southampton.

My love:—

Just a hurried line to thank you very much for your letters which I got to-day. Will write you again and tell my news. They are now waiting down below for me to pay off, so you must excuse haste as it is 5 P.M. and all want to get home. Just don't I wish we could see each other. I am sure you would say I have done wisely leaving off W——. I cannot say how much better I feel.

Good night! With love and a good big kiss,

    Yours, as ever,

                          Bob.

From Mrs. W——.

                            Salisbury.

My dear Mrs. Robinson:—

I am very sorry not to have answered your letter before, but this is to say I am intending to do it in person. I am coming to town to-morrow for just a night. To-morrow is quite full up, but I propose calling on you on Thursday morning, as near as I can say, between 12 and 1 o'clock. I hope it will be convenient and I shall find you in, if not you might send me a line. If you post it sometime to-morrow (Wed.) I should get it Thursday morning. If I do not hear I shall come as I suggest.

I suppose you couldn't settle to come down to Salisbury on Thursday. It would be nice to travel together, and you are coming, ain't you?

You will have lots to tell me.

        Yours in anticipation,

                          T——.

From Miss T——.
The Grand Hotel.
Manchester, Friday 18—.

Dear Mrs. Robinson:—

No doubt you will think I have forgotten my promise to write, but I have so little to tell except about the horrid weather that I thought it was not worth while troubling you.

I am leaving Manchester to-morrow, Saturday, for the country house of my friends, then I shall get some driving and bicycling if the weather will allow, both of which I enjoy very much.

I have been very disappointed lately as I had hoped to see some of my friends here, but the one I wanted to see most is away ill. However, I hope to see him before I return to London. I am not returning for another week, during which time I suppose you will be having a very good time. Hope you have had good news about your dog. I feel sure he cannot be lost. If you find time to write to me next week, I enclose you my address. It will be useless to add how delightful it will be to hear from you.

With kindest love, believe me,
Sincerely yours,
J——.

From Miss T——.
Russell Square, London.

My dear Mrs. Robinson:—

I hope you do not think I have forgotten you, for

I must assure you that is not the case. For the last two months I have been so unwell with a very, very bad cold, that at last Mrs. F—— went with me to Brighton for a week. The change did me good.

Dr. C—— has left London for Rome. We were quite sorry when he left. Mr. Q—— made such a noise that he was asked to go. For my part I was sorry, I liked him; but the great Mr. N—— said he must go, so he went. Dr. R—— has stayed here twice since you left. How is your dog getting on? Do write me a long letter full of news about yourself and doings. Everything is just the same here. Miss A—— has gone to her house at Southsea, so there are very few staying here now.

Hoping you are well and with much love, believe me,

Your friend,

J——.

From Miss L——.

Grand Hotel.—Alfred Hansen.

Naples, le —— March ——, 18——.

My dear Mrs. Robinson:—

You will doubtless be surprised when you open this letter, but I want to send you a few lines to ask you how you are. We sailed from New York the tenth of January to spend the winter months in Italy, but return home the end of June. I meant to have written to you before leaving, but it always amuses me how at the last one is always rushed. We had a very rough passage until we reached Gibraltar. Out from there to Genoa it was perfect—as smooth as glass. We spent a week at Monte Carlo, then joined the Misses T——s in Florence (they came over in October). After ten days there and two days in Rome we came on here. The weather is perfect, windows open and delicious sunshine to-day. We spend a few weeks in this vicinity and go back to Rome for a short time. Mr. L——, being a good sailor, has left us for three or four weeks and gone to Egypt—he joins us again in Rome.

I hope you are contented with your new home, and most earnestly wish that you are.

Pat the dear ponies for me. I think they would like the feathers the ponies wear in Florence. We often speak of them.

We all join in kindest regards to you.

Very cordially,

M——.

From Mrs. H——.

Honolulu, Saturday 17th.

My dear Mrs. Robinson:—

I was very glad to get the good interesting letter from you and to know that you have crossed in safety that great imaginary line we learn of so vaguely in our early days in our geographies. Miss L—— and Miss B—— left two weeks ago for the Volcano House to visit Mr. and Mrs. Ross. They expect to return the 24th. Last night two very bright young ladies took the room next to me. They came from Portland, Or., on a sailing vessel, and in thirty days. One is a Bostonian. They were ready to go to church this

A.M., when the captain who brought them down appeared with horses and carriage and they have just returned now at four o'clock from a long drive. I have had forty callers, been to one five o'clock tea and one garden party which was very picturesque—tea handed under the cocoanut palms. The people are delightful. I have such fine people at my table, Mr. S——, Vice-Consul, his wife (who treats me like a sister), and his beautiful daughter, who will marry early in January. I enjoy taking a stitch now and then in the trousseau. Dr. and Mrs. M—— and my son complete the party. My boy left the Pacific Club so as to be with me. I felt the sacrifice was too much, as none of us consider the food extra here, but there is no better place. People do not like the hotel for long. My son has been suffering from a carbuncle, which kept him in bed three days. He is very well now and greatly enjoyed your descriptive letter, about the "ex-cook," etc., etc. It must have fallen to your lot to really be the party leader. I have had ten letters from the States. This morning an American warship, the "Yorktown," came in and brought the good news of Morton's election in New York State. Everything Republican by an overwhelming majority. Mrs. Dr. M—— and I have taken in three different kinds of services to-day: Episcopalian, Presbyterian, and to-night a tent service by an Evangelist. Do you think we will have an overdose? There is so much here of interest all the time I am not going to tell you of—you are to come and see for yourself.

I must say good night as I am tired enough. My son and Mr. J—— send greetings. Tell me when you arrive and whether your brother and you knew one another. I guess you will be glad to see land.

Your friend,
C——.

From Mrs. H——.

Honolulu, May 19th,.

My dear Mrs. Robinson:—

As I am a "shut in" now, my friends are likely to get their letters answered, as the "China" is due to-morrow en route for San Francisco, on the tenth. I was taken with a violent attack of nausea and have had to keep pretty quiet until now. I will go to the table to-morrow. It has been very nice to have my devoted son for my physician and I am sure every one will spoil me if they keep on. My room is full of flowers, fruits and one basket arranged so artistically, and then such jellies and nice things. I am only allowed to have liquids.

Yes, it is a charming spot here and we have had delightful receptions and parties. A fine musicale is to be given this evening. The "Art League" has an opening Thursday, the 21st. Tourists come and go, and there is a good deal of life. Mr. and Mrs. B—— called a few nights ago and were very sorry not to have seen more of you.

My son is well indeed now, so much better than when you saw him. The young ladies keep him busy and he has a good time. I am thankful he seems well. I do not know whether I would forever like perpetual green. There is no anticipation of crocuses, jonquils, tulips and the bright upshooting blades of grass, and I own I like snow and ice, skating, toboganning, skeleton trees, etc., etc. I hear the season has been a hard one, though, so I am quite glad I was here. I get good news from home, so I am happy with my son. I am glad your pets and all were in good order. Your place must be delightful in summer. I must not get too tired, so will have to say "Aloha nui," in Hawaii—a big love. If my son were here he would send kind memoires, I know. He is dining at Wikiki with Dr. H——

C.——.

Boston.

My dear Mrs. Robinson:—

Yes, here I am back once again under the old flag. I did not want to come at all, and during these cold days I sigh for that land of beauty, for such it was. The last part of my stay did not agree with me, and I lost flesh, and the M. Doctors said I would not live there two years; but I would not believe it and I did not want to leave that dear precious son, but the more I tried not to come the more I was made to. The people said I should not, and yet here I am, and this is the first week I have been at all like myself, and now I do not write much or do much but be lazy. I was unconscious three days on the ocean. I rested at the Occidental Hotel, S. F., and then came by Denver & Rio Grande, reaching here October 25th. I lost my old room and am temporarily settled, as I was not able to go about.

We had quite a time at Honolulu during the cholera scare. We were quarantined twelve hours at

San Francisco and before we left fumigated. My son was quite well when I left or I would not have come, but since took a little cruise about the island as a guest of the officers of the "Bennington" man-of-war, and it did him much good. Dr. M—— took charge of his practice, Mrs. M—— went to Japan for three months and was charmed. If I could have afforded it I would have gone too. That is a trip you must have. Yes, we had a jolly evening together. My son moved out of that house Jan. 1st and went on the next street alongside of the Club House. Has a much better and a larger and pleasanter home. Is it not dreadful for me not to be with him? But living is so expensive there and I am not fit to keep house. I feel now farther away than I did before going, as I see how long it takes to get there; but such is life. Everything I ever loved is taken out of my life. I did not stop on my way home anywhere. I have had such insomnia and just begin now to sleep. I owe so many letters, but cannot write yet as I once did, but to-night made up my mind to answer yours if some others waited longer. I liked the people at Honolulu so much and had good times. I went twice to the Pali. You remember our good drive there? I had a picture of dear old Diamond Head sent me as a gift. Consul M—— lately returned from the States with his bride, and Minister Willis and wife gave him a grand reception. My son said all the belles of Honolulu were out in finest style. They did give such pretty receptions. So many came on the "Australia" when I did to spend a year in the U. S. to get toned up. Lieutenant J—— has been made major; he goes with my son to his new home. It would be nice to live in California and spend the winters in Honolulu. If my son were here he would have several messages, as we often talked about how nice you were. I am glad we met. I am sure we will meet again some time. Good night, dear.

Lovingly,

C——.

From Miss C——.

New Zealand, Sept. 6th.

Dearest Mrs. Robinson:—

It was the sweetest surprise I received this year when your letter came. I really thought you had forgotten us altogether. Next time you write you must send me your photo as you promised. I often look at your photo on the mantelpiece and wish you back again. Never a day passes that I do not think of you, because you are always in sight. Mr. H—— keeps travelling up from the South and down again, so we see him pretty often. He will be glad to hear we have heard from you. Mother and E—— went down to see Mr. F—— one day when the steamer was in and he told us he had heard from you. E—— and I go to the dancing class every Monday, and it is very enjoyable, but it will be all over soon now the summer is coming on. We shall be very sorry, for it used to help pass away the week. I am going out to M—— next Tuesday a week. You remember where I went when you were staying with us.

I think you had better send over a few hundred dollars and then we will be able to come and see you in your lovely home. It would be grand fun. Mr.

T—— comes to the house as usual and wishes to be remembered to you.

We had a Mr. J—— staying with us not long ago and we gave him your address, so you might see him. He would just suit you, I guess, because he is very fair, with a lovely complexion and very nice looking. You could not help but fall in love with him.

When are you going to take another trip to Auckland? I am anxiously awaiting your return. I suppose you will come here for your honeymoon soon. My mother has some shares in gold mines, so when we make our fortune we are coming over to see you and then you can accompany us back to A——. I would like to see your house with you like a fairy in it.

Believe me to be ever
Your sincere friend
G.——.

Do not forget to send your photo, because I want you in my own possession to gaze upon sometimes when lonely.

G——.

From Miss C——.
One year later.

Auckland, May 16th, 18—.

Dearest Mrs. Robinson:—

I am almost ashamed to write, because it is such a long while since we received your last letter. I thank you very much for those papers you sent me. I found them very interesting. We have E—— married now. They were married in April on Easter Monday, at 8 o'clock in the morning. I expected to hear of your wedding before this and am waiting patiently for your photo, which you promised me long ago. We delivered your letter to Mr. L—— directly it came. I knew the handwriting directly I saw it and expected my photo as well. I have not seen Mr. F—— since you went away, but have often watched the "Monowai" come and go from Auckland. Has that Mr. J—— called on you yet? I think it is high time he found you by now. I hope you won't break his heart, if you have broken other hearts before.

Do you know, Mrs. Robinson, I wrote you a letter a mail or two ago and forgot to post it. Was it not clever of me? And then I was always going and going to write until here I am at 11 o'clock writing when the mail closes at 1 o'clock. My mother and I often have a talk about you, and we wish you would come to Auckland again. We cannot know too many friends like you. E—— and I had our photographs taken in our bridesmaid frocks. You know, E—— was married in the travelling dress, so our dresses are winter frocks to match. We have some of the same boarders we had when you were here. Mr. H—— comes and goes; he is travelling and is generally away for a month and back for three weeks before he starts away again. I have not seen Mr. L—— since that day we saw you off.

I must now very unwillingly conclude. With best love and hoping to have a long letter and photo from you soon.

G——.

From Miss C——.

Auckland, Nov. 27th.

My dearest Mrs. Robinson:—

I received your most welcome letter some time ago and have been going to answer it every mail, but have not succeeded until this one.

We are all going to the floral fete to-morrow and I wish it had been to-day, so I could have told you all about it. I am sending you the Christmas number of our Graphic; it might be a little interesting to you, and with it I wish you a very merry Christmas and a happy New Year.

E—— is still living at home. I was simply charmed with your last photo; it is such a good one, and by this time you will have received E——'s and mine. I hope you like them.

The mail steamer has just come in a short time ago, so there is plenty of time. I suppose Mr. J—— has not called on you yet. I do not know what has become of him.

We had another German who would have suited you had you been here and he fell in love with your photo. Before he went away he said, should you turn up to tell you to wait until he came back. His name is Dr. F., a nice fellow; you could not help liking him.

Auckland is very busy just now with mining, and some of the people are making their fortunes, but we do not happen to be one of them. Worse luck!

I suppose you have been to see "Trilby"? We went to see it played by an American company, and it was splendid, and the opera house was crowded every evening they played here. I do wish I were going to see you in the "Mariposa." To-morrow she sails. How delightful it would be. Wait until we make our fortune at mining and then you will see us all.

My mother says she will write you by next, and if there is any fresh news she will tell it to you.

I will now close. With love from all I am,
Your sincere friend,
G——.

From Mrs. C——.

Auckland, May 16th, 18—.

My dear Mrs. Robinson:—

You will be thinking we have forgotten all about you, but it is not so. We often think about you and talk about you. By this mail you will receive some of E——'s wedding cake and card. The marriage took place in the new St. Paul's church on Easter Monday, at 8 o'clock in the morning. We had a reception here afterwards, and then the happy couple caught the 9.35 train for Whihoto and were away a fortnight on their honeymoon. They are very fond of each other and I am sure will get on well together. E—— was married in her travelling dress and she looked very nice. G—— was bridesmaid and E—— second bridesmaid.

You will remember Mr. ——. He took you and me for a walk one Sunday down the wharf.

I suppose we will be hearing of your wedding next and you will tell us who the happy man is. I have not seen Mr. F—— for a very long time, and I have not seen Mr. L—— since you left. We forwarded his letters always to him, and I am sure he would be pleased to see you back in Auckland, as I am sure he spent some very happy evenings while in your company. But I suppose you have forgotten all about your old friends by this time and have a number of new ones. You will remember Mr. H——, the Scotch gentleman that sat next to you at the table. He is still with us, and Mr. T—— calls to see him quite often, as usual. Mr. and Mrs. S—— are still here, and we always have a good number staying here; we like this house better than the other. There is nothing talked of here but gold fields—there is a boom. G—— wants to go and spend six months with you. I tell her she would be spoiled by then, that she would not care to settle down after that.

Now, dear Mrs. Robinson, with the hopes of hearing from you soon, I remain your friend

J——.

We will be better pleased to see yourself rather than a letter. I think you would enjoy another trip now.

———

From Mrs. B——.

Belleville.

My dear Mrs. Robinson:—

Indeed I had not forgotten you, but had given up all hopes of ever hearing from you again. I am sorry to hear of your loss, but you seem to have been having a gay time since.

You ask me how many little ones I have. Did you not receive a photo of my little girl about a year or a year and a half ago? I sent one anyway. I have another little darling since, also a girl, six months old, so you see our family is increasing. Our home is getting too small for us. We are going to build this summer and hope by fall to be in a home of our own. When we are nicely settled I am going to send for you to come and visit us and hope you will not refuse to come. I think the summer will be the nicest, as we have a lovely little steam yacht (the prettiest in the bay for the size of it), and we could make it much pleasanter for you then.

Mr. B—— is well, like myself, and we have nothing to grumble about. I shall be so glad to see you again. It will seem like old times.

You must have had a delightful trip. I suppose the steamer you went to Australia in would be a little ahead of the "Burnly." Oh! will you ever forget that trip? I never will.

I hope now, you will write again soon and let me know how you are getting along. If you have a photo of yourself, I would like to see how you look. Must close as it is getting late.

    Your sincere friend
           F.——

  From Mrs. L——.

    Russell Square, London, Dec.

Dear Mrs. Robinson:—

I was so pleased to hear from you and learn that you had reached home safely and found all well. What a pity you cannot find your dear little dog. I fear you will have to console yourself with M—— now, and

I am very glad he is better and that you like him. You will be sorry to hear Miss —— has been very ill with influenza, but I am glad to say she is much better and hopes soon to get out. We spent a very quiet Christmas, as so many have gone away for the holiday and will not return till next week.

Dr. H—— was here the beginning of the month, and I expect him again about the 7th. You must excuse this scribble—I let my housemaid go for a holiday and she has not come back, and it makes me very busy.

A—— unites with me in much love, wishing you a very happy New Year.

Yours very sincerely,

L——.

I wish you would visit London again before very long. Come in the summer and I think you would like it better.

Mangakahia, New Zealand, March 12th.

Dear aunt Alice:—

I thank you for your welcome letter which I received last week. I am glad to see you are well.

You say the ground is white with snow. Here it is summer and everything is green. We had such lots of peaches this year and blackberries. Fanny and I often bathe in the river; we can swim a little.

We are going to a bible meeting to-morrow night about two miles from here. I have a horse of my own now—its name is Napoleon; it is a roan color. We have a fat pup, a Gordon setter; its father took a prize at the last show.

We will be so glad when you come to see us. With much love from all,

From your
Dear Niece,

8 years old.

From Miss E——.

Brooklyn.

My dear Mrs. Robinson:—

I hope you have not forgotten your late companion of the cabin. I wanted very much to come and see you this week, but was only at Suffern a day or two. I have got some work to do now, which will keep me very much, too much, in fact, occupied; but shall try to come over and see you some afternoon and chance finding you in.

Has M—— recovered from the effects of his voyage? Did you send the tiny doctor something for his stateroom? I have been looking around for an idea. Of course, you are going to the horse show, being one of the "smart" crowd and, of course, I am not, as I shall not have time. New York shops are fine and goods so cheap that I wonder at Americans buying in London.

If you still remember me, write.

Yours very sincerely,

E——.

Brooklyn.

My dear Mrs. Robinson:—

Thank you so much for the kind little note. I wish I could come out soon and answer it in person, but cannot yet awhile manage it.

They expect people to work like horses in this city. I saw that the H—— had come and gone and imagined that some one's heart was beating faster the while. But take my advice and do not forget who plies to and fro 3000 miles away on the Pacific.

I am sending you an "idea." It is easy to picture you queening it in a like creation, so I cut the picture out—but must suggest that it is hardly suitable for an Atlantic or a Pacific steamer. I hope the little bow-wow will remind you of the miniature doctor of the M——. I am in danger of forgetting to redeem my promise to him. Would it matter much, think you?

Keep a tiny corner in your memory for me so you won't look too surprised and say, "Excuse me, but I haven't the pleasure, etc., etc.," when I do appear at P——.

Sincerely yours,

E——.

From Mrs. D——.

London, June.

My dear Mrs. Robinson:—

We arrived here yesterday after a very pleasant voyage. I feel sure it has done H—— good, although at times he feels his rheumatism a little, but think the salt water baths did him good. He was not sick, but I was for about three days but was up all the time. I changed my cabin. Went in with an actress; she had the best cabin on the ship. We had a lively time.

You remember the young lady in blue those gentlemen were seeing off. Well, she became engaged to a fellow on the voyage. H—— and I want to thank you for the nice time you gave us in New York the last day we were there. I am sure it was very kind of you, and also to get up at that unearthly hour of the morning. Poor Will, how he did look! I felt so sorry for him. How I wish you and he had come with us. We were very comfortable; the captain and his officers were particularly nice and the stewardess was more than nice. She looked after us all so well.

Last night we went to a music hall—enjoyed it immensely. My friend met us. Think we will stay here until Monday, then go home. How pleased they will be to see us. You must excuse this scrawl; am writing in my friend's office, and he and H—— are talking. The fashions in hair dressing and hats are very different from N. Y. They wear a large fringe nearly half way across their heads; then they set their hats on that it looks too comical for anything—and such large hats! But there are a lot of fine women. London is a wonderful place.

H—— joins with me in love to you. Again thanking you for your kindness, believe me,

Sincerely yours,

From Mrs. D——.

London, August 26th.

My dear Mrs. Robinson:—

Dad was delighted with the picture you sent him. He nailed it up over the fireplace in the kitchen beside New York's prettiest girl. You remember we got it with the Recorder. He said he would rather see her alive—the one you sent, I mean. Did you see the enclosed in one of the papers you sent me. You did not mark it, so thought perhaps you did not see it.

Suppose Mrs. B—— will soon be going to see you. You would look a swell at Mrs. W——'s. Am pleased you went, because I know you like that kind of thing and could hold your own and look as well as any of them.

Should think before this that you had been down to New York. Did you call on Mrs. W—— or M——, or was it too hot? I hear in New York it has been very, very hot. Did you have time to see W—— H——? If so he would tell you about the Brooklyn folks. What a queer thing you do not hear from your brother. It is getting time you heard, because the time is passing on. It will soon be time for you to start, October will soon be here. After we have seen you then we will be off to earn some more dollars. A—— has just come in to show me a large basket of mushrooms that he has gathered; he gets such a lot every morning. Our people are busy with the harvest. H—— has been on the stack two or three days. He is so brown—I think it is doing him more good than it is me.

The weather is something awful—rain every other day regularly; I am cold nearly all the time.

How is your heart? How does your housekeeper get along, also James?

H—— joins me in love to you. Hoping soon to see you, believe me,

Yours sincerely,
L——.

From Mrs. D——.
London, Sept. 25th, 18——.

My dear Mrs. Robinson:—

We are staying at my brother's for a few days, so your letter was forwarded to me and I have just time to write you before the postman gets here.

You say you are going to start on your journey the first week in October, but you do not mention the name of steamer you intend sailing on, or if you are coming to Liverpool or Southampton.

If you have time write me directly you receive this letter, letting me know that I can meet you. If you have not the time to write, telegraph me either from Liverpool or London and let us know just where you are. We shall be so disappointed if we fail to see you. We intend returning to the States the last week in October.

With love, in which H—— joins, believe me,

Yours truly,
L——.

THREE YEARS LATER.

From Mrs. D——.

Brooklyn, Sept. 15th, 18—.

Dear Mrs. Robinson:—

You say in England it is cold, you have to put your coat on. Well, here it is just the reverse; it is what I call muggy, keeps you in a perspiration all the time.

A few days since it was cold. I was a little surprised to hear you liked London so well. Have you yet found a house to suit you? It will have to be some way out of London to be cheap. The places we spoke to you about are Frascati and Cafe Monica—the former is the one.

I don't suppose for one moment that is the right way to spell it, but that is as near as I can get to it.

You must have had a lovely time going over. I thought you would like that ship. Suppose you will come back same way.

What luck you had at cards! That beats anything. Even H—— has better luck than that. I was to tell you he has seen about the pictures and would send them by the next mail to you.

We have been to all the seaside places this summer. They have opened a place called Bergen Beach, but I do not think it will ever come up to Coney Island.

We have our card parties every Saturday night and enjoy them very much.

How did you like the Alhambra? And did you

go to the Pavilion and Palace. Do they dress in London anything like in New York?

The boys wish to be remembered to you, and H—— joins with me in love to you. Believe me,

Sincerely yours,

L——.

From Mrs. D——.

Brooklyn, November 2d, 18—.

My dear Mrs. Robinson:—

Your kind letter to hand Saturday morning. Thank you very much for your kind invitation to come and stay a week with you. I am afraid I could not manage a week, but will be pleased to come for a few days. If convenient we could come on Saturday. Nelson called on us Saturday morning. What a big boy he is. He thinks he will like to go to school; it is, indeed, very kind of you.

It is too bad you could not have waited for the H—— to come home in. You would have had a good time. H—— said you looked well and that you had such a lovely cloak. Why don't you come over some Saturday and have a game with us? We play every Saturday night till the small hours. I usually go to bed about 12 o'clock and leave the others at it. My toothache is better, thanks.

The boys join with me in kindest regards to you. Let me know about Saturday.

Sincerely yours,

L——.

From Mrs. T——.

Wellington, Sept. 27th.

Dear Mrs. Robinson:—

I must ask you to forgive me for not replying to your kind letter before this, but have had Capt. T—— an invalid since May. He had cataracts taken out of his eye; it has been a very tedious operation. It has been my work attending to him. He is now able to attend to his duties, and hope the worst is over. We were all very pleased to hear from you and that you are well. No doubt your trip to New Zealand did you much good. A change of scene and climate is beautiful to every one. Another trip would brighten you; it's just as well to take all the pleasure you can when you are alone. Do you like black servants? The white ones here are a great trouble. Have you sold your house? You said you intended doing so. You should take another trip to New Zealand before you take another house, and you will know where to find us. We should be very pleased to see you.

I wish I could be near you—I should enjoy a chat. We are very quiet folks, but you would be welcome. I thank you very much for your kindness in wishing to send me anything from the States, also wishing to receive any friends for me. I thank you very much indeed.

I have no likenesses now—will send them when we have some taken. I hope the worst is over with my husband's eyes; it has been a very anxious time for me. You will forgive my apparent neglect of you.

We have had a very fine winter here. Just now everything is looking like spring—green and fresh to one's eyes. I have been in the house a great deal this winter. Are you still having fine weather? There is plenty of rain here to gladden the farmers and rather too much wind. Wellington is a windy place; it keeps up its name in wind—"Windy Wellington."

I hope this may find you if you have not changed your home. Captain T—— and my son send their kind regards to you. We all felt it kind of you to remember us. If you are coming to New Zealand again let me know.

I must close. With love and best wishes from,

        Yours sincerely,

                Jean.

P.S.—Will be pleased to hear from you.

                Chicago, Ill.

My dear Mrs. Robinson:—

Your letter of September 25th came duly to hand and I shipped you by express on same day the stirrup, which I hope reached you in good order.

Several things in your letter set me to thinking (a very little makes people think sometimes), and still my thoughts would never have satisfactory result. I endeavored to learn from your letter whether you considered there was a greater satisfaction in being Mrs. Robinson than being Mrs. Hutton, and I vow I am in a state of doubt this minute.

For one thing I am glad to see you are becoming economical, or at least restricting expenses, and it is plain that you are beginning to realize that matrimony has a practical as well as a sentimental side. When you sell that team I don't think you will invest in another one like it in a hurry.

From what you tell about inviting the poor young lady to visit you I am inclined to believe that with your other good qualities you are something of a philanthropist. I would be tempted to become a total orphan, poor and friendless, for the same reward myself.

We have an almost entirely new lot of boarders at the hotel now. Mr. and Mrs. W—— are still there, but expect to go housekeeping soon. Mr. and Mrs. S—— have left, and although there are five people at our table, Mr. N—— and myself are the only males, there being three young ladies to assist us in forgetting the cares of this life. Are they handsome? Oh, no! Homely, just about; two blondes, one brunette—two talkers and one decidedly quiet, been married and, of course, is suspicious of men. I don't blame her.

By the way, I hope you have not forgotten the little matter of champagne for Thanksgiving. Mr. N—— and I are counting on that to drink your good health and prosperity, but if you don't send it, will drink your health just the same.

When you write again tell me all about yourself and every one else in whom you think I am interested.

Yours truly,

C——.

New York, Sept. 18th, 18—.

Dear Alice:—

Your letter to me at Hanover and that of yesterday are both received, and the former would have been answered before had I not expected to get home sooner and waited to write from here.

I only got back Saturday night from Hanover; was very well while there and the weather was fine and cool enough to stir about in as much as one felt inclined to. There was a cattle show at Marshfield (really an exhibition of all farm products, and races to boot), which I attended one day. Got the livery man to drive me down with a fine pair of grays. He knew all the by-roads and wood roads and took me through some of them on the way down. Next day an old fellow who lives on the main road, near where we turned off, came up to Hanover and, meeting my driver, said he would just give a dollar to know who went past his house the day before with a spanking pair of gray horses. He said they were driving like the devil, turned off into the woods and went off down a road nobody ever thought of travelling. Guessed they were pretty d——d well set up and doubted if they ever got to the cattle show where they were probably bound.

So you see the reputation a man gets for gratifying his love of the beautiful and taking a romantic secluded road in place of the dusty highway.

I am glad that Mrs. W—— concluded to take the long drive, and hope the weather will not put a stop to it.

You need not look for me just yet. Next month after all the equinoctial storms and blows are over we ought to have some fine weather, and then if I can get off and you can conveniently take me in for a few days I should like to come.

As to the brandy, you could not have put it to a better use than to brace James up for the drive, but I will send you a couple of bottles of whiskey and the same of brandy to make up for it.

As ever, I remain,

Your friend.

www.ingramcontent.com/pod-product-compliance
Lightning Source LLC
Chambersburg PA
CBHW032046230426
43672CB00009B/1492